THE SPITFIRE LUCK
OF SKEETS OGILVIE

THE SPITFIRE LUCK
OF SKEETS OGILVIE

From the BATTLE of BRITAIN
to the GREAT ESCAPE

KEITH C. OGILVIE

VICTORIA • VANCOUVER • CALGARY

Heritage House Publishing Company Ltd.
heritagehouse.ca

Originally published in the United Kingdom by Fighting High Publishing, under the title *You Never Know Your Luck: Battle of Britain to the Great Escape: The Extraordinary Life of Keith "Skeets" Ogilvie DFC.*

CATALOGUING INFORMATION AVAILABLE FROM LIBRARY AND ARCHIVES CANADA

978-1-77203-211-6 (pbk)

Cover and interior design by Jacqui Thomas
Cover photographs: Spitfire, no date (*top*), and Skeets and Spitfire, 1940 (*bottom*). Collection of A.K. Ogilvie

The interior of this book was produced on 100% post-consumer recycled paper, processed chlorine free, and printed with vegetable-based inks.

We acknowledge the financial support of the Government of Canada through the Canada Book Fund (CBF) and the Canada Council for the Arts, and the Province of British Columbia through the British Columbia Arts Council and the Book Publishing Tax Credit.

Canada   Canada Council   Conseil des arts   BRITISH   BRITISH COLUMBIA
          for the Arts   du Canada   COLUMBIA   ARTS COUNCIL
                                                          An agency of the Province of British Columbia

21 20 19 18 17   1 2 3 4 5

Printed in Canada

CONTENTS

FOREWORD

On Battle of Britain Sunday, 1998, a small ceremony took place in the RAF chapel at Biggin Hill, the site of one of Britain's key defence aerodromes during that extraordinary time. It was attended mainly by old men and women who were survivors of those events and all that had happened in the world since, along with younger family members of some of the RAF's famous 'Few.' Following the ceremony, the members of the group moved slowly—some by choice and some by dint of their age—to the rose garden at the side of the chapel. There, in the brilliant sunlight and green of the English countryside, some of the ashes of Alfred Keith Ogilvie were laid to rest. There were solemn words and no few tears for those attending. There were fond memories, too, and a great deal of laughter, quieter than it might have been in past days, but rich and full even so.

Since that ceremony several of those who gathered at this famous site and for a drink after have also passed on. Time is taking its relentless toll on a generation whose particular adventures have not been repeated, and are not likely to be repeated, thankfully, among their children. With their skills and spirit, these men and women bought a form of peace, for at least a generation.

It is hard to think of them as young. They are our parents, these people who resided in London, going about their normal business as bombs fell around them—and who flew, sometimes filled with terror and rage and deadly intent, in marvellously supple and beautiful machines, often against overwhelming odds. We know them from Sunday dinners, from family spats and Christmases spent in sparkling living rooms. It is somehow not possible to imagine them, not just being youthful, but experiencing these unbelievable events and living to tell about them. Yet there is a wonderful and ever-growing body of work published that recounts the high adventure, disaster and gritty determination to push through the insurmountable and unimaginable. Sadly, these records are the last gifts of a generation that will soon pass from us.

I have always known about my father's wartime diary, documenting his experiences in the air. And many times I have heard him talk to admirers and biographers, storytellers and interested historians about his own exploits. It never seemed to me to be real, somehow, because he was always, first and foremost, simply my dad, someone who was more than happy to be just an ordinary guy with a family he loved and a job he liked. Even the enormous scars on his shoulder and back were of themselves unconvincing, just part of who he was. He was modest but open, always ready to share his experiences, but like most of his cohorts not wanting a particular fuss made over him. He always thought others deserved it more, that he was too ordinary.

My mother was the same. Although she was right there in London, working with the RCAF as a photographer and living under the falling bombs as the Blitz and all that followed unfolded in history, she has always stepped out of the light of my father's experience and downplayed the contribution she made and the things she did as unworthy of mention. She remained more or less healthy ('as good as can be expected, under the circumstances') until her death in early 2014, remembered it all, and was altogether too modest about her own contributions to her country during the war, and to our family in the marvellous peace that is all I and many of those of my generation have known.

To me, it is all of a piece. The adventures in the flying diary and the stories of hiding naked under the grand piano as the bombs fell are punctuation marks in lives that flowed and came together and ended up bringing my sister Jean and me with them. They deserve to be told together, as these lives unfolded over a few brief, significant years. That is the real purpose of this project, not just to talk about the extraordinary but to celebrate the ordinary too, as being extraordinary in its own right.

How do you write about a life? Two lives? It seemed relatively straightforward at first, given the written record my father kept of some of his adventures, and the enormous amount of information that's available about the times through which he and my mother lived. But historical facts and observations are one thing; doing justice to real, living people with whom you have spent much of your life is entirely another. It is one thing to describe the intricacies of airborne combat or the impact of bombs falling on London; it is another to understand intimately the feeling of adrenalin coursing through your body as tracer bullets fly past, or you listen to the 'whump' of explosions marching closer and closer to where you are actually standing. In these circumstances we can do little more than use our imaginations to place ourselves in their shoes. The words in this account come, whenever possible, from the letters, scrapbooks or spoken memories of my parents. Some come from others who were there at the time, and who recorded the precious memories that expand, supplement or illustrate the experiences of these two; yet in the end it is a story not about others, but about them.

Shortly before my father died in 1998, as I travelled through Ottawa on my way to a new job on the west coast of Canada, I had the good fortune to be able to spend some time with him. He was very uncomfortable physically, thin and a bit absent-minded, but still willing to talk and insisting on his modest role in the great scheme of things. On one of the last occasions I spent with him, we were talking about his life, and after a moment of quiet—I didn't know if he'd fallen asleep—he said, simply, with a bit of wonder in his voice, 'You never know your luck.'

You never know your luck.

Indeed you don't.

Keith C. Ogilvie

PART ONE

FROM HERE TO THERE

1

THE OTTAWA BOY

For a mediocre and only moderately interested student, Alfred Keith Ogilvie spent a lot of time in school. It was less the challenge of learning that held him there, though, and more the opportunity to enjoy a sporting life. He excelled at football, making a name for himself as a star halfback on many of Glebe Collegiate's Eastern Ontario Secondary School athletics championship football teams, both senior and junior.

Somewhere in his younger years, Ogilvie had come to the conclusion that the first name given to him by his parents really didn't suit him. He relegated the unliked and unlamented 'Alfred' to being forever an initial at the start of his signature, taking on his middle name, Keith. But even the preferred version of his formal name was soon overtaken. His nimble ball carrying on the football field quickly earned him his lifelong nickname, 'Skeeter,' later shortened to 'Skeets.'

His academic performance at Glebe also secured him something of a reputation, if not quite in the same league as the football achievements. It is best illustrated by an event that took place many years later, after the family had moved back to Ottawa following Skeets's eventual retirement from the Royal Canadian Air Force, when his son, also named Keith, was sitting on the first day of school at that same Glebe Collegiate, in a grade 11 maths class. The teacher, Abe Sonley, a tall, scowling and seemingly ancient gentleman possessed of bushy white eyebrows and an unruly head of white hair, was walking from one desk to another and watching as students wrote down their names. He surprised the class of thirty-odd new students by returning to the front of the classroom and repeating the names of every one, without an error. Furrowing his brows further, after a thoughtful minute or two he turned his full and discomfiting attention to the younger Ogilvie and asked sharply: 'Did your father go to this school?'

'Yes,' I answered, surprised, for I was the son in question.

More deep thought. Then Sonley said, half smiling and half seriously, 'If you're as bad at mathematics as he was, you might as well leave the class right now.' A hard act to follow!

His modest mathematical performance notwithstanding, Skeets continued to play football after graduating from Glebe, first with St Pat's College and then with the University of Ottawa teams. While his academic record at those institutions remains unknown (and is probably somewhat suspect), his name appeared in the newspaper coverage of the academic leagues on many occasions, becoming well enough known in the athletic circles of the national capital that he was asked to turn out with the Ottawa Rough Riders of the (then) Big Four of the Canadian Football League.

Unfortunately, the dream of a professional football career did not work out. By 1938 Skeets had joined the traditional working world, initially as a cashier with a local brokerage firm, O'Hearn and Co. It must have been a relatively interesting environment for him at the time, since it gave him a lifelong interest in the stock market. Small-scale investing became something of a hobby in his later years and his naturally conservative approach to finances left him in the enviable company of those who were able to benefit sufficiently from their long-term dabbling in the markets to enjoy their retirement years without financial worries.

But that was a long way off for the young man, who still lived with his family in their Glebe home. The Ogilvie kinfolk were long-time residents of Ottawa. Keith's uncle Clarence was the city clerk for a number of years and his father Charlie—never Charles, at least to family and friends—was a usually affable railroad engineer who made the daily trip from central Ottawa, up the Ottawa Valley to Pembroke and back. It was a time when rail reigned in the transportation world. The tracks on which the nation's goods and passengers were carried cut through the heart of Ottawa, terminating at that time downtown at Union Station, beside the Rideau Canal and opposite the Grand Trunk Railway's flagship Chateau Laurier Hotel. The tracks spread east and west along the corridor that now carries Ottawa's principal motorway, the Queensway, not far behind the Ogilvie family home.

The Ogilvie house was close enough to the east–west tracks that you could plainly hear the rail activity, or walk a couple of blocks to watch it if you were so inclined. There were some fascinating diversions offered by the proximity of this complex. The circus would occasionally come into town to be set up in the Auditorium, since torn down and replaced by the YMCA, but located at the time just across the tracks and down a few blocks from the Ogilvie home. Young boys like the Ogilvie brothers could go and watch the many mysterious pieces from which the circus was constructed being unloaded from boxcars—especially those most exotic of circus animals, the big cats, bears and other creatures, that rested most of the year in the imagination.

The house had been the family home from the early 1900s. It was built in what was then a working-class part of the Glebe neighbourhood, a pleasant enough place to raise a family of three thriving sons despite the proximity of the rail lines. You could fish or canoe in the canal at the end of the block and the schools were an easy walk away. The boys were quite different but shared a positive and sometimes irreverent view of life. Keith was the middle son, always ready with a wisecrack. The eldest, Emerson, was a cocky 'know it all,' in the words of a close cousin, and youngest brother James was 'full of fun.' Emerson was also a football standout, actually playing with the Ottawa Rough Riders for a couple of years as a kicker.

Charlie and the boys suffered a great setback in 1929 with the sudden loss of the boys' mother Edith to a strange automobile accident. She was hit by a car at an intersection, got up and walked home, feeling out of sorts but not bad. She lay down to recover and did not get up again. They all felt the loss keenly. It didn't take long for Charlie, working hard for a living, to realize what a handful his three sons were for a single parent. He turned for support to an old friend of the family, Margaret Dixon, marrying her a couple of years later. It suited Margaret just fine, as she had always had her eye on Charlie, according to family lore.

Margaret's success as a stepmother was probably greater with the younger two members of the family, who seemed to accept her fairly readily, than it was with Emerson. For the other boys, and certainly for Charlie, she became a solid and central part of their lives, living with Charlie—and later as his widow—in the family home for the rest of her life. In their advancing years together their loyalty and love for each other were obvious, even to their easily distracted grandchildren—they could only be conceived of as a team.

Despite his essentially gentle nature, Charlie had something of a reputation for a temper that was slow to awaken but spectacular when aroused. At one point, he got into a difference of opinion with another worker at the railway roundhouse that was located not far from Pretoria Bridge, just around the corner from the Ogilvie house. Charlie was not a large man but he ended the disagreement by picking the other fellow up by the ankles and dunking him in a barrel of engine oil, pulling him out in the nick of time. He treated inanimate objects that offended him with even more ferocity. One of the family legends recounts how he commonly applied his railroad engineer's technique of testing the soundness of things by tapping them with a large ball-peen hammer. He was performing such a diagnostic investigation on the iron furnace pipes in the basement of the family home when a patch of rust flaked off on impact of the hammer, squirting hot water into his face and soaking him. There was no waiting for retaliatory justice—Charlie promptly beat the offending system, furnace boiler included, to death with his 'diagnostic' tool. There is no record of how long it took to replace the house heating system, or how the place was kept warm in the meantime.

Skeets may have inherited some of this temperament, but in him it was not at all near the surface. Perhaps his lifetime of experience taught him to manage his temper. While he could anger quickly, it was never malicious or spiteful, and always over just as swiftly. Perhaps it was partly that he never had a head for mechanical things and consequently didn't have the same kinds of encounters with recalcitrant objects made of hard metal. He was the kind of person who, unlike his father, had a toolbox that consisted of an ancient hammer (not ball-peen), a couple of screwdrivers with well-rounded ends and a pair of pliers that did double duty as a wrench or sometimes a hammer when that item wasn't immediately to hand. Most times he picked up a tool, Skeets could be relied on to cut or gouge himself with it, thus reinforcing the disinclination to mess with anything mechanical.

Absence of a hands-on mechanical bent notwithstanding, Skeets, and indeed the whole family, were known to be crazy about aeroplanes. They would rush out of the house whenever an aircraft was heard buzzing overhead. Aviation was still a fascinating novelty in the pre-war years, but

Skeets was particularly interested. His boyhood photo scrapbook includes pictures of Charles Lindbergh's visit to Ottawa in 1927. Lindbergh had been invited to help Canada celebrate its Diamond Jubilee on July 1, only six weeks or so after completing his pioneering transatlantic solo flight, and less than three weeks after returning in glory to the United States aboard the navy cruiser USS *Memphis*. The pictures taken by the eleven-year-old Keith focus not on the crowds but on the machines themselves. They must have seemed magically exotic to an innocent youngster as he watched more than 60,000 people greet the famed aviator on his arrival at a grass field on the site of what is now Ottawa's international airport. Lindbergh returned to Canada in his Lockheed Sirius monoplane in 1931, the year after he and his wife, Anne Morrow Lindbergh, set a coast-to-coast speed record in that same aircraft. It had now been specially fitted with floats for long-distance travel over water and was being tested in North America on the first legs of their long overseas trip. Ottawa was their first stop. Lindbergh and his wife again attracted crowds along the banks of the Ottawa River, among them the young Keith.

Skeets's childhood scrapbook sports several pages of other exotic and historic aircraft, even a gyrocopter he had spotted around the grass-covered aerodrome at Rockcliffe. He was clearly a frequent visitor to the place, always equipped with his Brownie camera. One page of the album is labelled in a youthful hand: 'Col. Charles A. Lindbergh, Ottawa, August 1931.' The pictures on this and the following pages must have taken almost a whole roll of film. They show the unique aircraft tied up to a float on the Ottawa River, being gassed up, the famous pilot and co-pilot talking with local flyers as they planned their next flight leg, then finally getting into the cockpits, taxiing out and taking off for Moosonee, the next stop on their epic journey to Asia.

By the time 1939 came around Skeets, now twenty-three, must have been chafing under the routine of working 9 to 5 in an office. Like the rest of the world, he was watching events in Europe and wondering how they would unfold. It seemed clear that Canada would be eventually drawn in, one way or another, and that spring he made up his mind to be part of whatever was to come, one day walking into the recruiting offices of the Royal Canadian Air Force (RCAF) to offer his services as a pilot. The RCAF was then signing up officers, a rank for which a college degree was a mandatory requirement. There were a few sergeant pilots in the service but they were rare and recruiting was not taking place in this category. To his disappointment, Skeets was turned down.

Discouraged, but still intrigued by the idea of a patriotic commitment that might include the larger romance of a flying life, he crossed the street to the British Royal Air Force (RAF) office. The RAF was preparing for the worst and had established its own recruiting centre in Ottawa. Unlike the RCAF, they were hungry for volunteers, regardless of formal education. They immediately responded to the interest of this healthy, capable Canadian. Skeets remembered being called by the recruiting office one Monday, having his medical on Wednesday, and being on his way to England two days later. He sailed on the passenger liner *Letitia*[1] on Friday, August 4, 1939. Just before he left, with seven other RAF recruits, his group was notified that they could transfer to the Royal Canadian Air Force if they wished. They consulted together, thought about it briefly, then decided to proceed as planned. It was the RCAF's loss, at least for the duration of the war. They were the last group accepted in the RAF—from then on, all recruits joined the RCAF.

There was never any discussion of the family's reaction, but it must have been painful for Charlie and Margaret to see Keith leave for an uncertain and risky future. Flying was itself dangerous enough, never mind the prospect of imminent combat. And it is difficult to imagine how much harder it must have been, less than two years later, when the other two sons, Emerson and Jimmy, left for Europe as volunteers with the 4th Princess Louise Dragoon Guards, a Canadian militia regiment that had by then been activated for wartime service in a reconnaissance role. Emerson was the captain adjutant for the regiment and Jim was a private. By then the war was in a bleak stage, and it must have been overwhelming for the parents, no matter how proud, to know their three sons, their only children, would be fighting on the front lines in countries in which none had hitherto even set foot.

Following his rather precipitous departure, Skeets took the time to describe his new surroundings, to admit his trepidation and to reveal the depth of his emotions in a quick and poignant letter to his parents. Written from the ship shortly after it set sail, the letter displays an extraordinary prescience about what the next few years would bring.

Donaldson Atlantic Line
T.S.S. *Letitia*
August 4, 1939

Dear Dad and Aunt Marg,

Greetings, salutations and stuff. The hour is now eight o'clock and I haven't been sick yet. Practically nothing to it.

These few hours on board have been just grand. The accommodation is perfect and the service excellent. As for the meals, you wouldn't believe them; they are so perfect. At four o'clock the steward comes around and with tears in his eyes begs you to have afternoon tea.

The other seven boys going are all kindred spirits and there isn't a lemon amongst them. Already we are bosom pals. I don't mind admitting that parting was a plenty shaky business, my doubts were many and deep but now I know that my decision was the right one. It is going to be a grand adventure and I am looking forward to it all. I'm sorry that I couldn't have said the things I wanted to on leaving but somehow there was a twelve pound shot-put in my stomach and an egg in my throat.

However poor this method is, I'd like you both to know that I have the grandest parents ever. Because Aunt Marg has never been a step-mother but a real mother or more, because she did more than a mother could have by stepping into a spot as she did.

As for Charlie ol' boy, if I am half the man that my dad is, I am a cinch to go a long way in this old world.

Don't either of you worry about Keithie. For the simple reason that you have always trusted me to use my own discretion at home, I am leaving without a thing that I would be ashamed of having you know, and I am very sure such will be the case while I am away.

It is grand for me to go, knowing that you both are so happy together. Your turn will come and you'll get the breaks that you richly deserve.

Well gang, there is a brawl coming off here shortly and as there is a lot of ground work to be done, I better get moving.

I will certainly keep you posted as time goes along and expect the same from home. So long for now. God bless you both.

Affectionately,

Keith

Keith and the other 'boys' on the *Letitia* quickly bonded into a Canadian contingent. One of those who joined Skeets on the passage to England was Eric Dewar, a close friend from Glebe Collegiate days. Eric was also recruited into the RAF, but to a darker destiny. In later years, Keith claimed, sadly, that Eric had 'killed himself' with his impetuosity. Returning from a mission and circling the field, Eric was reported to have been frustrated about the lack of clearance to land and finally dashed in at high speed, without permission, and somehow crashed on landing.

When the *Letitia* sailed, however, it was on the promise of bright adventure. Among Skeets's papers is a printed menu from the Donaldson Atlantic Line, labelled 'Farewell Dinner' and dated 'TSS *Letitia*—Saturday, 12th August, 1939.' It is signed on the back by Keith and his companions on the voyage: George R. Lambert, Brantford; Fred de Sieges, Winnipeg; Gordon P. Knifton, Parry Sound; Alan Bigelow, Halifax; D.A. (Doug) Smith, Halifax; Ernest Publicover, Halifax; and of course Eric Dewar. The new recruits were not the only passengers of interest, however. Keith, at least, made the acquaintance of some of the fairer sex on the boat, including two dazzling young twin sisters from Toronto, Monica and Veronica Mewburn. They would be friends for years, a status not always popular with Irene after she came into the picture. But that would be later.

2

AND THE WESTERNER

Irene Margaret Lockwood's defining characteristic for those who knew her well was always her pride in being a western Canadian. Her roots were firmly in the prairies and despite all the places she had been and things she had been through, she invariably cheered for the Saskatchewan team—or as a poor second best, any other Western Conference team—in the annual Grey Cup football play-off. She always considered herself something of a country girl, as some of her fondest childhood memories were of time she spent on the prairie farm of her grandparents, the Mitchells.

When Margaret and Charlie Mitchell came to Canada from Scotland to farm on their homestead near Cardross, Saskatchewan, they brought their daughters, Kate and Jean. Charlie had married Margaret in Glasgow after the untimely death of Margaret's first husband, and the father of her daughters. A son, Andrew, was born to Charlie and Margaret in Canada after the move.

The decision to relocate from the urban centre of Glasgow to a homestead in the unknown prairies of Saskatchewan can only be imagined as momentous. It would have needed an uncommon measure of courage and commitment on the part of Margaret and Charlie, and must have been an overwhelming shock to the two girls. Jean certainly never saw herself as a farmer—and nor, for that matter, did her sister Kate. The two of them at some point jumped ship from the farm and moved to Regina, in circumstances that will forever be a mystery.

What is known, though, is that Jean was an outgoing person, with many friends in Regina. One was Arthur Lockwood, a young Yorkshireman from Leeds who had come to Regina with his brothers to make his fortune building houses. The 'ship's lists' for 1909 record the arrival on April 16 at St John's, New Brunswick, of the *Empress of Britain*, out of Liverpool. Three of the Lockwood brothers were on board: George, listed as a carpenter, aged thirty; Walter, bricklayer, aged twenty-five; and Arthur, also a carpenter, aged twenty-three. A little more than a month later another brother, Charles Lockwood and his wife, Eva, both twenty-eight, disembarked from the *Empress of Ireland* at Quebec and made their way west toward a declared destination of Winnipeg. By 1911, perhaps following the available work, the four brothers had congregated in Regina and established themselves as a family construction company.

The timing was fortuitous. In 1912 the 'Regina cyclone'—still considered the deadliest in Canadian history—flattened Regina's wooden buildings, killing twenty-eight people, leaving thousands more homeless, and causing the equivalent of what would now be nearly half a billion dollars in damage. The Lockwood brothers, up to that point only managing to get by, suddenly found their skills in high demand. They pitched in to the rebuilding effort and together put up many of the well-crafted, classic red-brick single-family homes, and even some of the government buildings, that still endure in the city.

How and why Jean and Arthur got together as more than friends is another mystery. Perhaps Jean saw a man with skills and prospects outside the farming community; or maybe Arthur saw a pretty woman with whom he could settle down and raise a family. In either case, and whatever the motivation, Jean and Arthur were married on August 2, 1916. A little over a year later son Gordon was born, followed two years thereafter by Irene. Ever the lover of cold, clear weather, Irene must have got that from her birthday, a day when the prairie temperature dipped to minus 27 degrees centigrade!

The family went through several moves in the early years, but finally settled into a house on Pasqua Street, not far from the Regina city centre and close to the brothers' business. The young family developed its own circle of friends. Irene remembered Saturday nights as special, when the adults would gather in one or another couple's house for a sing-song. The children would come with their parents, excited by the prospect of a sleepover while the adults socialized downstairs.

But there was a darker side to the family life. Her parents may have been compatible in the beginning, but Irene didn't remember any open affection between them. She didn't recall her father ever putting his arm around her mother. Worse, she recalled many times when Arthur was goaded by Jean into a state of anger, to the point where he would literally foam at the mouth. He never laid hands on his children, but the frequency and pain of these incidents lasted in Irene's memory and no doubt stayed with her brother Gordon as well.

When Irene was on her own, it was different. She thrived in school, enjoying academic studies and athletics in equal measure. She made some very close friends, including Lal Bing, with whom Irene kept in occasional touch all her life. She treasured wonderful memories of the two of them dancing together again and again, losing themselves in the wonderful music of Ethelbert Nevin's lyrical piano piece, 'Narcissus.'

Irene took particular pride in her winning performances at the school track and field championships in Regina but, sadly, the joy of these achievements wasn't fully shared by the family. By the time she was coming into her own, her beloved brother Gordon was found to have epilepsy and his condition became an ongoing preoccupation for the family. She always remembered the day Gordon's diagnosis was given, and the shock it caused, 'like it was yesterday.' At the time, there was no effective medication for the condition and Jean did her best to treat her ten-year-old son according to the common knowledge of the day. They were hateful treatments for Gordon—trips to a horse farm to drink mare's milk, supposed to be good for strange illnesses, and having to wear a hazelnut around his neck, with a hole drilled in it and mercury dripped in through the hole. In the persistent shadow of Gordon's illness, Irene's own achievements often went unremarked.

There were bright notes, though. To escape the prairie winters (and perhaps to give Arthur some room), Jean and the children often spent their winter months in Victoria. They lived in Fairfield—not far from the cemetery where the painter Emily Carr and other icons of Victoria's history are buried—near the shores of the Strait of Juan de Fuca. Irene loved the time she spent in that bucolic city as a child and visiting family much later in life. Their Victoria home was a small addition to a larger house. The owner's granddaughter, Joan, was Irene's age and lived a few blocks away. The two hit it off immediately, sharing a special bond that only growing up as girls in the same neighbourhood seems to bring, whiling away many happy hours of make-believe on nearby Moss Rock. Long after Irene was unable to make the trip west, she continued to keep in frequent telephone contact with her best Victoria childhood friend.

The Lockwood family pictures of those days show a mischievous child with a perpetual grin, surrounded by generally unsmiling adults. Irene found it difficult to shed her energetic, tomboyish ways. One day she arrived home with a broken arm after falling from a basketball hoop at Margaret Jenkins School in Victoria. Her teacher, Miss Hunt, had whisked her off to the hospital immediately after the accident and when her worried mother came to fetch her daughter, now in a cast, Irene had to explain that she had climbed the structure to dislodge a ball caught in the netting, and lost her balance when she jarred the ball loose.

A favourite place was her aunt (actually, great-aunt) Mary's candy store on May Street, around the corner from the 'funny little' place, not much more than a converted garage, where the family stayed during their winter sojourns. Irene and Joan would visit the store after school and invariably be spoiled. It was a child's dream that turned into the fondest of memories—Irene always maintained that every child should have an aunt with a candy store!

However, home life was not always so easy or pleasant when her parents were together. As the children grew, relations between their mother and father became more and more difficult and finally, in 1932, confronted with the collapse of the economy and spurred on by his sharp-tongued wife, Arthur decided enough was enough. He returned to Leeds alone on the *Athenia*,[2] arriving back in Liverpool in November of that year and leaving Jean in Regina with two children and no financial support. Irene didn't remember any family discussion of the matter and her father never spoke to her about leaving. She didn't even remember him saying goodbye.

Whatever her own contribution to Arthur's decision, it must have been an especially rough time for Jean to be left with no regular income and two young teenagers, one of them ill with an untreatable condition. The medical establishment considered Gordon's disorder to be linked to his situation in Regina and the doctors felt he would be far better off in the English climate. Whether this diagnosis was really based on physical or mental considerations was irrelevant given the circumstances. About a year after his father's departure, Gordon left for England, under doctors' orders, to join him. He travelled with his Uncle Walter, Aunt Olive and nine-year-old cousin, Charles. The Lockwood family business seems to have been running out of steam by then, and in the space of a couple of years three of the four brothers were to make their way back to England.

Gordon's departure left his mother and sister alone, both missing him terribly but still desperate for money on which to live. Even with one less mouth to feed and child to clothe, it was a situation that could not last for a parent with no income. Irene and her mother were dependent for food on the family farm in Cardross. No help was forthcoming from the remaining Lockwood brothers, and Irene recalled having no money at all and having to 'scrounge for everything.'

There was repeated correspondence between legal representatives that began shortly after Arthur's departure, including an April 1934 letter from Arthur's solicitors saying that he was prepared to put his family up and support them as best he could, but warning that his income was 'meagre'— after all, Britain and Europe were suffering the same difficult economic circumstances as North America. Still, there was no way out for Jean and a year after Gordon's departure, to Irene's utter dismay, the mother took her fourteen-year-old daughter away from her friends and out of the school she loved and followed her delinquent husband to Leeds. After selling the furniture and settling outstanding debts, late that summer of 1934 the two travelled across the country by train, with barely enough money in hand to pay for passage on the *Duchess of Bedford*, steaming from Montreal.

These most arduous of circumstances notwithstanding, the distracting afflictions of youth were not to be denied Irene. An otherwise difficult situation turned out not to be a complete disaster for the young woman. Irene met and was temporarily smitten with a young fellow on the boat—ironically, a German lad. In light of the next few years of European history, she always wondered what happened to him.

The two women disembarked in Liverpool to a new life on August 17, 1934. They went directly from the boat and boarded a train to Leeds, followed by a taxi ride to Arthur's home, where he and Gordon were rooming with an older couple. Irene was overjoyed to be with her brother again. Before ever seeing him, she discovered to her delight that he had already picked up something of a British accent. When she and her mother arrived at the house, she called for Gordon and he replied from upstairs, 'I'm in my baaaath,' sending Irene into hysterical laughter. Her giggled reply, 'What's your baaaath?' became a favourite exchange between the two of them.

The reunion of their mother and father, on the other hand, was not a happy one. Although their respective lawyers had communicated about travel plans prior to Jean and Irene's departure, Arthur had developed cold feet at the last minute and instructed Jean not to come to England. But by then it was too late; all their possessions had been sold and Jean was determined to see things through. She later recorded that Arthur 'was most hostile and aggressive and told us to "get the hell out of it and work for a living." We left and Gordon insisted upon coming with us and we found some furnished rooms.'

Given the rancorous situation, there clearly was no possibility of reconciliation between the parents. Jean and her children settled eventually in a small, cold row house arranged for them by Arthur, who then charged them rent. It was a thoroughly uncomfortable and unhappy place in Irene's recollection, 'a hovel,' with shared outdoor toilet facilities at the end of the block. Arthur's spinster sister was Aunt Grace, an ironic name given the fervour with which she later took on her role—whether self-appointed or instigated by Arthur—of protector of the delinquent father. She insulated him from his family, keeping Irene and her mother at a distance and treating them very badly.

Jean described their circumstances thus in a letter to the British courts: 'My daughter was only fourteen, I had no occupation, very little money and we had a very, very difficult time with hardly anything to eat.' As the school year started, the teenage Irene was given the choice of going to school or looking for employment. The young woman recognized the straits the family were in. Seeing little income beyond the occasional small payment from Arthur and once again a family of three to feed, Irene didn't hesitate to pitch in. Not long after arriving in England, she went with her mother to Lewis's department store to apply for a job. She was under age but the family needed the money and the manager, a man by the name of Mr Breen, who Irene remembered with great fondness, agreed to hire her. He understood the family's state of affairs and simply said, 'Bring her in tomorrow.' Irene recalled that Breen had a lovely wife and twin boys. He was, in her assessment, a 'good man'—a meaningful appellation from the young and naïve girl who was trying to get into the workforce.

Mollie Ward was the manager of the cosmetics department where Irene, by then a very attractive young woman, was put to work demonstrating for Harriet Hubbard Ayer's line of cosmetics. Mollie was equally helpful and constantly supportive, despite Irene's recollection of being inveterately clumsy and often breaking things. The novice to the workforce met some 'wonderful people,' whose encouragement made all the difference in building her own confidence and knowledge at a very uncertain age, and in difficult circumstances.

With this kind of support, and no doubt helped by her dark-haired beauty, Irene did well, enjoying her first full-time work. The family of three slipped into the routines of their new existence, punctuated by the occasional exciting event. One of Irene's sharpest memories of her time in Leeds was the 1936 abdication from the throne by Edward VIII, who had been advised that he could not marry the American divorcee Wallis Simpson and still remain king. It was a time of 'terrible uncertainty' about the future of the country, according to Irene, who clearly had been drawn quickly into the daily dramas of life in Britain . . . but without having adopted the speech mannerisms her brother had found so easy to assimilate!

Another memory, a much sadder and more personal one, was the loss of her beloved Gordon in 1937, at the age of twenty. He went into hospital for what was to be a minor operation, a tonsillectomy, but something 'went wrong'—it was never defined—and Gordon died during what should have been a routine procedure. It is too easy in hindsight to speculate about the many and unhappy possibilities that could have attended the death. It was never fully explained to the family by the medical profession. Whatever the cause, the tragedy left the family in great shock and Irene terribly upset at the loss of her brother.

The funeral was a dark affair. The coffin, brought to the council flat shared by the two women, took up nearly the whole of the tiny living room of the row house. There was little support for the bereaved women, but a close friend of the Mitchell family, lovingly referred to as Auntie Nan, came from Glasgow to support them through their grief. She was wonderful, Irene said, providing flowers and even some 'comic relief' to get them back on their feet.

After focusing so much of her life on the treatment of her son's disease, it must have been a huge blow to Jean, as well as to her grieving daughter. In its own way, the loss probably brought the two women far closer together than they had been until then. Now they had only each other, no friends in what was still a new place for them, and had to face all the challenges of everyday existence with few resources of their own.

Irene made a good impression on her employers as she gained experience at Lewis's. About a year after Gordon's death, Mr Breen came in and said, 'There's an opening down in London with Harriet Hubbard Ayer, at Harrods.' It was a dream job, one that offered a great increase in salary and that would take her out of her unpleasant surroundings. Still, the young woman was filled with uncertainty at the prospect of leaving her mother alone in Leeds. She didn't tell her mother about the opportunity and instead thought about it overnight. When she came in the next day, Irene was prepared to turn the offer down. But when the manager encouraged her to go, she changed her mind and agreed. So at the age of eighteen, with some understandable reluctance on the part of her mother but no further hesitation of her own, Irene packed up her possessions and prepared for her first move away from home.

The story of the train trip south from Leeds was the stuff of family legend. Her mother, Jean, and Great-aunt Mary (of the childhood candy shop), who was visiting from Canada and staying with them for a short while, accompanied Irene to the train station and boarded the train (as was common in those days) to help her get settled. They were sitting in a four-person compartment when an older gentleman stuck his head in and asked whether he could occupy the fourth seat. Irene looked at her mother and great-aunt, who agreed. Irene sat on one side, Jean and Mary on the other, and their new friend, who welcomed the chance to chat, took the remaining seat in the corner. Their gentleman friend offered to buy them all a drink and they were happily sitting, chatting and sipping . . . when without warning, the train began to move away from the station.

The conductor came by and Jean stopped him, explained the situation and pronounced, 'We have to get off the train.'

He replied, 'You can't. This is the express to London.'

'But you have to stop at the next station so I can get back to Leeds. I've got a kettle on, and I live there!'

The conductor said simply, 'You'll have to cope with that when we get to London,' and continued on down the passage.

Despite (or perhaps because of) the circumstances, Irene remembered, their elderly male companion was 'priceless.' He kept up a stream of jolly conversation throughout the journey of about five hours, plying them with tea the entire way. But Jean was worried; she simply didn't have the resources to pay for a trip to London and back. So when they arrived in the capital, they went to the station manager's office to explain the situation. Jean, adopting an appropriately severe manner no doubt rooted in her Scottish Presbyterian heritage, delivered a memorable lambasting about letting people know what to expect, and giving them decent warning like they did in Canada where the conductor shouted 'All aboard!' to be sure that everyone knew the train was leaving. That tirade clearly burned in the ears of its unfortunate recipient. He was furious, but the application of Aunt Mary's diplomatic skills successfully defused the situation. Jean agreed to leave her name and address and said she would write to British Rail. She did just this, and provided their ever-helpful elderly companion's particulars as a witness that no warning had been given on departure from Leeds station. He indeed confirmed that there had been no 'All aboard!' call.

Jean and Aunt Mary got back on the same train, the same day, for the return trip. They were never charged for their journey. Not only that, but in her promised letter, Jean demanded—and got—a written apology from British Rail for the railway's failure to adequately caution them regarding the train's departure from Leeds!

In London and on her own for the first time, Irene was temporarily put up by the company while she looked around for somewhere suitable to live. She finally settled into accommodation shared with Jay Jacobs, another girl working at Harrods and who was judged by the store owners to be a suitable roommate. The two women got along well but, to put it delicately, Jay seems to have had a somewhat more worldly outlook than the young, naïve and easily disconcerted prairie girl from Leeds. Jay spent a great deal of time entertaining gentleman callers—always away from the flat, but with some regularity. Irene never figured out whether Jay was what might have been termed, in the vernacular of the day, an 'actress,' or 'just generous,' as Irene later put it in a wonderfully roundabout way. In any event, after about a year Irene finally determined to take her slightly bruised Scottish conservative sensibilities to rooms of her own. It was an opportune decision, for

Jean was ready to leave Leeds and the unhappiness it represented. Mother and daughter took a flat together, in Clapham Common, and once again Irene settled into the more or less regular life of a working woman living 'at home.'

However, the one thing she took with her from her life with Jay was her relationship with 'Chili' Chilcott. He was South African born, raised in Argentina and had been sent along with his sister Dora to England for finishing school. In addition to absorbing British manners, he seems to have been something of a rake. A charming and handsome member of Jay Jackson's circle, he occasionally came to visit and began to spend time chatting with the new girl. Irene admitted to having fallen in love for the first time. 'Oh, I loved him so much, and his family, especially his sister Dora, were wonderful to me.'

When she moved to London, Jean secured work as a dentist's assistant—finally with a small income of her own—but had to spend all her holidays travelling to and from Leeds, unsuccessfully issuing summonses for maintenance arrears. It was an unfortunate, nasty situation of family break-up—Jean refusing to divorce Arthur until he provided some guarantee of support to her and her daughter, and he refusing to acknowledge repeated court orders and judgments calling on him for support, even to the point of spending a brief period in jail. The result was the worst kind of anger and bitterness for the whole family, including Irene. When she learned years after the fact that Arthur had been killed in 1961 in a motor vehicle accident in Leeds—hit by a truck, apparently—Irene admitted she genuinely felt nothing . . . which, of course, led to twinges of guilt.

The solicitors informed Jean that Arthur had taken her out of his will, leaving his small estate in its entirety to his nephew. It seems most of his assets had already been transferred to Aunt Grace, probably to remove them from the view of the courts and to keep them out of Jean's hands. Finally, after much further correspondence between solicitors and across the Atlantic, Jean received a cheque for £300. It was the end of a sad chapter for the family, but at least it allowed them to move on with their own lives. But all this was to be in the future.

In the meantime, life in London was good. Irene loved Harrods and the work she was doing, had a boyfriend she adored and an active social life—what could be better? But life's small realities are not always in tune with the larger ones, and the gathering tide of European history would soon change the personal stories of Irene . . . and some 46 million other souls in Britain, and many more across the continent, as the summer of 1939 drew to a close.

PART TWO

PREPARATIONS
AND PARTIES

3

DE HAVILLAND SCHOOL OF FLYING:
THE ADVENTURE BEGINS

T he late summer of 1939 brought a whole new world to Skeets. After arriving in England, his orders took him to the De Havilland School of Flying in Hatfield, just north of London. He was determined to get the most out of this new episode in his life, and for reasons known only to him, decided to keep a diary of his time there. This document, and a similar one he kept to record his combat exploits, are the heart of the account that follows. They clearly reflect the joy and (sometimes) nervousness of being away from home, with a committed and energetic group of peers, enjoying the incomparable experience of learning to fly. And of course, the challenges of being back at school.

The cover of his diary reads:

A. Keith Ogilvie, Aug. 14/39
Hatfield, Hertfordshire
De Havilland School of Flying

Please send to:
C.E. Ogilvie
43 Patterson Ave.
Ottawa, Ont.
Canada

The forwarding address was always included in an obvious place, just in case. The entries begin, literally, right off the boat:

Aug 14, 1939

Arrived at Hatfield after one of the damnedest train trips I've ever encountered. From Liverpool, around 200 miles, we changed trains 5 times, one two hour jaunt in close contact with a hamper of fish. Quarters are quite good, I room with Bigelow, Dewar and Lambert along the idea of a fraternity. Today, Monday, was a perfect day.

The home—Longfield House—is about a hundred yards from the 'drome. This is a huge affair, hundreds of planes milling all over the place. This morning we were issued flying suits, helmets, parachutes, gas masks and odds and ends. Had a flip up this afternoon for thirty odd minutes[3] and flew vaguely in the direction of London. My instructor is P/O Reynolds, and seems to be a very nice chap not given overly much to talking, but means what he says. Spent most of the night getting unpacked and organized. Meant to go to bed early but I can see where our room is going to be a general hangout. The house contains eighteen chaps, many of whom are Canadian. Rather early to speculate but they all seem to be quite decent birds. We arise at 7 a.m. in the morning for P.T. [physical training] so it would seem a bright idea to turn in.

Cheerio.

Tuesday, Aug 15, 1939

Seven o'clock came damn early and P.T. at 7:30 was no fun. I can see where the pilots are going to be kept in good shape. We Canucks form the 'Dawn Patrol' and I was first up. Had two thirty-five minute hops this morning and had straight and level flying, along with climbing and gliding. A good day for flying, rather smoky horizon. Had lectures all afternoon and I can see where this ground work is going to be plenty tough. Have to learn the Morse Code for next Monday, shouldn't be too tough. We went for a swim, we have our own pool, pool tables, ping-pong, tennis, squash courts, damn near everything. Got a damn nice letter from Carm today which gave me my first touch of home sickness. Went to a hop at the De Havilland Hall which was a bit of a fizzle. Weirdest dancing I've seen in years—not worth a copper. Popped across the street to a pub, 'The Stone Hall,' and had a couple of modest beers though it could quite easily have blossomed into a jam session. We have to be in at 10:30 which is a dampener. Pubs blossom here at quite regular intervals and they are all very smart. We were all late, especially Biggy [Bigelow], but nothing came of it.

Wednesday, Aug 16, 1939

Our room was late for P.T. this morning and brought forth a gentle reminder from the instructor. We had lectures all morning and boy, I haven't written as much in years. Only had one forty minute flight this p.m. due to a smoky horizon. Did straight and level flying, a few stalls and gliding. Shot a game of billiards before tea which is at seven. Wandered down to Dormi House and saw my first television set. It was damned interesting, and we were all very much intrigued. Met a few Voluntary Reservists (VRs) and wandered farther afield to a swanky joint known as the 'Comet.'[4] I can't get over the number of pubs around here and they are all so smart. Haven't run across any of the fair sex as yet but I gather from the general tone of talk that the moral scale here is a few notches lower than our own. Some of the fellows are damn fine, others are drips, mostly fine chaps tho. We are in the 'Dawn Patrol' again tomorrow and it is damn near midnight so cheers.

Thursday, Aug 17, 1939

This early morning rising is not the wrench that it used to be but is nonetheless a tough struggle. The perfect weather still holds and this I gather is phenomenal—four good days in a row. Had two good flights this morning, 40–45 minutes. Handled the controls more than I have yet and tried a couple of takeoffs and horrible landings. Had lectures on machine-gunning this p.m. and it was a tough struggle to stay awake. Flying in the morning makes you horribly sleepy. Some classroom with the bombers and all sorts of craft droning by the window. The flying goes on from dawn 'til dusk and night flying later. We have had a few pep talks on discipline today and things are getting tougher. Got a welcome card from Hurdy[5] today—gawd, he seems far away just now.

We wandered down to Stone House for a couple of quick ones and then retired at a modest hour.

Friday, Aug 18, 1939
The good weather still holds good. Really remarkable. I attended lectures this morning for a while and then I had a spell in the Link Trainer, a really remarkable machine on the ground which does everything a machine does. It is especially adapted for blind flying. Invented by a Canadian and made in Gananoque, incidentally. Had a forty-five minute flight this morning and made a horrible hash of everything.

Had moving pictures of care of an aircraft after dinner and had a devil of a job keeping my eyes open. This was a common fault and can be blamed on flying. Had another forty-five minute flip this PM and things went a bit better, but were still no hell. This brings my time up to 5 hours 15 min. now. Should be getting somewhere soon. Drew my first pay and find that I have around $3.00 to run next week on—every time you turn around it costs money here. Had a swim with Eric after work (?)[6] and we wandered down to the London Aero Plane Club dance. It was too late to go in so we returned home early after visiting the Stone House for a couple. Got two nice letters from Muriel and one from Aunt Marg. I wrote one to the Manchester menace and hit the hay early.

Saturday, Aug 19, 1939
Usual PT at 7:30, played with a medicine ball for a change. Lectures this morning were on the 'Care and Feeding of an Aero Plane'— get the spelling of aeroplane—we were informed, nicely of course, that we Canadians would have to learn to speak English if we were to get anywhere on the exams. Was reprimanded by Reynolds my instructor for not shaving—quite an oversight but nonetheless an unforgivable sin. Knocked off at one today, and spent a quiet afternoon lying around the swimming pool. Tonight a few of us wandered afield to St. Albans, about 4 miles from here, in search of something to do. Certainly did not find it and sat in a beer garden downing a few. This has been a cruel disappointment, this beer

situation—it is miserable stuff unless one drinks imported Pilsner, which runs into dough. Alan, Jimmy Beasely and I sat around here until turned out at the ungodly hour of ten. The whole country folds up around this hour as far as I can make out. We were home and in bed at eleven on a Saturday night. Could I stood [*sic*] it? Ricky and George got led astray by the two 'Bobs' and spent a miserable evening romping around the countryside. Got a letter from Fred Smith today.

Sunday, Aug 20, 1939
Sunday it is, and a brief respite from P.T. Just lazed around all day and accomplished nothing. This afternoon I wandered over to the pool and splashed around for a time. Met a couple of gals there who were no hell and saw a gorgeous vision in a white satin bathing suit. Oh me! This evening was spent in a quiet bit of messing around. Went over to the Comet, thence to the Stone House, taking in the Old Fiddle on the way. Got nowhere rapidly and as it is now midnight, I'll finish wasting the day by turning in.

Monday, Aug 21, 1939
No P.T. this morning so we slept in til 8:15, then had to rush like hang. Lectures this morning on machine gunning and wireless. Had two thirty minute flights this afternoon. Did a few landings and takeoffs which were miserable. Can get the feel of level flying o.k. but the rest comes a bit hard. We just got in ahead of a big thunderstorm—the first bad break that we have had in the weather so far. It cleared up after tea however. The weather changes very quickly here and you can get caught napping quite easily. Got a nice letter from Mary Martin, a very pretty Scotch girl I met on the *Letitia*. Wrote her a reply, also one to Muriel. I have so damn much writing to do I can't get organized. The weather cleared up nicely after tea so a bunch of us wandered down to the London Aero Plane Club for a couple of quick ones. They close the pubs so darn early here—10 o'clock to be exact—one can get nowhere quickly. We had a bit of fun kidding a couple of the English lads along. They seem to think that in Canada we are waging a con-

stant battle against bandits and redskins—maybe they are right. We were home early and in bed before midnight.

Tuesday, Aug 22, 1939

Back into the groove with the usual P.T. this morning. The exercises are really very soft and it is all a valuable waste of time. The weather was a bit mucky this a.m. so we all had a go at the Morse Code again. Later on, Lovelock, our lecturer, sprung a bit of a quiz on us and rather caught the boys napping, including yours truly. It cleared up this afternoon but our flight was out-stick handled and got more lectures—what a job to stay awake, it was cruel. Eric and I went to a barber's. He missed his calling, he should have been a blacksmith, or maybe he was. I look as though I have been hit by lightning. Had a dip in the pool before tea at 7 p.m. After tea the urge for studying was lacking so one sallied forth lightly touching at the 'Comet' and the Stone House. Met Bob Ullmar's guardian—a girl of 29 and very nice too—had a short jaunt in a Mercedes. Came in on time, 10:30, and listened to a few fair bands.

Had a bit of scragging around and a few beds were dismantled in the process—no bones were broken, however, so everyone was happy save George, whose bed was demolished by 'Jumbo'[7] and Bob. Lights out around twelve, I hope.

Wednesday, Aug 23, 1939

Another perfect day. Everyone is afraid to breathe for fear the spell will break and the rains will come. We had lectures all morning and for a change they went quite well with me—I stayed awake nearly the whole time. After lunch, I had two flights, one for 25 the other for 45 minutes. Did some spins—they were fun—and then back to the only landing and taking off business. They were only fair and I'm sure my landings were horrible. It is getting vaguely near solo time, but I've a lot to learn. We got issued with light-weight overalls for flying tonight, and they are fine. The others are too heavy for this weather. Went for a plunge after flying and at night Eric and I went for a walk and stopped only for one quick one at the Stone House. We were home very early—10 o'clock.

Got a nice letter from Muriel today, sixteen pages.

I'm trying to get up enough energy to write Hurdy, now. I'm so darn weary. Guess I'll start it now. All sorts of rumours coming through here now on possibilities of an air raid—home was never like this.

Thursday, Aug 24, 1939

Much the same routine today. Due to unsatisfactory weather, there was no flying. Have had only one flight this week so far. Everything is creeping into a war situation again. We had extensive drill in the use of gas masks in one lecture. Everyone is quite calm but the signs all seem to point to a flare up at a short notice. We would be for it here because of the De Havilland factory near by.

Eric and I did a bit of a pub crawl tonight but once again the early closing hour nipped things in the bud. Had a round of bridge as a night cap.

Friday, Aug 25, 1939

Another murky day, with lectures all morning. Later on, however, we were called out to fly in semi-rainy weather. This is the first time we have flown in poor weather—a rather ominous sign, I should think. My instructor was called back into the RAF today and I got a new instructor whom I like much better, although my flying wasn't any better. Just did a few circuits—I have eight hours now, and I should be learning something. We were given cards for our dugout in case of a bomb raid and anti-aircraft guns are being placed around the field. Very cheerful thought this—I suppose the next few days will tell the tale. None of the boys are particularly worried, just don't seem to give a damn. Wandered up to the 'Comet' and got a bit involved with some of the army boys who are camped near the aerodrome. They are certainly a mad crew, and we all wandered home feeling fairly happy about the whole thing. Drew another week's stipend today, I certainly won't get into much trouble on my weekly allowance here. Got a letter from Hurdy and I sent him one.

Saturday, Aug 26, 1939

A grand morning today and 'A' flight—ours—was first up. I had another new instructor today, a very decent chap, Hawes by name. Reminds me of the Massena Menace.[8] I wonder what Betty is doing now. Later on in the morning I had a go on the Link Trainer and didn't do so well—more lectures on navigation, a rather full morning.

Had an extremely lazy afternoon. Eric, Biggy and Bob Williams and I lazed around the swimming pool for utter lack of anything else to do. Started from the London Aero Plane Club and had a couple of rum swizzles. From there we sallied forth to Hatfield where a 'swingeroo' was in progress. It was some party. The dancing was weird, the music terrible, and the girls down there really make me long for the old home crowd. They were definitely on a lower scale. Anyway, we all had an edge on and it helped to pass another Saturday night. By and by a party should be sneaking up on us.

Sunday, Aug 27, 1939
A day of rest and not a day too soon.

After diarising a rather dissolute day of swimming and playing squash, Skeets returned briefly to the important matter at hand, and the reason why he was there, for the time being at least enjoying both his days and his evenings. The newspapers had been full of headlines about Germany's expansionist activities. The Nazi–Soviet non-aggression pact had been signed a few days before and there were clashes reported between German and Polish troops along the Polish border. His premonition, duly recorded, would soon turn out to be disturbingly accurate.

The war situation continues to look plenty dark. Next few days should tell the tale.

Monday, Aug 28, 1939
A welcome rest from P.T. this morning. Had another new instructor this morning. This makes four, it's getting to be a habit. I made some horrible landings although I think I'm getting close to the solo stage. Eric soloed today and made a good job of it.

Went over to the pool after work. Stayed in tonight for the first time and got some Morse Code with the aid of Doug Smith. Wrote a letter and sent a few pictures home. All in all, it was merely a routine day.

Tuesday, Aug 29, 1939

A usual day from P.T. to afternoon flying which I made a mess of. Seemed to do everything wrong today. Only had twenty-five minutes today with Berg, a new instructor, rather young and nervous. Played a couple of sets of tennis with George L. and then swam. Stayed around the house all night tonight and accomplished nothing, in fact it ended up in a gin party in our room. Got a letter from [older brother] Emer and sent one home, along with some photographs.

Wednesday, Aug 30, 1939

Today's routine grind was broken by two momentous events, two veritable milestones in my career. With utter disregard to the importance of their appearance, I'll put them down briefly as:

The appearance of a vague line of down on the upper lip. This is a mere whim on the part of Ricky and I, in fact of the majority of boys in the house. Time will tell.

My first solo came as a great surprise in view of my lousy landings of late. Whereas it wasn't good, it wasn't bad. The thrill was unlike any other I have ever experienced. On the first circuit I bounced her and scurried across the 'drome like a startled deer. The second landing was no hell but at least I got it down. Today I am a pilot.

Wandered over to the Aero Plane Club for want of anything else to do and saw a lovely girl—for a change. Something must be done about that. Her name is Peggy Hellman. Wrote a letter to Muriel and am about to hit the hay at the ridiculous hour of eleven—despite the appearance of Jumbo, our 6'4" of English manhood.

Thursday, August 31, 1939

Eat, sleep, fly, lectures and repeat. The same old routine goes on. War seems quite near now. Preparations around here are quite extensive. They have overlooked nothing. The planes and the aerodrome have effectively been camouflaged, search lights and anti-aircraft all over the place. Stepped into a bit of a jam session over at the Comet tonight. My instructor was there—he is a swell chap, quite young and a thorough good head. 'Kid' Berg we call him. I got in under the wire—some of the lads were late and came in by way of a window.

Friday, Sept 1, 1939

Today's grind was broken by quite a bit of flying, 2 hours 10 minutes, of which half was solo. We are bound to get in a good deal of flying now. Britain just handed her ultimatum to Germany and it is certain to be refused. There can't be any doubt but what we are for it now. At least I'm damn glad that I'm not at home. I'll be doing the job here that I'd want to do, at any rate.

Tonight the whole country was 'blacked out' in more ways than one. The boys gathered around the old Stone House and the beer just simply gushed. No late passes were allowed tonight but everyone just straggled in at all hours anyway—no one gave a damn. Some of the boys did pretty fair jobs on themselves. Friend Bigelow, in our room, did a lovely job on himself. Who, me? Well, not badly—I wasn't feeling any agony. After all, war isn't declared every day in the week. The fat seems to be in the fire for fair now. A few days will tell the tale.

Saturday, Sept 2, 1939

Got my old instructor F/O Reynolds back today, and that means I'll have to be on my toes. He is damn good, tho,' and will no doubt make a flyer of me. Had only one 25 minute flight this morning as we were hampered by lack of planes—they are all being camouflaged, in preparation. As a matter of fact, everything around here is being camouflaged. Spent a quiet afternoon around the pool. After tea we wandered over to the 'Comet.' There we met one Mrs. De Havilland and her sister Miss Alexander, who later on became Gwen and 'Ga Ga,' respectively. She invited us out to her cottage for a bit of A.R.P. [Air Raid Precautions] work. George, Eric and I toddled along and we had quite a party. Drank a few spots and danced around the place, lots of fun in all. There may be more heard from this direction—I hope so.

4

WITH SERIOUS INTENT

The new routine of classroom lectures punctuated by the thrill of being in a cockpit and followed by exploration of the local night life was not to last. Just three weeks after his arrival in England the young Canadian and his fellow adventurers were abruptly reminded of why they had come. Underlying Skeets's somewhat laconic record of the news must have been the first feelings of trepidation, anticipation and probably some frustration at how far he still had to go to make his own contribution to determining the course of history.

Sept 3, 1939
Today is the day. While sitting around in our negligees at 11 a.m., we heard Mr. Chamberlain quietly yet dramatically announce that Great Britain was at war with Germany. This looks like the beginning of the 'Great Adventure.' A few minutes later I saw a Fairey Battle bomber come in for a landing with his wheels up. No one hurt, but it rather messed up the plane.

At 11:30 there was a general air-raid signal given and we sat around in the shelter for forty minutes until it was proven to be a false alarm. Almost too much, all this coming at once.

Settled down later on and wrote a letter home, and one to Marj.[9] Wandered up to the Comet as usual, and consumed copious draughts with Jumbo—thence to bed around midnight. Everything is blacked out here, of course, and all our windows are covered with tar paper-like material. Such a country.

Irene was caught up in the drama of that day as well. She too remembered everyone listening to Chamberlain's broadcast on the radio, and recalled that one of the first things that happened after the shocking news of a formal declaration of war was the sounding of air-raid sirens. She had two experiences with air-raid shelters during the war that made her resolve never to go into one again. They were not places for someone who suffered from claustrophobia. Speaking of this incident, she later said, 'We went down to the shelter once and nearly threw up and turned around and came back up. We never went down again, so we never did get to know the neighbours.' Why nearly threw up?

> Oh, it was just awful. Same as when the war first started, on September 3rd, Mother and I were living in a place on Clapham Common . . . Mother had been told to go into the church across the street, should there be an air raid warning. So we went into the church across the street and there was screaming, babies crying, women fainting and really scared people, who were scaring everybody else. I just said to Mom, 'Sorry, I can't stay here, I've got to go,' so I went back into the house . . . and never went into another air raid shelter until we got to Chalmers Place and we had been asked by other people to go into the shelter. It was so horrible, so we came right out . . . for the same reasons, and it smelled . . . it was pretty scary [outside the shelter]. We lost all our windows.

For Skeets, it was a different focus from the fears of the civilian population, for whom destiny was moving beyond their own control, and who would become the passive recipients of so much of the pain of war. He reverted to the long routine of learning how to fly, punctuated by the inevitable incidents among his classmates, parties and letters from home.

Monday, Sept 4, 1939
Grr! At 3:30 last night we were awakened by the air-raid signals and staggered away up to our trench cursing 'Jerry' every step of the way. It was again a false alarm . . . this is too much. Jerry opened up things, however, by sinking a passenger ship, the *Athenia*, sister ship to the *Letitia*, the one we came over on. A dirty piece of work in all. British bombers bombed Berlin . . . with pamphlets, and lost a plane doing it. Actually things haven't started to move as yet.

Here, we carry on as usual. I had four flights today, two solo, and am starting to feel like a flyer now. The lectures this p.m. were killing—it was agony to stay awake. Had a plunge in the pool and met Gwen De Havilland there. Over to the Comet with Eric and Jim Beasely for a couple, and now at 10:15 I'm washing out. If Jerry comes tonight, I'll resent it!

Tuesday, Sept 5, 1939

Rather a busy morning at lectures today, right up until one o'clock, and nearly two hours flying this p.m. Time is up to nearly 20 hours now, with only 3 solo, however. Today was a bad day all in all. Palmer piled a ship into a fence taxying and hard luck Knifton made a bad landing, ending up on his back. He wasn't hurt himself, but he certainly messed the plane up. The cross country hops all went astray. It was definitely a poor day all in all. I had instructions in low flying and also how not to low fly. It was great sport hopping a very few feet over the hedges and stuff. I'm about to break all rules by staying in tonight. I ate too much for tea this evening and have felt waterlogged ever since. The war news is at nil—no one seems to have done anything, as yet. I think I'll write Muriel and then hit the hay.

Wednesday, Sept 6, 1939

Spent a tough morning sitting on the bench waiting for a flight. Actually got half an hour in eventually. Sat through hours of lectures and had to undo their evil effects by rushing over to the Aero Plane Club and wrapping myself around a few. Old Lovelock burst a bombshell by informing us that we will have our A Licence test tomorrow. Speaking of bombshells, we were hauled out of bed and spent an hour or so in that cursed bomb shelter again this morning. Once again, it was a false alarm, although actually enemy aircraft did approach the coast but turned back. Six Blenheims landed on our field and made a very pretty picture when they left again. They were all loaded for bear, all right. After tea, Biggy and I wandered over to the lecture room and absorbed a spot of knowledge. Later on we wandered over to the Comet and once again absorbed a spot or so. Another day has gone by the books.

Thursday, Sept 7, 1939

Lectures all morning, and quite a spot of solo this afternoon. My time is up over five hours now and I should be getting a test for this time. I was slightly reprimanded by my instructor—who incidentally is a new one, Dufort—for taxying across the aerodrome instead of around it. Practised steep banks, which are a lot of fun. Wrote that exam and found it quite easy. Got a letter from Carmel today, and one from Marg H. Actually, I had a letter to her in my pocket which I promptly mailed. It is now shortly after nine and the four of us are all in for a change. There isn't actually much to do tonight. These exams next week loom up rather formidably. However, there is still a spot of time. This is the quietest damn war I've ever been in. Things are quite slow to get going but one of these days, things are certainly going to pop. Oh well, we have nearly a year before we will be in it. A heartening thought, that . . . and so to bed.

Friday, Sept 8, 1939

Time marches on. Reynolds, my instructor, went away on a cross country flight with Ernie P. so I had a plane all to myself this p.m. and had a grand time just messing about. Old Ricky lost the aerodrome and finally ended up in a field near Whitering [*sic*], some 65 miles from here. He made a good landing all right, and is going to stay there overnight. The festive spirit was strong upon the boys tonight so we wended our way up to the Comet and all drank a bit more than usual. I wasn't feeling any agony by the time we arrived back here.

The declaration of war stirred something patriotic in Irene as well. She resolved to make her own contribution and gave her notice to her employer. She received a lovely and very complimentary letter from her regretful employers:

Harriet Hubbard Ayer Ltd
130 Regent St., London W.1.

8 Sept 39
To Whom It May Concern
Miss Irene Lockwood has been in our employment as Permanent Demonstrator from the period commencing March 1937. Miss Lockwood has at all times proved a most conscientious and active

worker. Not only does she take a keen interest in her work, but her sales ability cannot be improved upon, having a quiet and charming disposition she has been able at all times to make friends with her fellow workers in the stores and thus gain their support. We cannot too highly recommend her for work of a similar character, and wish her every success for the future.

But it was not to be work of a 'similar character' that defined Irene's new direction in life. Instead, she joined the Postal and Censorship Branch of the newly established Ministry of Information[10], with responsibilities for reviewing and censoring letters. This would be her contribution to the war effort for the next four years.

Meanwhile, Skeets was continuing his diary entries:

Saturday, Sept 9, 1939
Lectures part time this a.m., then I had one short flight with Forbes, then we had to 'wash out.' We got a bit of a pep talk on the lighting system at the house and were also informed that we are now Acting Pilot Officers in the RAF Reserves. Exactly what it means, I don't know, but it ensures that we will all get our training before we are piled in. It also means that we will be in uniform before too long. Had rather bad news in the form that Nifty is going to get the air. It seems that poor old 'Hard Luck' just won't ever be a flier. That cuts our 'Legion' down to seven. Ricky wandered in in time for lunch and took a good natured razzing from the gang. He had a good time, however.

Lay around the pool all afternoon, as I didn't have much energy. Tonight we wandered a bit afield and took in the 'Comet,' the Cherry Tree, and finally the Bull, the last being quite a dump. We drove in blackness nearly all the time. The blackout is nothing if not complete here. Got home in one piece and retired in good order.

Sunday, Sept 10, 1939
Spent an entirely lazy morning doing nothing more than actually getting up, having breakfast and then retiring in good order. As a matter of fact, there have been mornings when I have felt better. However, something in the climate here seems to do away with a

hangover. Spent an afternoon of penance by playing a few games of squash with Eric, wherein he mopped the court with me. Topped this athletic achievement off by diving into the pool a few times. So far, so good, but as the evening wore on, our steps once more strayed 'Comet'-ward and I rather went on the beer wagon again. Three nights in a row is almost too much, the more so with the mid-term exams looming up. However, next week will be reform week . . . I hope.

The familiar routine of learning and seeking relief from learning starts to seep into the diary. Flying, particularly preparation for combat flying, requires the pilot to have access to an enormous amount of information in order to deal with real or imagined challenges and emergencies of all kinds. This means long hours of repetition, in the cockpit and in the classroom, expanding the envelope so that when something happens, the survival chances for the pilot lie with something other than sheer luck. They were flying six days a week at this point, weather permitting. It didn't always; Skeets noted, 'weather continues somewhat cool and nasty—fine one minute, and raining the next.' In any case, the routines were settling in: flying when they could, studying occasionally (hardly a routine), and spending dissolute evenings, mainly at the 'Comet,' as a counterpoint to the focused activities of the day. But with each day came a bit of progress. In addition to recording the long, repetitive process of learning to be a competent pilot—and those post-curricula elements involving the many pubs around the De Havilland airdrome—Skeets's record from time to time highlights events of special interest.

Wednesday, Sept 13, 1939
Lectures all this morning and two long solos this p.m. Got caught in a rain storm and it was good fun. I had the aerodrome well in sight, so I stayed up for a while and finally came in, making an atrocious landing. It must have been from ten feet, but it was three point so I let it ride. Jim Beasely got lost in the storm and flew around for nearly three hours before coming down in a field. Everyone fully expected to pull him out of a tree or something, and everyone breathed a sigh of relief when he came in, or rather came down, OK. He had to stay

away overnight. We wandered by instinct over to the Comet. Quite a fair party boiled up and we ended up in the kitchen here. There was a bit of ragging later on and a near riot might have developed, but it blew over after a few hot words. One of these days I'm afraid that there will be a bit of trouble here. Maybe not.

Heard a strong rumour today that we are going to Egypt rather than Montrose. It sounds good, but I'll believe it when and if it happens.

Thursday, Sept 14, 1939
Today is a famous day in history, being my twenty-fourth birthday. Had some good flying today. Did my first loop, a couple of spins and side slip landings. It was darn cool up at 3,000' and the clouds were quite low. It is damn baffling flying in them as you haven't any idea what is going on—at least I haven't. We drew up a squash ladder and I won my first match—a rather soft one—against Ernie P., who is even worse than I am. It will be fun later on, as it is a good game. Eric Trouard, an English lad, got lost in a cross country but made a good landing in a field. Darn near got some studying in, but on the news that we would get a respite from exams till next week we (Eric and I) promptly betook ourselves to the 'Comet' where we exchanged uncomplimentary remarks with Gwen the barmaid. Quite a good institution, this idea of barmaids. We left at closing as usual and returned home in good order.

And from time to time, the seemingly light routines were interrupted by a dose of reality.

Monday, Sept 18, 1939
Truly a black day in history. Lovelock up and sprang our exams on us; the result is bound to be a slaughter. Yours truly certainly took a licking. Had my RAF test this p.m. and didn't do too badly, I don't think. Just routine manoeuvres: turns, steep turns and a spin. Went to the local cinema—and I did say cinema—with Eric and Bob M. Pictures were Brother Rat which I had seen and Tail Spin.

Not too bad, and it served to pass the evening . . . almost. There was just time for a night cap, and so to bed.

Tuesday, Sept 19, 1939

Did my first acrobatics today and enjoyed them very well. Had F/O Weighill as instructor and he is one of the best. Did loops, rolls and roll off a loop. Quite an enjoyable flight all in all. At night we got our old bridge foursome working. Biggy and I vs George and Eric, and continued our feud where we left off on the boat. They added a few points to their lead making it 1,550. Jim Beasely got the air today, bringing the total up to three. He is a Canadian but enlisted here. It has been coming to him for a long while but he is a good kid, if rather dumb, and we hate to see him go.

Wednesday, Sept 20, 1939

This was a black day. I couldn't do a thing right. Tried some aerobatics and damn near tore Betsy in half trying a roll and ending up in a power dive at 150, which is too fast for a 'Tiger.'[11] My landings were gawd awful. I had to gun it twice before I could set it down.

Of course Reynolds, my old instructor, had to see it and was slightly caustic. Jack Brockway, a V.R.,[12] piled a ship up quite badly in landing in a gusty wind, but was unhurt. Rumours flying around predict a purge at the end of the week. Spent another evening in, it's getting to be a habit.

Thursday, Sept 21, 1939

Went on a cross country triangle today with Brown, my instructor. It was quite interesting and kept me damn busy trying to watch my instruments, the compass and read my maps at the same time. By the time I'd find a point, it would be gone. However, it all goes under the heading of experience. Went to the 'flicks'—and I do mean movies—with Eric and Bob M. Son of Frankenstein was on picture, nothing better to do than that. Finally broke a three day fast by going over to the Comet and having a night cap. Early to bed again tonight. Incidentally, today was the first day of our P.T. man's holiday, so for two weeks we'll get an extra hour's sleep.

Friday, Sept 22, 1939

Today opened with a grand surprise when I discovered that I had passed all my exams. In fact, I was the only one of the Canucks to get them all. I just got over the line in the whole works so it can well be seen how lousy the marks were. Some ten of the boys, including George, Eric and Biggy are up before Pike[13] tomorrow and no doubt will get the old pep talk. Actually, these exams don't mean much more than an indication as to how much we don't know. The real thing starts two weeks from Monday, so the near future will bring forth some great old brain bending.

Had some instrument flying under the hood and some rolls, but only had half an hour in all. I was to go on the triangle solo, but poor weather fixed that. A very quiet evening tonight, we barely got over to the Comet before it closed. Tomorrow Eric and I are going into London to see Ronnie and her twin sister.[14] Sure hope it works out OK, a bit of action would be in order now.

Saturday, Sept 23, 1939

Visibility was fairly thick this morning but I had a circuit with Hawes and then half an hour solo. Next week I get a new instructor as Brown is going away on leave. Eric and Biggy and I grabbed a rattler into London at 2:20 this p.m. Biggy just came in for something to do. There may be worse trains in the world than the English, but I very much doubt it. We spent most of our time trying to outguess the tunnels. We would plunge into one and just get the windows up in time to get out of the tunnel again. We finally gave up and left them up. As we approached London, I was amazed at the number of balloons in the barrage. They were just like flies—they say that there are 6,000 of them and reaching up to 20,000 feet, making a damn formidable barrier. Finally we arrived in London and spent one hell of a time trying to find Ron.

Contact was established and we had a grand dinner in a somewhat smart flat in Mayfair. Ron's sister is a good egg and we clicked quite easily. She is quite pretty and a barrel of fun. We sat around and had a few drinks until midnight, then decided to go out (and have a few drinks) to a night club. We went to the Embassy and had a super time. It wasn't too expensive—15 shillings a couple 'couvert' charge, and 22/6 for a bottle of Rye. It was quite crowded and the 2' by 4' dance floor was very reminiscent of the Gatineau on a crowded night. When we got there at 12, a band was playing and when we left after four it was still playing. Two bands alternate and consequently the music is continuous. I haven't danced so much in years. Both girls were superb dancers. One band played ordinary dance music and the other was a rhumba orchestra. Eric and I were initiated into the intricacies of the rhumba and had a barrel of fun. It is wonderful rhythm and I nearly wore myself to a frazzle. We left feeling no agony whatsoever, and went back to the flat where we whipped up some bacon and eggs . . . except that there were no eggs. Ricky and I pulled out and got into our room about five. We stayed the night at a small flat—a rooming house Monnie (Ronnie's sister) recommended. All in all, a good start for a weekend.

Sunday, Sept 24, 1939, London
Sunday dawned bright and clear . . . also early. Our landlady came in with breakfast at 9:30. After that and a warm bath, the din in my head abated somewhat. We sallied forth and made a tour of inspection of Hyde Park. Surely there is no other place quite like Hyde Park. Pigeons are there in swarms. There were at least five or six soap-box speakers, some reviling Hitler, some the government, others just spreading the light. There was even a female supporter of the League of Nations. Everyone stands around and listens to their burble and no one gives a damn. Smack in the centre of the park were four very efficient looking anti-aircraft (guns).

Ricky and I had a nice lunch at Lyons on the corner, then tottered over to see the gals. We sat around and then went over to the Empire Cinema where we saw an Andy Hardy picture. Back to the apartment for tea and thence, after a suitable pause, to the Danish restaurant for dinner. A spot of chatter and a final drink and we left quite under control with fond farewells and stuff. We found King's Cross without too much trouble and arrived home around 12:30. All in all, it was a damned fine weekend, by far the best yet in this country. It cost us around 25 dollars each; we gathered that we used ten taxis, and a good time was had by all. This Monnie is a mighty attractive girl—hmmm.

Monday, Sept 25, 1939

Back to the grind again. Had a new instructor today, F/L Wills, a middle aged, quiet spoken chap who seems to be very nice. He does not believe too much in cross country stuff or aerobatics but believes in smooth flying. He also believes in lots of solo, which suits me fine. Finally got around to getting my hair cut; another few days and I would have needed an anaesthetic. Spent a quiet evening around the house tonight and retired at an early hour.

Tuesday, Sept 26, 1939

A perfect morning which we ('A' flight) spent in close contact with Morse Code and Gun, Browning. This p.m. was also fair enough and I managed to get in two hours solo, which brings me past my thirtieth hour. A long letter from home today (by Air) says that everything is under control. Emer's Regiment is still idle and Jim has not yet got in the navy.[15] Another quiet evening spent in barging around the house, and so to bed.

Wednesday, Sept 27, 1939

Today was indeed a red letter day in this boy's calendar. I was up around 4,000 feet doing aerobatics, and gradually lost altitude to 2,000. I pulled old HV[16] into a stall turn and cut the motor too soon, and stopped the prop. The only thing to do was to dive like hell to try and start her, but outside of a protesting whoosh, it wouldn't give. There didn't seem to be much future in this manoeuvre, so I levelled out and started to glide in. The only damn thing in sight was a hay field, so in I went. Betsy hit with a hell of a smack, bounced and took a wheel off on a rut. Things happened fast after that and I ended up hanging by my straps, upside down. Poor old HV was a mess, and I was lucky, not even a scratch. I wandered in the police station and started explaining then, and kept on explaining till dusk. I think I was lucky, but I did make a mess of things after all. I suppose the powers will take a poor view of this business. Oh well, it all goes under the heading of experience . . . yowsah!

An article dated Saturday, November 25, 1939, from the Bristol *Evening World* on 'Teaching the Pilots of Britain's Great Air Armada,' includes some pictures of the training techniques and equipment employed to introduce new pilots to the mysteries of aviation. The article is preserved in Ogilvie's scrapbook. One of the pictures shows Tiger Moth G-ADHT and includes the handwritten notation: 'This is the bus I soloed and later on cracked up. Poor old HT. It was taken quite near our school.' A bit of poetic licence for the folks at home, surely—in fact, according to his flying log book he soloed in ACDG and 'cracked up' ADHV, as recorded in his diary entry.

Thursday, Sept 28, 1939
The sun broke through today (figuratively that is). I was reprimanded gently but firmly and was asked not to throw His Majesty's property around like that. It seems that this sort of thing is tolerated—up to a point. We were issued with heavy equipment —gloves, socks, teddies and the smartest half-Wellingtons, fleece lined. It would seem that we are being prepared for a cold climate such as Montrose in Scotland. The rumour still persists that we might go to Egypt—oh, boy.

Had a good grilling in the air with Wills today, as I expected, then he let me go up for forty-five minutes alone. I'm glad to find that it doesn't bother me at all.

Went to the 'flicks' tonight and saw *The 39 Steps*.

Time marches right along, and there is only a couple of weeks left here. Actually, I'll be glad to get moving into a zone of more action. This place is just commencing to get me down a bit.

Friday, Sept 29, 1939
A most uneventful day, didn't even crack a plane up today. Even the fact that today was payday failed to arouse much enthusiasm in the ranks. Went over to the Comet for a night cap and thence to the Stone House for something to eat. This necessitated breaking in after hours, but Jumbo had a key and a successful entry was effected.

Saturday, Sept 30, 1939
Flew to Halton and back solo this p.m., a distance of 21 miles. Hardly a record breaking flight, but it was my first effort at solo

flying by instrument. Everything was under control. Didn't do much this p.m. save play Ricky some squash, in which he still continues to beat me. This evening we went in St. Albans for the sole purpose of going to a cinema. The idea was OK but Ricky, Alan and I got sidetracked into doing a 'pub crawl' in which we visited some 12 establishments. We came home feeling no agony, but quite under control. This English beer is quite mild, never get anywhere on it.

Sunday, Oct 1, 1939

Began the new month in the right spirit by going to Church and taking communion. A tremendously old place, beginning some time around 1240. This afternoon, I took a solitary stroll through a big park on Lord Salisbury's land. A big castle there has long been converted into a hospital. This district here is evidently steeped in tradition as must all places be in this country. Spent a very quiet evening in the house, wrote letters and things and continued our bridge feud—Biggy and I vs. George and Eric.

Monday, Oct 2, 1939

Flew my first triangle solo today, some 80 miles or so. Visibility was very good and everything unfolded itself according to calculation. It was quite good fun and I enjoyed the 70 odd minutes that I was up.

Went into the local picture house and saw Bing Crosby in *East Side of Heaven*. The music in it brought back fond memories of the 'Blonde Bomber'—the kid still packs a wallop.

Long awaited Canadian mail finally came today and made the boys all very happy. I got 3 from Muriel, 2 from Norm, 1 from the family and 1 from Margaret H.

Tuesday, Oct 3, 1939

A long cold morning in the lecture room, during which time we had Lovelock on the 'Effect of Controls' all morning. There is still quite a lot of work to be done as we should be leaving here in two weeks. Flying was tricky today as there was a gusty wind and intermittent rain squalls. Several of the boys had rather close shaves. I nearly landed on top of a plane myself. Time is getting up close to 50 hours now, which is the time we should get in here.

Spent a very quiet evening in the house, as did most of the boys.

The next day, flying was cancelled altogether, with the promise of desperate weather for the remainder of the week.

Thursday, Oct 5, 1939

Today was a repetition of yesterday's dismal day. Rain washed out flying again, and once more we spent the day in the lecture room. Looks as if the good old English weather is starting to come into its own.

After supper, George, Eric and I wandered down and spent the evening with four Canadian chaps who have an apartment down the avenue. We had quite a chin fest about this and that. We also had a cup of coffee, the first that tasted like coffee in this country. Their apartment is cluttered up by dozens of drawings by this artist chap around here who draws aeroplanes for us. He is really a wizard and can draw Petty drawings to the exact likeness. We have a couple coming up which should brighten up the room a bit.[17]

We left around half past eleven and avoided a forced entry by one of the lads letting us in.

About four this a.m., big Jumbo roused me from my slumber with a shower of boulders and I had to go down and let him in.

Ronnie and Monica invited us into London for the weekend so against our better judgement I guess we will go in, Eric and I.

Friday, Oct 6, 1939

A bit of a break in the weather, but our group was out-stick handled nonetheless; we only got in half a day's flying, with huge bunches of lectures. I resent it!

They took our tailors' names for uniforms today so that is the first step in the right direction.

They are filming a picture here now called *Training of a R.A.F. Pilot*. No doubt, Hollywood offers will soon come pouring in.

Spent a quiet evening in tonight and managed to get a spot of work done.

Saturday, Oct 7, 1939

The urge to romp and play was strong upon us again, so Ricky and I contacted Ronnie and Monnie and met them in town. We managed to spend plenty of money and had a swell time. I believe I vaguely tied one on and Eric wasn't suffering any pain either. We went to a club called Willerby's, which is a very smart one. They have a West Indian negro band, not as native as American, but they can still hit the groove.[18] Margot's husband has an interest in the club, and if it weren't for this hopeless war it would no doubt do very well. We rather tore it down, in a mild sort of way, and wandered back to the flat and had some food. Finally tottered in around 5 sometime. We stayed at the same place on Robert Adam Street, which is most handy.

Sunday, Oct 8, 1939

We got up at a reasonable hour and decided that we both felt very ordinary. Had lunch at Lyons at Marble Arch and took a walk through Hyde Park. We are very charmed by the open air speakers who babble on about a variety of subjects from Communism to 'The Light.'

After lunch, we went over to see the ladies and took them to see *These Glamour Girls*, a very smart American picture full of fast cracks which most of the English audience missed. Did me good to see a good film again. We went back to the apartment for tea and they also had an English officer. He was a bit of a drip but not painfully so. We left early and arrived back at Hatfield damned near dead, but I suppose it was worth it!!

Monday, Oct 9, to Friday, Oct 13, 1939

This painful week could be known as the week of the big push, culminating in five exams on Friday. Most of the evenings were spent if not actually studying, at least in thinking about it. On Monday, we had Morse and armaments. The first Morse I made a mess of, but the next effort was OK so I got it. Also got 75 on armaments, which was the average mark. The exams on Friday were not too bad and I figure I got them all but one—engineering.

On Friday night we had a party for the instructors and it was a fair brawl. Our instructor—Brown—did very well for himself and told me that he has recommended me for twin-engined work. This suits me all right as the glamour of a single seater is not all it is cracked up to be.

I stayed on the beer wagon and was well under control, though some of the boys got well oiled.

Flying was curtailed most of the week by lousy weather. It rained nearly every day.

Somewhere I caught a mean cold, which is nearly taking me apart.

Saturday, Oct 14, 1939
A thoroughly miserable day—rained all day and night. I retired to bed in the afternoon and beat the racket that way. Went to the movies with Doug Smith. I saw some horrible picture or other.

Then an entry written across the lines, to the effect that 'This diary business is too much work.' The next entry is nearly a year later. The accounts that followed were rewritten in a cleaned-up fashion in a separate diary, but in some ways lack the raw excitement of the original reporting.

5

FROM STUDENT TO FIGHTER PILOT

The only record of Skeets's departure from basic flight school and subsequent activities is his pilot's log book. This shows a final flight in a Tiger Moth on October 20, followed by a signing off by C. Pike, chief instructor of the De Havilland School of Flying (Hatfield) and a rating as an 'Above Average' pilot. Total flying time was under sixty hours, about half of that solo.

Skeets's marching orders took him to multi-engined training. He must have had a couple of weeks off, no doubt using them to good advantage to celebrate the end of the first phase of his training with those of his cohorts who had, like him, successfully navigated the basic part of the course.

The next log book entry shows a first multi-engined flight in an Anson on November 9, 1939, at No. 9 Operational Training Unit (OTU), Hullavington. The Avro Anson was originally built for maritime reconnaissance but proved to be more useful as a multi-engined trainer, and became the standard across the British Commonwealth Air Training Plan.

After only two hours listed in the 'passenger' column and a further two and a half hours of dual instruction, Ogilvie went solo for the first time in a multi-engined aircraft. From then until the last log entry for No. 9 Flying Training School, dated May 7, 1940, his training was intensive and almost exclusively on the Anson. In a letter home, Skeets described the feeling as he learned to get comfortable with these larger, more powerful machines:

> I wish I could fly over Ottawa in my big, twin-motored job. I still have to laugh when I look at myself piloting that big tub around. I thought I'd faint when I first looked in the cockpit. It seemed

beyond my comprehension that I'd ever be able to fathom out what all the instruments stood for. Now it is merely routine. You have a drill to run through. A good look around to see if there is anything coming in to land, slap on the super-charger and 3½ tons of metal goes into the air.

He went on to describe the cosmopolitan character of his fellow recruits:

The RAF, in fact, is composed 60 per cent of pilots from the colonies, nearly one third are Canadian. Often in the mess we have a couple of Canadians, a South African, a New Zealander, an Aussie or two—even an Englishman occasionally crops up. The colonials always get along well together.

By this point, Ogilvie had been picked as a potential instructor and began a new course of flying (the 66th Flying Instructors' Course, 7th War Course) on May 15 at the Central Flying School, Upavon. This exposed him to a number of single- and multi-engined machines, including the Hawker Hind biplane (and variants), Avro Tutor biplane and Airspeed Oxford aircraft. But in the end, it was not what Ogilvie had hoped for. As ever, he was in luck—at least, as far as he was concerned—for he managed to, in his own words, 'evade the fate of an instructor by the strangest combination of circumstances.' The best account is in Frank Ziegler's charming and brilliantly detailed book on the history of Skeets's wartime 'home,' 609 Squadron:

That Keith Ogilvie joined 609 at all seems to have been partly fluke, partly skilful manoeuvre . . . After completing his service training on twin-engined aircraft . . . his 'dreams of fame and fortune via the shot-and-shell route were abruptly dashed' when he was posted to Central Flying School as an instructor. There, however, it turned out that the 'wonderful elderly gentleman' who was his flying partner was a buddy of no less an officer than 'Boom' Trenchard,[19] and when the latter appeared on one of his ubiquitous visits, 'an impassioned plea on behalf of the young fella from Canada who had come all the way, etc.' was successfully made, and the next step was to the first O.T.U., formed from the survivors of No. 1 Squadron after the Battle of France.[20]

It turns out that Skeets's 'buddy' was none other than Lieutenant Colonel Robert Smith-Barry, about whom Trenchard himself said: 'The great Smith-Barry! He was the man who taught the air forces of the world to fly!' Smith-Barry, moving toward his mid-fifties by the start of the Second World War, had played an incredibly important role in pioneering training techniques and actually teaching First World War pilots. He had flown with Trenchard in that war, retired and then rejoined the RAF at the outset of the subsequent global hostilities to serve as a ferry pilot and instructor. Skeets and Smith-Barry, a 'remarkable old fellow' in Skeets's words, regularly played pool together in the evenings. Skeets would often 'beef' about not wanting to be an instructor. While Smith-Barry never said anything, he clearly absorbed the lack of enthusiasm his younger colleague was feeling. However, Skeets eventually received a posting to a Flying Training School at Southampton and resigned himself to his fate.

At the end of the course, the group prepared for a graduation parade that was to be overseen by none other than Lord Trenchard. With his usual wry wit, Skeets described the awe this exalted personage inspired: 'He had more rings on his arm . . . he was Marshal of the Royal Air Force, with four Air Commodore's stripes on his arm.' They duly had their parade, but at the end the commanding officer called Skeets into his office, and tersely said, 'You're to stay here. Your posting has been cancelled.' Skeets had no idea what was going on, but found himself alone in the mess that evening with Smith-Barry, after all the other graduates had left the base. They were playing their usual game of pool, and the older man said, 'Well, aren't you going to thank me?'

'I don't understand, sir, what for?'

'You didn't want to be an instructor?'

'No, that's the last thing I wanted.'

'Well,' said Smith-Barry, 'I was talking to my friend "Boom" and told him that this young fellow had come all the way from Canada to get into this thing, and he's reluctant to be sent home as an instructor.' 'Boom' had said, 'We can do something about that,' and the posting was cancelled, right then and there.

It had been Skeets's great good fortune to have been paired with such an illustrious mentor, and it was probably due in no small part to his enthusiastic and personable character that Smith-Barry interceded on his behalf with Lord Trenchard. Who said nothing good ever came of playing pool?

While the behind the scenes details of this transaction may be somewhat questionable, the result was the desired one, for after another week of waiting Skeets left to begin fighter training at No. 5 OTU, Aston Down[21] on July 28. It was a brand new training school, part of No. 12 Group Fighter Command, with as yet no students and no organized curriculum or equipment. The instructors were, in Skeets's words, 'a group of chaps from the RAF's No. 1 Fighter squadron that had just been chased out of France. They arrived back with what they could wear and what planes they could save. But they were a wonderful group of chaps. They all became very important pilots as the war went on.' At this point, however, those in charge were completely unprepared and suggested Skeets take a week's leave and go to London. He said, 'I've just come from London and don't have a penny to my name!' This clearly elicited some sympathy as they told him, 'Well, hang on here and we'll give you some flying.'

Although he was trained on twin-engined aircraft and had taken the instructor's course on this type, they gave him time on the single-engined aircraft they had. He was checked out on a Harvard on July 28 and given three hops in a Master, then the next day taken out to a Spitfire. His recollection was a rudimentary and somewhat shaky introduction:

> They said, 'It's the same as everything else, wheels go up and down there, flaps up and down there, away you go . . .' I got into this thing and opened it up, and just rocketed into the sky, hardly knew what was going on. I couldn't get the hood closed, and had to hold it with one hand and come around and make a landing.

It was a fifty-minute flight, recorded as 'flying practice' in his log. His feelings at this momentous event can only be imagined, and are hinted at in a later comment to Ziegler about this 'day of days.' The fabled Spitfire was light years beyond anything on which he had had his hands to that point, and it must have been with some satisfaction that he could reflect on his failed attempt to join the pre-war RCAF. Now, a year later, here he was at the controls of the most powerful, nimble and lethal aircraft in the world.

It took some getting used to. Skeets described it as best he could in a letter to his family in Ottawa:

This business of coping with a Spitfire is coming along nicely now. The terrific speed no longer scares me to death. The first few days I don't mind admitting a little shaking, but I have the swing of it now . . .What ships! My first three trips were damn near my last. You open her up and the thing rockets into the sky while you are getting your wheels up, airscrew adjusted, throttle set. By the time you look around you have lost the blasted airdrome [sic].

Throttle right back and coast along at 250 mph. We get the feel of it and get a bit cocky. We go up to 10,000 feet for some aerobatics. A loop is the easiest so we pick up speed to 280 and pull back on the stick. We climb straight up and on the top encounter a horrible 'high speed stall.' The damn thing shudders unbelievably and just before it spins, the horizon appears over your head and it drops in a nose dive.

So much for that. Next we try a slow roll. Pick up speed, stick hard over and she rolls onto her back, hold it there and around it comes . . . in theory. But somehow we balled it up and down it comes in an over the vertical dive. Diving around 350 we pull out too quickly and everything goes red—a blackout. Ease it out gradually and it quickly clears . . . If you suddenly try to change your path of flight, everything goes blotto. The idea is just stay within the blackout stage.

And then we find we have lost 5,000 feet in a second or so. Back for a landing and we drift in at 100 mph. They are not hard to land and we set it down gently like a brick. Taxi over to the tarmac and just sit there.

I never used to perspire, but when I get out of these babies I am absolutely soaking. Two hours a day in these thunder buggies and you are poohed right out.

His log book for the next few days shows flights in a Hurricane as well. But time was limited; with the pressure of massive German attacks on the RAF's facilities, especially their fighter stations, and the accompanying casualties to the defending squadrons, the pace of training increased accordingly to get every possible resource into the operational theatre.

Ogilvie's final training log book entry on August 15 brought him to a grand total of just under twenty hours in high-performance fighters, all gathered in the space of a couple of weeks. This entry was one of four for that day, totalling three and a half hours in a Hurricane practising '#1 & 5 attacks' and formation flying. This was also the day the Luftwaffe flew 1,786 sorties, its biggest effort during the whole of the Battle of Britain. There was clearly some urgency to get as many trained resources into the operational theatre as possible. Skeets's log book was certified that same day by the officer commanding 5 OTU. With some 155 solo hours under his belt, the entry notes him as being 'above the average as a pupil,' and is followed by a general comment: 'A Canadian true to type—should do very well.'

Training concluded, and on the verge of becoming an operational pilot, Skeets was asked where he wanted to go. He opted for the all-Canadian squadron, Douglas Bader's, but was advised there were no vacancies—they didn't need replacements at the time. Instead, he was sent to a Spitfire squadron, No. 609, at Middle Wallop. In his account, Ziegler says: 'So far as the West Riding Squadron was concerned, it was Canada's best-ever contribution. After thirty years Darley still remembers him as "very pleasant, most courteous and well-spoken," as well as a "keen and capable pilot."'[22]

RAF 609 'White Rose' Squadron was based at Middle Wallop, Hampshire, as part of 10 Fighter Group. No. 609 was an auxiliary squadron, equivalent to the army 'Territorials,' but was blessed with a line of strong and highly competent leaders and talented pilots. It was to become the first Spitfire squadron in Fighter Command to score 100 air victories. No. 609 had been at the sector station of Middle Wallop since July 1940. It came there in May that year from its first significant wartime location at Kinloss in northern Scotland, via Northolt, where it was assigned to bolster London area defences after the end of the 'phoney war.' It was here that the squadron got its first real taste of aerial combat, and of losses. It was now that the full understanding of what lay ahead sank in for the young pilots of the squadron. In his own wartime memoir, pilot David Crook, another 609 pilot, describes how he noticed on coming to Northolt from a period of leave that, 'A great change has come over the Squadron . . . The old easygoing outlook on life had vanished, and everybody now seemed to realize that was not the fairly pleasant affair that it had always seemed hitherto. The general mood now appeared to be one of rather grim determination.'[23]

Following the heavy attacks by the Luftwaffe on Portland and on convoys in the English Channel, in July 1940 609 was posted from Northolt to the sector station at Middle Wallop. Air Chief Marshal Dowding was unhappy with the use of his fighters to protect convoys, for many reasons, not least of which was the potential for greater loss of pilots and aircraft from battles over the sea, given the lack of air-sea rescue facilities. He viewed protection of the land targets as far more important, but was overruled by the Air Ministry.

To make things more challenging, 609 was given further orders to move on a daily basis from Middle Wallop to the satellite station of Warmwell, near the Dorset coast, from where it could be directed more quickly into defensive positions. At first, the squadron operated from tents with an almost complete lack of sanitation and eating facilities. In the words of John Dundas, 'Warmwell possessed . . . the two chief characteristics of a forward station—action and discomfort.'[24] The situation was eventually somewhat alleviated by delivery of mobile latrines and some rudimentary cooking equipment, but remained some distance from the ideal.

As Crook had noted, morale was low. This was one of the first things the new commanding officer, Squadron Leader George Darley, noticed when he arrived in June 1940, and he 'told the pilots in no uncertain terms that they were a miserable and ignorant bunch who needed to pull their fingers out and start learning the lessons from Dunkirk very quickly indeed. The old pre-war auxiliaries—the weekend fliers—had been shocked.'[25]

However, by the time Skeets had settled in enough to make his first flight as a member of an operational fighter squadron on August 19, 609 had under Darley's leadership come out of its funk and had made its own substantial contribution to the early days of the Battle of Britain, in particular the aerial action on August 13, Adlertag (Eagle Day), when the Luftwaffe set out in force to destroy the RAF. Based on the experience of this day and the valiant efforts of the RAF's pilots and crews over the following week, Churchill was moved to rise in the House of Commons on August 20, the day after Skeets joined his new squadron, to make his famous speech that included the line, 'Never in the field of human conflict was so much owed by so many to so few.'

The newcomer was, by the standards of the squadron, an 'old man,' all of twenty-four years in age, nearly twenty-five—almost as mature as the new CO, who was twenty-seven. Although 609 was in the middle of intensive combat, Skeets's flight log shows that he was given ten days of practice and familiarisation flying. Arriving with nearly thirteen hours in Spitfires or Hurricanes, he flew another twelve hours around Middle Wallop before being thrown into combat operations. This was only slightly more than many of his peers, some of whom had as little as ten hours in fighters when they were sent to their squadron assignments. The lack of combat training and the result of this inexperience was often devastating; Dowding pointed out that it was one thing to be a qualified pilot and quite another to be considered combat ready. At this point, Fighter Command was losing 120 pilots a week, a thoroughly unsustainable loss rate. The unofficial but often referred to rule of thumb was that if a pilot could last out his first week in combat, he was likely to survive for quite a long time with his hard-earned experience.

Not only did Skeets last out his first week, but he had a good run in the next phase of his adventures—and duly recorded it for posterity. He first kept a rough diary, then rewrote it when he had an opportunity to do so, expanding on the memories brought back by the initial draft.

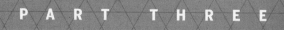

PART THREE

HEIGHT OF THE BATTLE

6

INTO THE FRAY

Please forward to:
C.E. Ogilvie
43 Patterson Ave.,
Ottawa, Ont.
Canada

A. Keith Ogilvie, P/O
609 Squadron (Spitfire)
Royal Air Force
Aug 20, 1940

HEYTESBURY, *Nov 6, 1940*

It has been an idea for some time now to keep a rough log of activities in a squadron with a view that some day it might be of interest to me or someone to read back on those hectic days of London's first mass air attacks. It never got past the idea stage until now when the weather has deteriorated and leave is more frequent, and time on my hands may thus be used up. I shall try as best I can to record these impressions as they occurred to me at the time.

On Aug. 19th, 1940, having successfully evaded the fate of an instructor by the strangest combination of circumstances and as successfully having missed being posted to a twin engined squadron, I found myself with orders to report to 609 Squadron flying Spitfires and stationed at the moment at Middle Wallop, Hants, near Salisbury. I had hoped to go to Doug Bader's 242 Squadron, the all-Canadian

Squadron in the RAF, but as there were no vacancies, any squadron would do. It turned out later how kind fate really was to me.

This squadron in common with all 600 squadrons is an Auxiliary squadron and its pilots and most of the men were originally drawn from their peace time occupations to form this squadron representing the cities of Leeds and Bradford in the defence of their country.[26] When I arrived the auxiliary touch had already been considerably thinned out and on the line-up of pilots were three Americans, two Poles and now a Canadian so that we resembled an international brigade of the Spanish war rather than an English Auxiliary Squadron.

My first ten days or so were spent in uneventful formation flying and doing practice attacks interspersed with unwelcome sessions as duty pilot.

According to Skeets, the duty pilot 'sat in the middle of the airfield with a Very gun and fired off cartridges to guide pilots coming or going,' a somewhat less than interesting pastime even for the admittedly green newcomer. The flying, however, offered greater challenges, even without the spice of combat. The reference to 'uneventful formation flying,' for example, was a bit of a typical understatement. Formation flying in fact entailed the utmost concentration and a great deal of practice to get it right. In a post-war interview, Skeets admitted that 'flying beside the leader at 200 mph requires a bit of judgment, so help me. After a time, though, you can fly and do turns with your wing about five feet from the leader and the three planes act as one.'

His flight commander, Frankie Howell, took him up to try to show him some of the tricks of dogfighting. Frankie told Skeets, 'Just stay on my tail.' Skeets described what happened then:

A couple of zips and zaps, and he'd be gone. I'd get on the radio and say, 'Where are you?' and he'd say, 'Just look behind!' and there he was, sitting on my tail. I figured this was going to be a short war for me, if the Jerry pilots were anything like this.

His log goes on:

During one of these days when I languished in the duty pilot's hut the squadron had a most successful day repelling a dive bombing attack on Portsmouth. Coming out of a thin layer of cloud the boys could hardly believe their eyes when they encountered a milling mass of Ju87s, the dreaded 'Stuka.' This type of plane, used with such success by Jerry in Poland and Holland against no air opposition, was a gift to our eight gun fighters. The boys waded in and after a ten minute skirmish downed thirteen German planes, for no loss. 700 of these planes were withdrawn and sent to the 'Muddle' East.[27]

The squadron was not too well off for pilots and had little or no time to train the raw recruit from an O.T.U. I was soon OK'd as operational and took my place in the roster of pilots.

That the squadron was shorthanded is abundantly evident from A.K.'s log book. He was coming in as a replacement pilot. From his first flight with 609 on August 19 through to September 7, there were only two days without an entry of one or two flights recording various patrols. Yet, they still seemed to be going lightly on the 'new boy.' The squadron diary shows 609 responding to another Luftwaffe raid on Portsmouth on August 24, a raid that killed more than 100 civilians. The squadron didn't fire a single round but had a couple of machines damaged. Skeets was involved in practice flying that day, according to his log. The same was true on the 25th, when 609 again acquitted itself superbly, shooting down eight Me109s and 110s without a loss. However, 609's forward operating base, Warmwell, was that day a main target for the Luftwaffe's attacks on British airfields and was hit by a number of bombs. Almost 100 enemy bombers were engaged in the raid, but they were fortunately intercepted by one of Middle Wallop's Hurricane squadrons and prevented from doing more than minor damage.

On August 30, 'A' Flight, of which Ogilvie was part, 'put up a terrific black, practice flying,' in the words of John Bisdee, already a member of the squadron when Skeets arrived, and destined to be a lifelong friend. 'We were all over the place, Ogilvie spun off the turn into a beam attack and the result was a huge lecture from Frank' (Flight Lieutenant Frank Howell, the flight commander). They consoled themselves that evening at the Square Club, followed by more 'rye and dry' at the Mucky Duck.

The only other trouble Skeets managed to get into during this period was caused by a burst tyre on landing, on September 3. Shortly before he made his approach, another pilot, American Pilot Officer Mamedoff, burst a tyre on his own aircraft, hit a ridge and nosed over, writing off the propeller. Flight Sergeant Tich Cloves described what happened subsequently in his own diary: 'Plt Off Ogilvie L1065 also burst a tyre and got into a waggle, somehow managing to write off both mainplanes. Perhaps he thought that as he was a Canadian he would be neighbourly and follow the lead of the USA.' There is no mention of the incident in Ogilvie's flying log book, but the aircraft number is correct so there is little doubt the incident took place. Given the circumstances of combat, these relatively 'minor' accidents were often promptly forgotten.

On the 4th, John Bisdee took Skeets up to patrol Radstock. Bisdee's own diary describes a fruitless search for enemy aircraft, something that did happen from time to time: 'Chased all over SW England after a single Dornier, which unfortunately got away without us seeing it.' Skeets's diary reflects on these 'learning opportunities':

> Our patrols covered the important naval ports of Southampton and Portsmouth, but with the increasing strength of German raids on London our patrols carried us usually to Northolt and Brooklands while the squadrons there were engaged. The Luftwaffe was quite interested in and paying more than some attention to our fighter stations at this time. Several times the keen eyes of Squadron Leader Darley or Frank Howell saw signs of revelry in the distance, but we were never called upon to leave our sector and engage.
>
> In one of these trips I came close to never seeing action, due to my stupidity. We took off for the channel and started climbing steadily. I turned my oxygen on but after a brief flick it registered zero. I figured I'd stay around for a while in case it was not a high patrol, but at 20,000 feet I began to get a little worried. I looked around and found I was very much alone, and clipping along about 100 feet above the Channel. This was all I wanted to know. I turned for home and landed, a plenty shaken guy. A pep talk from the CO on trying to fly without oxygen did not increase my self-respect. Live and learn . . . if you live.

The squadron saw little action on patrols on September 5 and 6, but September 7 marked a turning point in the Battle of Britain. After concentrating for two weeks on attacking airfields and facilities defending London, almost all in 11 Group's territory, the Luftwaffe had had a devastating effect on Fighter Command's resources. Ziegler noted the scope of the damage: 'During this desperate fortnight 11 Group's twenty-two squadrons lost 466 aircraft destroyed or severely damaged, 103 pilots killed and 128 severely wounded. Some squadrons had been almost wiped out.'[28]

No. 609 Squadron, based in 10 Group's area, was less affected and spent much of its time in local patrols. In any case, though, the Luftwaffe failed to follow through on its initial successes. After an accidental bombing of London by a miscalculating Luftwaffe crew on the night of August 24, Churchill had ordered several nights of limited retaliatory raids on Berlin. These strikes at a civilian target in Germany enraged Hitler to the point of redirecting the Luftwaffe to refocus its bombing action on the city of London, at great cost to the population but to the great benefit of the RAF, which was able to take advantage of the diversion to rebuild. This difficult decision by Churchill—no doubt taken with full knowledge of the potential consequences—would stave off the possibility of being defeated in the air long enough to turn the tide of the war to Britain's ultimate benefit. However, the loss to London and its populace was enormous. On September 7, the capital faced its first major attack of the war—over 300 bombers and 600 fighters in the first two waves, all watched by Luftwaffe Reichsmarschall Hermann Göring himself from Cap Gris Nez, near Calais. No. 609 Squadron, on patrol over Windsor, was sent to respond as the fires in the East End docks raged and the bombers began to return home.

Skeets was sitting in the crew room in the dispersal hut with the other pilots on standby. The weather was good, around 70 degrees Fahrenheit, few clouds about and good visibility. The ring of the operations phone with the scramble order cut the reverie of the pilots, who ran at the double to their aircraft, parked close to the dispersal hut. By the time they were in their seats, the fitters and riggers were already there, strapping them in, while others rushed to pull the chocks away. Engines ticking over at around 1,200rpm and the slipstream already blowing the grass flat, the aircraft trembled as they waited to form up on the leader and taxi out to join the fray. The excitement Ogilvie must have felt would be justified; it was the first time he would fire a shot in anger. His diary picks up on this rapid transition to full operational status after the initial quiet period of patrolling around their home base.

However, this blissful state of non-action could not last forever and on Sept. 7th I saw my first action. About one o'clock, the bell went and orders came, 'London,' '20,000 feet.' We arrived over our sector and were encouraged by the radio announcing 200 plus coming in our sector. To say I was not excited would certainly be a fallacy but I'm sure that I was not frightened, mainly because there was too much to be done before entering the scrap: routine checking of instruments, turning on gun sights, gun button to fire, etc. were all calming and reassuring factors.

I well remember seeing what seemed to be a cloud of little black beetles crawling in towards us, and there was no doubt but that they were headed our way. We were given orders to engage and positioned ourselves as best we could in the sun to one side and above the bombers. I was third in the leading section[29] and following S/Ldr Darley and Mike Staples I half rolled and dove in on a beam attack on a formation. This type of attack strikes the enemy where they are least protected and consequently most vulnerable. 'Mike' Staples, I think, must have hit one because he pulled up and over, giving me a clean shot at his belly. I opened fire and hit it for a few seconds and he fell away. That was all I saw of him because in my excitement I found myself directly in the centre of the formation and receiving no little attention from the rear gunners. I did the obvious and dove straight down collecting only a hole in my wing and tail as I went.

Another pilot involved that day, Flight Lieutenant Peter Brothers (then with 257 Squadron), provided a similar perspective on this type of action.

It was quite impressive, meeting this black cloud of aircraft, all piled up like—as somebody else described it—'the moving staircase at Piccadilly Circus.' They would be up in their hundreds, with the bottom squadron leading. They'd be stacked up behind, as well, with the fighters sitting on top. One thing I remember from those early heavy raids was the density of the rear-gunners' fire. They'd put up a sort of barrage that you had to go through if you wanted to get in close—to about fifty or a hundred yards—

which was vital. The aim was to get the rear-gunner out of the way. There was nothing you could do to avoid it—you'd collect a few holes and just hope for the best.[30]

Skeets's diary continues:

Well out of range, I pulled up and saw the bombers haring for home. I was a bit sad about my first effort and climbed into position for another attack. As I prepared for another go, I was certainly surprised to see a yellow nosed Messerschmidt [sic] '109' drift across in front of me, and then another. By sheer blind luck I was in the sun to them and they either did not see me or figured I was another escorting fighter . . . had they come out the other side of me . . . but we don't think about that. I opened fire on the second one, which had a big number 19 on a silver background, and connected as he rolled over and dove, turning on his back. I got very close and emptied my guns as he streamed glycol, then smoke and finally a sheet of flame. This was a certain, and now out of ammunition I streaked for home. I could feel nothing except my insides were frozen and my heart was beating up where my tonsils should be.

The squadron had a good day and the score was six destroyed, six probably destroyed and there must have been many more carrying scars as they made for home. We had no casualties and only 'Aggie' [Agazarian] had a bullet in his oil and landed at Maidenhead. The squadron score is now sixty two aircraft destroyed.

His survival, and his victory over the Me109, were as much a matter of luck as anything else. He later described in more detail how the event unfolded:

After a squadron attack, it's pretty much everyone for himself, you attack whatever you can find. So I climbed back up into position again, hoping to do a little better this time, and turned to my left to go down again, and saw two Me109s doing the same thing, looking down to find a target. I didn't seem to be any more than 10 or 20 yards away from them. Two big yellow-nosed 109s, and I could see the pilots in their seats, looking to the left. If they had come out on the other side of me the war would have been very short for me, like one day. However, I swung my nose over and opened fire on the leader and the second guy rolled over, pouring smoke and glycol and disappeared. I didn't have enough experience to follow him. That was over, and I looked around the sky, and it's a funny thing, all pilots remark on this—one minute there are umpteen airplanes all around, and the next minute you can't find one. I couldn't find another aircraft anywhere. My fuel was getting down and I started heading home. It counted as a probable. Once you hit the glycol, he wasn't going to get home. I was so close, I should have blown him out of the sky. However, this was the first engagement . . . and you learn.

The squadron maintenance log recorded: 'Spitfire N3280. Returned to base, tail damaged following combat over south London 5:45 p.m. Pilot Officer A.K. Ogilvie unhurt. Aircraft repairable.' Bisdee reported to his own diary that 'Staples and Ogilvie were thought to be lost but turned up OK, which put us all in a good mood.' Staples and Ogilvie in particular, no doubt. Bisdee went on to say, 'We all celebrated the great day with cocktails at a party at Gordon Harker's house, Monkton, in aid of the Spitfire Fund. O. was full of his first day's fighting—my god, you learn more and more each time you go at it!'

Altogether, it had been a momentous day for Skeets. The flight log shows the combat took place on Ogilvie's second flight of the day, one that lasted 1 hour 50 minutes, very near the limits of the Spitfire, especially under the kind of conditions seen on that occasion. Ogilvie had to land at Worthy Down, a grass field some ten minutes' flying time from his station at Middle Wallop, to refuel for the last short leg of the day. The two holes in his Spitfire could be repaired at his home base. What was most interesting, though, was that he came to this first combat without having gone through much of the usual aerobatic and gunnery training fighter pilots usually received. The art of deflection shooting—that might have allowed him to hit the leading Me109 he was actually aiming at—was something he would have to learn and refine through repeated combat experience.

It appears the preceding three weeks of continuous patrols, culminating in his first combat with one 'confirmed' and one 'probable,' brought Skeets to a few deserved days off. The weather for the next week was reported as bad, although the Luftwaffe continued its bombing campaign regardless. Skeets's next flight was on September 12, again taking up patrolling duties. Bisdee's diary entry for that day reports that the weather had turned for the worse, which he felt was a good thing as it would reduce the risk of invasion by Germany. That evening he 'took Ogilvie into Salisbury, where we visited the Rose & Crown, and met Bill Williams and Baylis.'

Things were moving quickly in the air war over this period. The tactics the Germans now employed over London had evolved from a series of separate attacks to a concentration of 300 to 400 bombers in two or three consecutive waves. Air Vice-Marshal Keith Park, commander of 11 Group, charged with the fighter defence of London, changed his response strategy accordingly. On September 11 he ordered his controllers to scramble squadrons in pairs and instructed his fighters to adopt a looser strike formation of four aircraft in line abreast. Spitfires were to attack the high fighters and Hurricanes the bombers and lower escort.

Despite the changed response, on the 14th—'Black Saturday'—the RAF lost twenty-nine fighters to the Luftwaffe's twenty-five, prompting the German High Command to commit itself further to an air supremacy strategy. No. 609 Squadron was not engaged that day, although Skeets's log shows an instrument practice flight in a Spitfire and a trip to south Gedney and back with Leading Aircraftman (LAC) Cohen in the squadron's Magister, for purposes unknown. It was also Skeets's twenty-fifth birthday. There is no record of a party.

7

BATTLE OF BRITAIN DAY

The next day, Sunday September 15, the weather was ideal for massed Luftwaffe attacks. Both Park and Prime Minister Churchill anticipated something significant and settled into 11 Group headquarters' operations room, located in a bunker at Hillingdon House on London's west side, not far from the RAF headquarters proper. Churchill watched the subsequent action with an unlit cigar in his teeth, in deference to the limitations of the bunker's ventilation system.

The date of September 15 is now commemorated as Battle of Britain Day. On this day in 1940, No. 609 Squadron—scrambled to meet the departing bombers—was the lone squadron from 10 Group to participate in the massive dogfight over London late that morning.

Sept 15, 1940
Over London again and the Jerries are really throwing everything in now. We were ordered to intercept a heavy bomber formation headed for Northolt. 'Butch' MacArthur identified them as Dornier 215s and then led us in on a head on attack.[31] The 215s turned out to have an armoured shield of Me110s in front as a spearhead. Armed with four cannon, the Mes poured out some stuff and we broke down and away. The plane beside me took a direct hit and went down a flamer. It turned out to be my room-mate, Geoff Gaunt. I came back up and saw several dogfights going on around and about. I was looking for an opening when five 'vics' of three 109s went over directly on top of me tailing the bombers. Damn good thing for me that they didn't come down. I saw a Dornier

215 diving below and alone. A break for me, and I attacked him from the beam. The rear gunner fired back but packed up on my second attack. The third time I got in close and saw a fire in his 'glass house,' just as two of the crew baled out, one narrowly missing going into my prop. It was an incredible and terrifying sight to see the bomber spin slowly, suddenly the tail snapped off and then the wings and the wreckage plunged into the heart of London. I learned later that it landed on a jeweller's shop by Victoria Station.

Skeets summarized that morning's experience in a letter home, written shortly afterwards. He called the disintegration of the aircraft under his guns 'a most amazing and terrifying sight. I could see fire in the Dornier's cockpit.' The pilot of the Dornier, Oberleutnant Robert Zehbe, and two crew members were killed. The two German parachutists landed on the Kennington Oval, according to Ziegler, 'fortunately without disturbing any cricket, whereas the main part of their aeroplane arrived in the forecourt of Victoria Station, and the tail-unit (as is recorded in the Squadron's war diary) "just outside a Pimlico public house, to the great comfort and joy of the patrons."' The bulk of the wreckage demolished a jeweller's shop and damaged the Victoria Station restaurant, where thirty women were taking shelter in a basement room. Trapped by the wreckage, they had to be freed, luckily uninjured, by a party of men who broke in through a locked door at the other end of the room. They came out with their knitting and raised a cheer for the RAF. They were most worried about the state of their lunch. One was quoted as saying, 'After we had taken a look at Jerry, we tidied up the mess he had made.' That pretty much says all that needs to be said about the attitude of Londoners for the duration of the war.

Other newspaper articles describe this most public dogfight of the war, with Londoners standing in the streets during the lunch hour and cheering wildly as they watched the flaming enemy aircraft fall to the ground. The whole episode was photographed and recorded in the London *Daily Mirror*, who presented original copies of the photographs to Ogilvie. One shows the Dornier falling on and near Victoria Station, at the corner of Wilton Road and Terminus Place, with the tail and wingtips missing, with an unidentified fighter in the bottom of the picture. Another reveals the tail section falling separately to land on a rooftop in Vauxhall Bridge Road, while others display the wreckage being checked by rescue personnel. The proof of his contribution was in the 16mm camera guns that were synchronized with the Spitfire's eight .303-calibre machine guns. They clearly show pieces of the aeroplane flying off, and crew members baling out, as the Dornier is caught squarely by a lethal blast before falling to earth in pieces. Ogilvie noted in his combat report that two other Spitfires had also attacked the Dornier.

8

A ROYAL NOTE

The bomber was thought to have tried to bomb Buckingham Palace, but Skeets thought it more likely the pilot was simply jettisoning his bombs and trying to get away. Whatever the case, the bombs caused minimal damage when they fell in the courtyard of Buckingham Palace. Queen Wilhelmina of the Netherlands was standing on a balcony watching the air battle. She was staying in London for the duration of the war and, along with other Londoners, was following the action from the ground. Queen Wilhelmina put her gratitude for the aerial action they had witnessed into concrete terms in the form of a personal note to Skeets, which is now in his diary. It reads as follows:

> Dienst Van H.M. de Koningin,
> Der Nederland
> 82, Eaton Square
> London S.W.I.
> 17 September, 1940

I am commanded by Her Majesty Queen Wilhelmina of the Netherlands, to convey to you Her Majesty was most gratified to see from Her London House a German bomber shot down by an eight gun fighter during the air battle in the morning of 15th September.

Her Majesty would be very pleased if Her congratulations should be conveyed to the Squadron concerned in this battle and to the pilot who shot down the German aircraft.

> Signed Major General de Jonge Van Ellemeet
> Aide de Camp on service.

To: The Air Ministry,
London.

The note was forwarded to 609 Squadron from Fighter Command, along with another, ordering that no publicity should be given to it.

The original write-up in the latter pages of Skeets's flying school diary contains a more businesslike and detailed report on the day's action:

Combat Report, Sept 15, 1940
I was Yellow 2, in 'A' flight. We were ordered to attack heavy bomber formation headed for Northolt. A head on attack was a failure, came up on one side, saw many 109s pass over me tailing the bombers. Saw lone Dornier 215 and made beam attack, experiencing return fire. One grazed tailplane. Another Spitfire joined in, on second attack pieces came off and could see a fire in glass house. Crew jumped and bomber went into spin, broke in half and crashed over Battersea, London.

However, the account of the day's action was not without controversy, as was the case with many of these events. Ogilvie always acknowledged that there were probably several people who could have shared responsibility for this 'kill.' In addition to the other Spitfires that Skeets acknowledged were part of the attack, Sergeant Pilot Ray Holmes of 504 Squadron claimed he was out of ammunition and had actually rammed the Dornier, then baled out of his Hurricane over Chelsea. Richard Collier, in his book *The Few*, credits Sergeant Pilot Ginger Lacey with downing a Heinkel that was supposed to be 'the only bomber that dropped bombs on Buckingham Palace.' So there is naturally great confusion about all this. In 2004, some of the wreckage of Holmes's Hurricane was dug up during a street rebuilding exercise in central London, and was put on display at Leicester Square as part of the 'West End at War' exhibit, then subsequently preserved at the RAF Museum.

Ian Darling, a Canadian journalist and author, wrote a book[32] that in one chapter recounts Skeets's experience on September 15. Darling's research included examination of camera gun footage taken from Ogilvie's aircraft. In a letter to the Ogilvie family, he wrote:

The film from [Skeets'] Spitfire at the Imperial War Museum . . . shows several scenes when [he] was attacking the Dornier. It also shows what appears to be the tail of the bomber breaking away.[33] This scene is intriguing because [he] is in front of the Dornier. Interestingly, the film of the tail leaving the plane starts with the tail in the air, having left the plane. Just what occurred in the seconds before [he] switched the camera on is something that will never be known with absolute certainty.

Darling goes on to say that he believed Skeets was 'both accurate and modest when he wrote . . . that several pilots were involved in the attack. I spoke to the staff at the museum about the film and they confirmed that there is no way to be absolutely certain what occurred during that couple of seconds before the bomber started to break up.' Then he brings the incident into the present:

> You may also be interested to know that the Dornier scraped against the granite at the base of Victoria Station when it crashed and that the scuff marks remain there to this day. I went to the customer service department at the station, introduced myself and asked to speak to anyone who knew about the Dornier coming down at the station. I met a person who is like a promotion manager and he took me to where the Dornier ended up. He showed me how rough the granite is in one area and how smooth it is about 30 feet away . . . The part of the station where the plane came down is now a pub, so it is easy to find.

At the time of the action, however, the uncertainty about just how much credit Skeets deserved for this victory was hardly an issue. After rearming and refuelling, 609 Squadron was again ordered into action around 2:30 that same afternoon, just after the enemy had crossed the Kentish coast, and arrived at the action only in time to intercept the bombers from the Brooklands–Kenley patrol line as they returned from their mission. Skeets's diary resumes:

> In the afternoon, we intercepted some 20 Dorniers tearing for home off Hastings. We were too late for the main body but there were two stragglers and my flight took one each. On our 'kite' my attack was the third and it was starting to go down, though the rear gunner was still firing and hit my wing. The bomber just came

to pieces and two of the crew jumped. On 'B' flight's attack, Mike Appleby was leading but the boys were so excited they peeled off from the rear first, and when Mike started to go down, he found himself last in line. He was some burned up. This one crashed on the beach.

I followed a parachutist down to the sea and took some film of his descent. He waved quite wildly, probably figuring that he was going to be machine gunned. He landed about ten miles out and I doubt if he was picked up at all as there was nothing in sight.

The squadron was credited with four destroyed, four probables and several damaged, bringing our score up to 66 destroyed. The total for the day was officially reckoned at 185 Jerries definitely downed.

Unfortunately we learned that Geoff [Gaunt, Skeets's room-mate] went straight in [at] Kenley for our only casualty.

Skeets never again mentions a room-mate in his diary. Most poignantly, Gaunt must have intended to keep a diary himself but never started it. It fell to Ogilvie to do so, and his personal record was borrowed as a reference by Frank Ziegler when the latter was writing the 609 Squadron history. Ziegler describes the provenance of the actual notebook thus:

I have before me as I write two 'RAF Large Note Books, Form 407.' One bears the name 'S.G. Beaumont.' On the cover of the other the name 'G.M. Gaunt' has been deleted and that of 'A.K. Ogilvie' substituted. It is recorded that at Middle Wallop they shared a room, and it is clear that Gaunt never had a chance even to begin his diary. But Ogilvie did, and when he was posted missing in 1941 it was forwarded to an address in Ottawa written on the fly-leaf. Thirty years later it has been sent to me by its Canadian owner—who after all survived.[34]

Skeets later summarized the nature of friendship in these perilous times: 'People came and went, you know. You'd lose some. You'd get to know a guy pretty well, then all of a sudden he wasn't there any more. You just sort of got used to it. We had some guys who came to the squadron, and went missing on their first trip. You just didn't know—if your luck ran out, it ran out.'[35]

The date of September 15 had seen the arrival over England of the largest aerial armada the Luftwaffe was able to muster; it also led to the RAF's most exaggerated claim of victories in the whole of the Battle of Britain, some 185 enemy aircraft. The squadron's declaration of four aircraft destroyed was accurate, but the final tally for the RAF as a whole was 56. Yet there is no doubt that many of the returning German aircraft suffered damage.

In any case, it was a near thing for the RAF. Fighter crews, barely down from the morning's intensive action, were faced with over twice as many aircraft in the afternoon. Fighter Command was stretched to the limit. A famous anecdote records Churchill turning to Park in the 11 Group operations bunker—as the plotting table once again filled with markers and lights showing engagement of Fighter Command's pilots—and asking, 'What reserves have we got?'

'There are none,' was Park's answer. But by early evening, when Churchill and Park left the bunker, the sky was clear, calm and empty of aircraft.

Skeets's log book credits him with a 'D.O.215 destroyed.' The squadron's record of victories shares the kill with Pilot Officer J. Curchin, but also notes that it was 'claimed by numerous RAF fighters and crashed at Victoria Station.'[36] It was a famously public victory, brought to all Londoners via the publication on the front pages of many of the capital's papers of the pictures of the doomed aircraft, tailless and without wingtips, plummeting vertically to the ground. The incident came to characterize for many Londoners what Winston Churchill later described as 'one of the great days . . . the most brilliant and fruitful of any fought upon a large scale by the fighters of the Royal Air Force.'

Not long after, Skeets wrote to his younger brother Jim about the incident, but the letter is just as interesting for the broader perspective it puts on the experience of being in London on the ground during these raids. 'I'm in London on leave,' Skeets writes.

Eleven o'clock at night and a fine rest I'm getting. The sky is red from a fire Jerry has started somewhere and you can hear the bark of Archie [anti-aircraft] guns close by. The sky is criss-crossed with searchlights but the clouds are low and they can't pick out anything. And at home you are probably cursing at the mosquitoes.

A final footnote to this day took place some fifty years later, at an event commemorating the fiftieth anniversary of the Battle of Britain. Skeets was introduced to the Queen as the pilot who brought down the aircraft that had bombed Buckingham Palace. The Queen thought for a moment, obviously remembering the incident. 'It didn't do any damage, you know,' she said, 'as all the bombs landed in the forecourt.' There was probably more destruction done when the aircraft fell on Victoria Station and the adjacent shops.

Following this hectic day, Skeets seemed to adopt a more fatalistic attitude to the daily events. He later said: 'Things went on from there. If you were lucky, you came out on the right end of things. If you weren't, well, you didn't.' In any event, the following week was an anticlimax for Skeets and his fellow pilots.

9

LEARNING BY EXPERIENCE

Sept 16–23, 1940

This period was conspicuous for its lack of action. We had our usual patrols taking us over Croydon, Brooklands, and lower London but the Hun is still licking his wounds. That last party cost him some 185[37] aircraft of which the greater part were bombers, and he could never hope to keep that up. Poor weather also played its part and the only fun I had in this period was a dog-fight with three Fairey Battles who were also in a playful mood. We were very sorry indeed to lose our three American boys, 'Red' Tobin, Andy Mamedoff and 'Shorty' Keogh, who have gone to join the first American Eagle Squadron.

To this, his draft note in the flying school diary adds an ironic comment after recording the loss of the American pilots: 'Goodbye, leave.'

That week saw much-reduced activity by day as the weather was deteriorating into what Skeets called the 'good old English fall, with lots of rain.' It is likely also that repairs were needed to much of the German air fleet. Once again, the Luftwaffe's leadership failed to follow through on its momentary advantage, giving Park the opportunity to make further adjustments to his tactics that would increasingly prove to place the advantage with the RAF.

However, Ogilvie's reference to a 'lack of action' may be considered relative. The squadron history in fact records a raid by two aircraft on the Middle Wallop airfield on September 21. An observer noted: 'One appeared with a Hurricane on his tail and hurriedly dropped some heavy stuff behind the officers' mess, but only made some nice holes in the ground.' Nonetheless, it must have livened things up for the squadron, at least temporarily.

With the departure of the three Americans in the unit, the torch was also passed on to something other than the combat front: 'As far as New World wit and humour were concerned, this lone little Canadian took over the tradition founded by the three Americans, and especially 'Red' Tobin, who much to their own and their comrades' regret had departed to help form the first all-American Eagle Squadron, with which they and many others all tragically perished in 1941.'[38]

Sept 24, 1940

Long about tea time we were scrambled to intercept a raid headed for Southampton.[39] We saw ack ack fire over the Isle of Wight and proceeded there. My wireless packed up at a most inopportune time as I had to guess what was going on. 'Dogs' Dundas was leading Yellow Section and I stuck to him like a brother. There were about a dozen Do17s with a fighter escort, though I never did see the escort. I attacked a Do17 and had his port engine on fire. From about 20,000 feet he dove for the sea . . . and I gaily waited for the splash. Was my face red when he levelled off and went like a ding bat for home. I dove after him again and caught him about twenty five miles out to sea. Flying Betsy through 'the gate' had poured oil over my Perspex and I could hardly see to fire. He was right down on the deck and very difficult to attack. Nearly rammed him on one attack so I emptied my guns into him—or at him—and regretfully broke away. A stupid mistake on my part and I'm afraid he got home alright. The squadron was more successful and we claimed three Dos and a 109 destroyed with no loss. The score is now seventy Jerries destroyed.

Ogilvie's log book for this day shows '1 D.O.17 Probable.'

The next day, the target for the Luftwaffe was the Bristol Aeroplane Works at Filton, Bristol. A diversionary attack was launched on Portland, drawing much of Fighter Command's resources off the protection of the main target.

Sept 25, 1940

Today was party day again. At 11:30 we 'scrambled' to intercept a raid headed for Portland. Poor vectoring by Operations and we ended up in a long tail chase, catching them up only at Bristol. It was one hell of a big raid, I should think 200 bombers and fighter escort of all types, Dornier 17s and 215s, Heinkel 111s, Messerschmidt [sic] 110s and 109s. It was a bad show as Fighter Command had only three squadrons there to intercept.[40] The next few minutes were some of the most hectic I ever hope to get mixed up in. Just over the big aircraft plant and obvious target, we came out under the damn bombers. At this moment, the ack ack opened up for fair, at the same time the bomb doors came open on the bombers and the whole flaming issue dropped their bombs at once. How none of us was hit by a bomb or shell, I'll never know, but we finally got in position to attack.

Following Squadron Leader Darley, I was Red 4 and made a good attack from the beam. Sgt Feary saw one bomber go down, a flamer, from this attack. I broke away down and came back to attack a Dornier 17. I was giving him hell and both engines were streaming glycol when there was a gigantic 'pow' and a fine big cannon hole appeared in my right wing. A snappy glance in my rear mirror showed the whole thing full of a yellow nosed '109' and it occurred to me he didn't want to be my valentine. I shook him but not before he put another up my tail, one through my fuselage, exploding in my wireless set behind my back, and, as a final souvenir, one in my port wing, puncturing my tire. Certainly my closest call to date.

From the 609 Squadron website, an editorial comment: 'And after all that, this modest, courageous little Canadian from Ottawa still went on fighting.'

I had lost my Dornier so gave chase to the formation now stream-ing for home. Caught a chap close down on the water and made two beam attacks but could only get one engine smoking before my ammo gave out. He probably got home but I can always hope that he came down in the channel. 'Mick' Miller got a Heinkel burning and the miserable bastard deliberately turned and flew into a house. He should roast forever.

I nearly turned over on landing, but for a change I made a good landing and got away with it. The Squadron bagged six confirmed and five probable, boosting the score to 76. I could only claim a probable and a damaged.

A most unusual occurrence when John Newberry pulled out of a dive too quickly and bent both wings, tearing his seat clear loose from its fastenings. He hurt his insides and won't fly again. Strangely enough Osta [Ostazewski-Ostoja] did the same thing, causing the glass house to burst from the pressure and he didn't even black out. Tough babies, these Poles.

Serg. Hughes-Rees got hammered and made a forced landing with his wheels up in a field, but was unhurt himself.

Skeets's flying log claims '1 D.O. possible'; it also notes, somewhat tersely, 'two cannon shots in wing and fuselage. Wireless destroyed and tire pierced in Spit.' He would have been unlikely to know about the burst tyre before setting down, so it was probably a somewhat surprising—and very lucky—landing, especially considering the previous experience with a rupturing tyre on September 7, which ended up with both mainplanes having to be replaced. This time, he said, 'I was lucky, it just pulled me in a slow circle, didn't do any more damage than that.'

Flight Sergeant Tich Cloves clinically observed in his diary that 'Ogilvie returned peppered with bullet holes in both mainplanes and the tail unit.' And Ziegler noted that despite several dogfights during this one flight, Ogilvie was airborne longer than anyone else in the squadron.

Again from the unit's maintenance log: 'Spitfire N3280. Hit by Bf 109 during combat south of Bristol 12:00 p.m. Landed back at base on burst tyre. Pilot Officer A.K. Ogilvie unhurt. Aircraft damaged but repairable.'

On September 26, 1940, 609 Squadron intercepted about fifty bombers who made an effective attack on the Supermarine works at Woolston, shutting down Spitfire production for a time. In the ensuing action, Ziegler's squadron history says, 'once again Ogilvie was giving and getting into trouble.'

Skeets recorded this operation in his diary:

Today again we were 'scrambled' around four o'clock to intercept a raid headed for Southampton. We missed the interception and it tur-ned into a tail chase. My radio packed up at a crucial stage of the game and so I stuck close to 'Dogs.' He suddenly made a steep climbing turn and I surmised that there were Jerry fighters around. It was a good guess and I soon found myself playing ring-around-a-rosy with a silver grey 109. I was some pleased to find after a few minutes that at that altitude, 25,000', my little old 'Spit' could out-manoeuvre his 109 quite nicely. I got a deflection shot at him, he dove away and I lost him. Found and gave chase to a huge black Heinkel 111. I got in very close on his tail and pounded him pretty steadily. I could actually see yellow flashes as my [de Wilde phosphorous incendiary] bullets hit, but he soaked it up and flew steadily along. His rear gunner was no sissy and threw plenty back, bouncing a couple off my wings and putting one in the ammo belt of my incendiary gun, jamming it. He was still going strong when my guns went dry. I was so damn mad I could have rammed him . . . except I wasn't quite that mad. All in all it was a discouraging encounter for me, but the boys were in there for two Heinkels and a 109. Church got a Heinkel and 'Dogs' [the] 109.

During the action, Skeets's gunsight got covered with oil, probably from flying the engine 'through the gate' again, and he was frustrated not to be able to see well enough to ensure a good shot. He later said:

I emptied everything I had at him and he just kept on going back home. I couldn't do anything more. Once your ammo was gone, you couldn't do anything else but ram them, but I wasn't in that category. His plane must have been a sieve when he got home, but he got away from me, flying level over the water. I just didn't hit anything vital.

Bisdee's diary records that he 'went to MD with Ogilvie in evening. It was Bill Williams' birthday and he kept on standing drinks.' No serious damage was reported . . . at least to the participants. The aircraft Skeets had been flying that day was not so fortunate. Again from the squadron maintenance log: 'Spitfire N3288. Mainspar severely damaged by return fire from He 111 engaged over Christchurch 4:35 p.m. Returned to base. Pilot Officer A.K. Ogilvie unhurt. Aircraft damaged but repairable.'

On September 27, the target for the Luftwaffe was Bristol, and the attacking force was Me110s and Me109s acting in an experimental fighter-bomber role. The results were disastrous for the Luftwaffe, with 609

Squadron shooting down at least five enemy aircraft for the loss of one of their own. Skeets was in a front-row seat for the loss of Flying Officer 'Mick' Miller, who took the lead in the squadron's attack when the radios of both Squadron Leader Darley and his number two flight commander failed. Skeets was flying as number two to Miller.

> Business continues to be good and we were back on the same old stand. I had a lovely new ship that handles like a dream. A raid was headed for Portland but we missed it due mainly to the CO's radio packing up. We messed around for a bit, then headed for the coast to try and pick them up going out . . . and ran straight into a flock of Me110s who were waiting to escort the bombers back. These twin-engined fighters fly in a big circle to protect each other's tail with the four cannon in their nose. To break it up we attacked from the beam. I was number two on 'Mick' Miller as he led the attack in. One of the 110s turned out to get his cannons working on 'Mick' and for a split second they were looking at each other at a combined speed of 600 mph. They hit, head on. There was a terrific explosion, a sheet of flame and a column of black smoke. I caught a glimpse of a Spitfire wing flutter out of the mess and the tattered white remains of a parachute with something on the end. It was ghastly. Pray God I never see anything like that again. I was frozen, the explosion blew my ship up and over. I half rolled and came straight down to see a 110 floating by beneath me. A quick burst hit his wing tanks and he went straight down in a sheet of flame.[41] I looked around and saw two more 110s going down in sheets of flame and a third in a shallow dive which took him straight into the channel. The whole vicious action was over in almost seconds, with six 110s destroyed for our loss of one. We had a tremendous advantage once they were broken up—a twin engine job has not much chance against a single.

One that 'hurtled into the sea' was an odd victory, witnessed to the end by Skeets. He saw a 110 doing a slow glide downwards and turned after him, then heard another pilot say, 'Leave him, he's mine!' Skeets flew over and the two Spitfires formed up closely on the 110, which never altered its path. It slowly descended toward the Channel and when they got to about

100 feet, the Spitfires pulled up and watched the Messerschmitt continue straight into the water 'with a big smash.' The tail came up and the aircraft quickly disappeared beneath the waves. The pilot had obviously been killed or incapacitated, and the aircraft was simply going down on its own.

But despite the victories, it was not altogether a good day for the squadron:

> We are also unfortunate to lose gallant old 'Butch' MacArthur who blew his eardrums out in a dive and is through flying in combat. With the CO laid up we are now short of both pilots and planes.
>
> I find that slowly I'm learning a few tricks of the [dogfighting] trade, especially the value of conserving ammunition until close in. Live and learn, I suppose. The two certainly go hand in hand in this racket.
>
> I wonder where the hell all this rain is they talk about in this country? I could sleep for a week.

It was a typically modest understatement. Skeets had flown every mission after the events of September 15. He was in combat on four successive days between September 26 and 30, shot down or damaged four enemy planes and twice suffered serious damage to his own aircraft over this period. It had been only one very eventful month since he had joined the unit as an operational pilot.

The squadron's success was recognized the following day in a series of messages from some very senior people:

> **Addressed to No. 609 Squadron, etc. from A O C 10 Group**
> *p.877 28/9*
>   The C-in-C desires me to convey his congratulations on the excellent work of yesterday which was even more successful than that of the previous day in that the enemy was broken up and prevented from accurately bombing their objective.
> 1050. Jones B.

> **Addressed to 609 Squadron. Etc. From No. 10 Group**
> *p.880 28/9*
> *The following message dated 26/9 received 10 Group from the S of S for Air begins*

congratulations on your fighting yesterday—ends
1055. Jones B.

Addressed to 609 Squadron, etc. From No. 10 Group
p.889 29/9
A message has been received by the A.O.C. from Sir Stanley White
of the Bristol Aeroplane company through Lord Beaverbrook
commenting on the fine courage displayed by fighter squadrons in
breaking up enemy attacks on Filton on the 27th inst. Which he
says undoubtedly saved the factory from serious damage and heart-
ened and encouraged all the factory employees. He wishes thanks
and appreciation to be conveyed to all concerned.

Skeets's diary entries continue:

Sept 30, 1940
A brief respite of two days then cloudless skies again, forerunning
a visit from our playmates. First of all a 'stand by'—a monotonous business in which one sits in the cockpit all ready to go,
but usually never do. Next a phony scramble in which we took
off and landed almost right away. However, the third they say is
a charm and at 11:30 off we went pleasure bent to Portland. Ere
long, we tangled with a 109 circus and I found myself a playmate.
This was almost a mistake as this baby had too much stuff for
Junior and though he only got a fair deflection shot which floated
across in front of me, I never got a shot at him. However, the boys
were in there again and knocked down five, David Crook leading
the parade with two.

Again at tea time a raid came up headed for Bristol which we
were told to wait for but it never did materialize. However, there
were the inevitable 109s circling above us at 30,000'. They made
a mistake of coming down and again Crooky got one, also Novo
with a doubtful second. I didn't fire a gun all day and climaxed it
all by bursting a tire on landing.[42]

We were credited with six destroyed and the score mounts to
91. Business is good!

This day had seen the last of the big daylight raids by twin-engined German bombers against both London and industrial centres further west. The Battle of Britain was entering a new and, as history records, final phase.

Oct 1, 1940

Only one patrol today which did not bring forth any action. We were patrolling the Southampton area and we could see plenty of Jerry fighters over the Needles at altitudes from 30 to 35,000'. It is hopeless to try and get up there in a Spitfire whereas the 109s are very manoeuvrable up there with their fuel injection engines.[43] The mass bombing raids seem to be petering out in favour of these comparatively harmless fighter sweeps. Even these boys are not too keen to engage and always draw back over the channel when we go after them.

Oct 5, 1940

A break in the weather today and we had two scrambles, neither of which produced any action. We had a spot of excitement, however, when Novo got one wheel down and one stuck up. 'Ops' figured it too dangerous to land a Spit like that so he was ordered to jump. Novo was some incensed at this reflection on his ability but jump he did, the only casualty being a chicken when he descended on a chicken farm.

I flew my 300th hour today.

We got a new CO today, and two new Polish pilots. We were very sorry to lose S/Ldr Darley but he was promoted to Wing Commander and given a station at Exeter. Our decorations are coming through now and we were all pleased to learn that S/Ldr Darley got a D.S.O., with a D.F.C. for 'Dogs' Dundas, Frank Howell, and 'Butch' MacArthur. Each of these decorations was well earned and there should still be more to come.

Squadron Leader 'George' Darley was taken ill after his last flight with the unit on September 26 and on his recovery transferred, with a promotion to wing commander, to a new job as station commander. He was given an appreciative and emotional send off by his pilots. His successor was Michael Lister Robinson. Robinson would eventually find his own place in the annals of 609 Squadron's history, but the replacement for the enormously popular Darley now found himself facing a medley of seasoned veteran combatants. With his aristocratic background and arriving as he did from an assignment training raw recruits, Robinson seemed out of place at first. But he would not take long to prove himself in his first combat with the squadron.

One of the other new arrivals and one of two Polish pilots was Jan Zurakowski, who became a lifelong friend of Ogilvie's and later went on to become the chief test pilot for the greatly advanced but ill-fated CF105 Avro Arrow jet fighter developed in Canada in the late 1950s.[44] The other was Zbigniev Olenski, whose first name was 'much too difficult for English-speaking tongues . . . [and was] promptly changed by Ogilvie to "Big Enough."'[45] It was in fact Zurakowski's second tour at Middle Wallop. From August 14, 1940 until September 11, he had flown with 234 Squadron from the same airfield. No. 234 suffered such grievous losses over this period that it was rotated back to St Eval in Cornwall. Three weeks later, he was posted back to Middle Wallop to join 609, with 'Ogi,' as he called him, as his section leader. Skeets always felt 'Zura' was a big factor in his survival. 'I didn't have to worry too much when he was back there,' he told an *Ottawa Citizen* reporter in an interview on the occasion of Battle of Britain Sunday, September 14, 1968. 'He could spot the rivets on a 109 before I could even see it.'

Oct 6–14, 1940
A space in which I had four days leave and accomplished nothing during that time. I went down to Sherbourne to see Margot and heard a terrific dog-fight going on overhead. I learned later that it was our squadron and it must have been a good party, because the boys got five. However, my Flight took a caning and four of the six got knocked down. Serg. Feary, an old pilot, was killed. Mike Staples got an incendiary through the leg and had to jump for it; 'Dogs' got slightly wounded by shrapnel and landed at Warmwell; Frank Howell had to make a forced landing in a field.[46]

A lull has once again descended on activities aided by poor weather.

Our squadron strength was aided no little bit by six new pilots, P/Os Hill, Baraldi, Titley, Baillon, Chappel and Sgt. Mercer. When they all become operational things should look good for leave.

'Aggie,' 'Johnny' and I have applied to go to Greece, as there seems to be more doing there.

And a poignant postscript to that last entry, written later:

The CO talked us out of it on the old story of no experienced pilots left. Aggie was determined to go and he did. He was killed, as were most of the boys on that disastrous campaign.

It turned out to have been a good time to be going on leave, airborne action notwithstanding. The squadron history records a near miss when 'many pilots were nearly written off in the officers' mess, to which they had retired to drink beer and play billiards because the weather precluded all flight, when a sharp whistle of descending bombs caused much spilling of beer as officers hurled themselves to the floor, and two terrific explosions rocked the building to its foundations.' Ogilvie's timing was impeccable, and he never expressed regret at having missed that part of the adventure.

Skeets took advantage of the break to write to his cousin, Dorrie Armstrong, to congratulate her on her marriage. Subject to the wartime rules of censorship, he writes from '—[blank] Fighter Squadron, Some-where in England.' He provides little detail of his experiences other than to say,

We are on duty from dawn until dusk [and] it keeps [me] out of mischief . . . so much so that I have barely had time to see the little blonde actress I have been kicking around with. All in all it is not a bad life and I would not change places with anyone at home. Of course, I should hate to go on forever like this but it is a thrill at the moment.

This is the only mention in his papers of the 'little blonde actress,' so her identity will no doubt forever remain a mystery.

Oct 16, 1940
A surprise raid this morning in view of the poor weather. As luck would have it, I was spare pilot and did not have a machine. The boys had a brief dust up with some 109s over Southampton and were very lucky to get away unscathed as the Boche came down from the sun and had everything in their favour.

However, all went well and Novo and Aggie got one each, lifting the squadron score to 98, trembling on the verge of our century. It later developed that Dogs had fired a brief deflection shot at a 110 and by a fluke clobbered the pilot. The score at 99 . . . oh boy, a big party soon.

Oct 21, 1940
A five day lull broken only by two machine patrols searching for a lone Jerry recco job in clouds and occasional efforts at practice flying came to an end today. Frank Howell and Sid Hill came upon a Ju88 which had just machine gunned Old Sarum aerodrome and was hedge hopping for home. After an exciting chase along the deck they sent it into a field in flames near Christchurch. The complete crew was written off.

The 'century' party which followed this destruction of our 100th Jerry was a dandy and none of the boys was feeling any agony by the time the last cork had popped.

A recount shows that our score is actually 103, counting machines we have shared with other squadrons. I think we could safely add to this total at least half of our probables, so all in all 609 has made a considerable dent in Herr Goering's Luftwaffe.

In his own diary, John Bisdee recorded a 'shocking party in the evening—champagne cocktails of which we all drank many more than we had intended.' It was probably a good thing for everyone that the next day's poor weather precluded any further flying.

Oct 24, 1940
On a section scramble, Forshaw, Osta and Baillon came in contact with a [Ju]88. However, not only did he get away into a cloud, but his rear gunner hit Baillon's machine so that he had to jump, landing safely near Upavon. He has now been christened 'Bale Out.'

No extra points for guessing who gave poor Baillon that name.

Nov 1, 1940
We had four scrambles today, none of them productive of any action. On one, a squadron of 109s passed over us by about 2,000'

with their yellow noses gleaming but despite the advantage of height and the sun, they would not attack. It is of interest to note that above 25,000' the 109 is superior to our present Spitfire I. They can go up to 35,000' and appear quite manoeuvrable up there whereas the Spitfire will barely hold itself in the air at 31,000'. This handicap must be over-come if we are ever to engage them at this height. All this I explained at great length to a civilian who was displaying great interest at our dispersal point today. He said it would soon be overcome. Was my face red when he was introduced as Sir Archibald Sinclair, Secretary of State for Air. Oh well!

The rarefied air at these heights causes all aircraft to create a smoke trail and lucky for us eliminates the element of surprise. It is a fantastic sight to be behind the squadron and see each aircraft smoking furiously.

10

ACCIDENTS HAPPEN, EVEN IN WARTIME

While Ogilvie was revelling in the odd evening in London with his squadron mates, Irene was enjoying the company of her then fiancé, Chili Chilcott. Not long after her twenty-first birthday in November 1940, Irene was invited to come to Clandon, about twenty minutes from London by rail, where his sister Dora lived. Chili, Dora and her husband had been invited by a friend near Dora's home for cocktails. Irene was included and arrived on the train dressed to the nines in new, tailored pair of flannel slacks she had made herself and two fox stoles that were on loan to her from a friend. (She laughed that while walking through Bond Street in this garb, a local 'professional' warned her to 'Get off my beat, sister!')

The party turned out to be somewhat less formal than anticipated and after a few drinks, the host—something of a 'wolf,' Irene recalled—offered to drive her in his sports car the ten minutes back to Dora's, where she was staying, to change into something less dressy. The drive there was uneventful, but the return trip turned out to be a different story. Driving too fast around a curve on the gravel road, the friend lost control of the back end of the car. Irene remembered the roar of the engine as he tried unsuccessfully to correct the skid, and then nothing until waking up in hospital. She had been thrown out through the sun roof of the car and had hit a telephone pole; sliding to the ground, her legs had been run over by the car. The damage to her face from the impact with the pole was bad enough, but her legs were worse—the doctors feared for her ever being able to walk again.

This was the start of a six-month convalescence at Dora's, a time that Irene recalled with great gratitude. The Onslow Arms Inn became a favourite haunt, once she could get around. More sobering, London could clearly be seen as it suffered under the ongoing Luftwaffe attacks. 'You could see the bombs everywhere,' she said. 'It was sort of exciting—until you realized what could happen.' She recollected watching the flames on the night of one particularly heavy raid on the London docks and wondering about her mother, Jean, living in Clapham on the city's south side.

Even in Clandon they had the occasional run-in with errant bombers. Irene and Chili were in the living room talking with Dora and her husband, Andrew, one evening when bombs began to fall close by, probably released prematurely by a bomber under attack by fighters. They all squeezed into what they deemed to be the safest place in the house—the downstairs water closet, which was surrounded by stone walls on the outside—and huddled together until the danger had passed. An intimate but not very romantic evening, perhaps.

To the astonishment of the doctors, Irene's legs eventually recovered, and although she was scarred and plagued with aches and pains of various kinds for the rest of her life, Irene was never limited in her mobility in any way, at least as far as her family could see. She kept in touch with Dora until Dora's death in the early 2000s.

Skeets, meanwhile, was finding the pace of flying slowing down somewhat as the poor weather of that autumn set in, with one of the rainiest Novembers on record. His diary continues:

Nov 2–7, 1940
Leave, which I spent down at Heytesbury.[47]

Nov 10, 1940
One scramble today, bags of 109s on top of us as usual but no action. They must only be a sort of training flight that comes over. Olenski had a crash landing turning on his back, but was unhurt. Aggie crashed into Dogs before we took off, making it an expensive day on aircraft. We were sorry to hear that David Crook is leaving us to go to CFS[48] but it is a good thing as his wife is expecting a little one.

Nov 25, 1940

Two weeks unbroken by any sign of activity. Occasional sorties by two aircraft but never an engagement.

Mike Appleby has gone to CFS and will become an instructor. George Titley blew his eardrums out pulling out of a dive and I'm afraid will be lost to the squadron, if not for good, at least for some time. Old Olenski is also in hospital with four ribs cracked in a car crash.

The English rain and short days slowed down the frenetic pace of activity for the whole squadron. Ogilvie's log books show mainly short flights around the base, along with the occasional patrol.

Nov 27, 1940

On a scramble today 'Dogs' Dundas spotted ack ack fire over Southampton and on investigating saw a Ju88 haring for home. He gave chase and finally got in range, only as they crossed the French coast near Cherbourg. He had the port engine on fire and it was blazing down the fuselage as it went down in a slow spin. I think it could be safely assumed as destroyed. Two more DFCs go to Johnny Curchin and David Crook. The new CO, Michael Robinson, has also been 'gonged.' Practically an all star squadron.

Nov 28, 1940 [Flying Spitfire X4590, PRF]

What a black day this was for us. It started when we were informed that we had been transferred to Warmwell on the South coast, just when we were nicely settled for the winter at Wallop.

Coupled with the preliminary steps of moving we had some 150 Sandhurst cadets milling about the place. In the midst of the chaos we had one scramble which was fruitless. A little later we had a second one and over the Isle of Wight saw some fifty smoke trails coming in in line abreast. They broke up and milled around and it looked like the usual hide and seek game.

Skeets later recalled that they were flying at altitude, patrolling up and down the English coast, around 25,000 feet:

There were smoke trails coming from behind and our control told us a few "snappers" were flying up and down the other side of the English Channel, doing the same thing we were doing. That day I was the weaver. We used to have two guys weaving behind. We were to yell 'break' if someone came up. We were flying along like that when out of the corner of my eye I saw a big yellow nose come down our contrail. This guy came right behind us, I yelled, '609, break!' I broke, and I was lucky . . . I got a bullet through my tail and one through my wing, went into a spin, and came back up.

His diary described the rest of the action:

I was Yellow 3 and was weaving merrily behind keeping an eagle eye above when I caught a glimpse of three 'yellow noses' in my mirror. They were obviously crack pilots by their tight formation and strategy. I gave the warning and dove as the centre Johnny opened fire on me and was speeded on my way by a cannon shot up the fuselage, and a second through my prop. We heard 'Dogs' say that he had clobbered a 109 and that is the last we heard from him. There must have been a second one on his tail. Paul Baillon was also clobbered and jumped. I followed him down to the sea about twenty miles off Bournemouth but he must have been hit because he gave no sign of life. At any rate, he was not picked up. On top of all while I was circling the spot one magneto packed up and I sweated blood before I reached base with the engine vibrating badly. What a bloody day!

It developed that the Jerry Dogs got was Von Wick, leader of the Richthofen squadron, who had destroyed some 56 planes to date. I have a horrible feeling that I was damn near his 57th. Poor Dogs, the award of a bar to his D.F.C. has just come through.

Skeets tersely described the squadron's return to base: 'Dogs never showed up. He was our leading pilot at the time, he had something like 16 victories to his credit. He was just a wonderful chap, but didn't come back.' In fact, when Dundas was shot down, his tally was twelve aircraft destroyed, two shared destroyed, four probably destroyed and five damaged.

Unusually, the German English broadcast admitted that their big ace had been shot down, and that his number two had in turn brought down the victorious Spitfire. Von Wick's fifty-sixth victory had been Paul Baillon. John Dundas dispatched Von Wick shortly after and was himself wiped out by Rudi Flanz, one of Von Wick's wingmen. In short order, three pilots, including two of the war's top aces, had been shot down and killed, an ample demonstration of the speed and lethality of the aerial war. Baillon's body later washed up on the coast of France.

To add insult to injury, the squadron was next day moved permanently to Warmwell, out of the relative comfort of Middle Wallop and into tents. The pilots' battles now included the wet, blustery English winter weather as well. Ogilvie had two flights that day, the first of twenty minutes, 'Wallop to Warmwell,' and the second a squadron scramble with no result.

11

THE BATTLE MOVES ON

November had seen the end of the Battle of Britain, fought mainly in the air. With the staggering losses experienced by the Luftwaffe,[49] Göring left France in November and turned his attention elsewhere. The two key figures in Britain's extraordinary aerial defensive effort, Dowding and Park, were moved to other duties. They are generally acknowledged by historians as having brilliantly and successfully directed the resources of the RAF in the most critical and dangerous period of the war, at least for Britain. In recognition of this, Dowding's office has been preserved at Bentley Priory, Fighter Command's wartime headquarters. Park went on to confirm his outstanding leadership by directing the successful air defence of Malta in 1942, in the RAF's second biggest air battle of the war.

Their successors were less revered. In his excellent account of the Battle of Britain, author James Holland says: 'Sholto Douglas (who replaced Dowding) is now largely forgotten, having commanded Fighter Command during a period of endless fighter sweeps over France in 1941 and 1942, which achieved very little and cost far too many lives and aircraft.'[50] This judgement would have some resonance for Ogilvie, given his subsequent experience.

Meanwhile, there was also a steady and endless stream of activities on the home front in support of 'our boys.' Margaret, Skeets's stepmother, helped to establish the Patterson Avenue Group of the Canadian Red Cross Society, which was initially constituted on November 28, 1940, with a founding meeting held at the home of a Mrs Young. Fourteen of the local ladies were in attendance, along with two representatives of the Red Cross Society who explained the work and requirements of the organisation. Tea was served and initial contributions totalling $2.25 were collected. The proceedings and contributions were all duly recorded by Margaret, the meticulous former bank teller and secretary to the group, in a small black book.

These small, seemingly insignificant, contributions flowed in from all over Canada and steadily added up. They provided a reliable and invaluable stream of assistance in the form of food and clothing that were sent to men on active service and those incarcerated as prisoners of war. Skeets himself would eventually benefit from this patriotic largesse, collected pennies at a time. But in the meantime he was regretting an embarrassing and considerably more expensive loss to the war effort:

Dec 2, 1940
Swat me! Leading my section in after practice flying, I came in down wind and was so busy watching them I forgot to watch myself. I overshot a bit and my ship slid on the wet grass through the hedge and is a near write-off. Woe is me!

Ogilvie's flying log book speaks for itself, with a large, heavily lettered comment signed by Squadron Leader Michael Robinson, CO of 609 Squadron that reads: 'Error of judgement.' Flight Sergeant 'Tich' Cloves gave the incident a bit of context in his own diary:

We never had to wait long at a new camp for a pile up. Plt Off Ogilvie landing X4588 overshot and careered through the aerodrome fence; nice effort. Pilot uninjured, aircraft beyond unit capacity to repair. Plt Off Ogilvie was very peeved with himself, saying how stupid it was to wreck good aircraft in this manner when we were so short; exactly.

The following day, December 3, was little better. Again, 'Tich' Cloves provides the perspective: 'Plt Off Ogilvie X4173 found his engine coughing etc whilst on patrol and lobbed down at Exeter. He made his usual long landing; went off the runway and got bogged down in the famous Exeter mud. He was rescued and eventually returned to base without further mishap.'

Dec 5, 1940

Led Yellow section in an escort job over the Channel while a Harrow dropped strings of small parachutes. Some sort of experimental job it was.[51] Novo has been awarded his D.F.C. There should be another coming to Aggie then we will have to work on a new batch.

Dec 19–24, 1940

A long period of inactivity featuring only squadron flying practice and general fooling around. One day Aggie and Novo caught an Me110 snooping around and sent it into the sea for our 104th victim. I flew the adj. up to London one day in the Puss Moth and managed to get lost in the balloon barrage while looking for Hendon, but everything worked out OK.

This entry was written on Christmas Eve, 1940. Skeets's log book entry for the following day, Christmas itself, shows an uneventful fifty-minute practice flight. There is nothing to suggest a warm festive dinner was served to the pilots and ground crew in their tents at Warmwell.

Dec 31, 1940

Comes the end of the year with nothing exciting to report. Christmas and New Year went by most uneventfully. The days were spent striving to keep warm in our damn tent. The weather turned quite cold and life became a bit grim at times. The nights were occasionally spent in riotous living. When life became too unbearable at this darn camp we would wander afield, occasionally to Bournemouth, Weymouth or Dorchester, but on the whole early to bed and reluctant to rise was the key note.

Jan 6, 1941

Nothing to report save that I have finally caught up with this diary, and can perhaps add a bit of local colour to it from time to time.

In January 1941 Frank Ziegler arrived to become 609 Squadron's intelligence officer. In his squadron history, *The Story of 609 Squadron: Under the White Rose*, he describes being introduced to some of the pilots at the dispersal marquee, including 'a little, monkey-ish, wise-cracking Canadian named Keith Ogilvie.'[52] Shortly after, the duty flight was scrambled, returning some time later with the pilots complaining that it turned out to be an RAF aircraft. Ziegler described the post-mission conversation thus:

> 'Just a bloody old Hudson,' said Johnny (Curchin), reseating himself at the chess table. 'The silly clot went into cloud, and we chased him for ten minutes before we could see it wasn't a Dornier.'
>
> 'Better get the new Brains to teach you some aircraft recognition,' said Keith Ogilvie, the Canadian, slyly. 'Did you know you were supposed to do that thing, Brains?'
>
> 'I didn't,' I replied, appalled at the idea, 'and for heaven's sake don't call me Brains.'

But the name, of course, stuck.

The squadron was released shortly after this conversation from active standby; the pilots leaped to their feet and made for the exit to prepare for a night on the town, courtesy of the mayor of Dorchester, who was holding a dance at the Corn Exchange in honour of the unit. Pilot Officer John Bisdee, known to A.K. as 'Bish,' was driving Ziegler and others to the event in one of the shared vehicles the squadron somehow managed to come by and that everyone in it seemed to use. Again, Ziegler describes Bisdee's navigation: 'With supreme confidence he drove at great speed up and down the country, not at all perturbed that it was dark and that he had only a hazy idea of where the camp was. "Funny, you know," he said, "how lost one can become on the ground. I've pin-pointed the place often from the air."'

By the end of the month, everyone, Skeets included, was experiencing the boredom and angst of relative inactivity.

Jan 23, 1941

Sometimes I think that I should have joined the Foreign Legion. I've had only one day's good flying this month. Four trips in a Spitfire netted about three hours flying. A week's leave did nothing to swell my flying time and did much to deflate my bank balance. About four days ago, the rains set in with a vengeance and our dispersal point has taken on the appearance of a naval yard rather than an aerodrome. I'm afraid a submarine might sneak in and torpedo the squadron. As it is, the field is quite unserviceable for flying.

Perhaps the only bright spot on the horizon is that we can move into our permanent hut now and out of that wretched tent. We were sorry to hear that Aggie [Agazarian] has been transferred out to Greece at his own request. At this moment I envy him. At least he'll see some action. Our four Polish boys have received the Polish M.C.

Jan 27, 1941

Sitting here glumly watching the rain, it could be any day of the past two weeks—rain or near rain every day. Conditions absolutely unflyable, life is very dull indeed. Frequent nightly excursions as far afield as Bournemouth but more often Weymouth did little to relieve the monotony. Handcock was transferred to an O.T.U. by way of a surprise. Poor old Paul Baillon was found off the coast of France as we were informed through the Red Cross.

Feb 1, 1941

At last, the sun came through after almost two weeks and I finally got some flying in, if only in the Puss Moth when I flew Mrs. Owen back to Wallop. Come to think of it, this is my first woman passenger. Feel somewhat brittle today as a result of a mammoth party at the tank corps mess at Bovington. Everything remains very quiet, no visits from Jerry.

Feb 18, 1941

Just back from a riotous seven days leave in London and find things unchanged. Novo making a practice attack on a friendly aircraft suddenly found it to be a Ju88. He damaged one engine before it escaped into a cloud. We have also got three new pilots: P/O Williams, Sergs. MacSherry and Rigler. Once again the hot breath of an OTU is panting for a pilot and though the job carries two stripes, none of the boys wanted it at any price. The names went into a hat and I'm afraid Johnny Curchin got stuck. Johnny is on leave and he'll lay an egg when he hears. It is getting much too close now; I'll be so disappointed if I have to leave the squadron before the Blitz.[53]

12

A BIG MOVE: BIGGIN HILL

Skeets finally had reason to 'celebrate':

Feb 24, 1941

A big day this; gone are the days of sitting around wailing in this dead beat dump for something to happen, because it has happened. The squadron has been moved to Biggin Hill, the number one fighter station in the country. Just outside the London balloon area, about twenty miles from the centre of the city, our new playground will be that stretch known as 'Hell's Corner,' the Dover Straits. We flew up in squadron formation, Bish and I bringing up the new pilots in the rear and all arrived safely, save for Sgt. Mercer who ran off the runway and turned over. Here we found a real fighter station; during the London Blitz it was badly beaten up, stopping some 300 HEs [high-explosive bombs] in one day. However, the station has accounted for some 600 Jerries destroyed. We relieved 66 Squadron and took over their Spitfire IIs, which are faster than ours and can romp around at higher altitudes. We found a spot of trouble getting used to landing and taking off on the concrete runways but soon got the swing. All in all, everything looks very promising. We have lost old Frank, who has been given a squadron at Filton.

When he announced the move to Biggin Hill, the CO also informed the squadron that Frankie Howell, one of their most experienced flight leaders, was leaving for a promotion and that four of the (now experienced) Poles would be transferred as well. He went on to remind the unit of Biggin Hill's pedigree as the front line in the air war. Planning a suitable departure from Warmwell, the squadron did a flypast of their old base while Bish and Ogilvie led the newer recruits directly to Biggin. Ziegler describes the Mercer incident in typical understatement: 'One of the sergeant pilots . . . turned over at the end of an unaccustomed concrete runway and wrote off not only his Spitfire but a civilian worker's bicycle. . . . Civvy very peeved and wanted a new one . . . we should have offered him the Spitfire remains in lieu.'

The famous South African pilot, 'Sailor' Malan, was the wing commander flying at Biggin. He wasted no time in putting 609 into the air on its first operational sortie the next day, after the ground crews had figured out how to operate the new Coffman starters on the Spitfire IIs the squadron had inherited. It was (perhaps fortunately) a quiet patrol, but a good chance to get used to the newer aircraft.

Feb 26, 1941

We lost no time in getting going here. We were scrambled on a job escorting bombers over Calais. We were all a bit excited at this job, our first across the channel. We were top guard and flew at 30,000' above 92 and 74 Sqns, which in turn were above a couple of Hurricane squadrons protecting 23 Squadron's Blenheims. It was a perfect day, excellent visibility and smoke trails above 25,000'. From that height the channel looks like a stream and we were soon across. Over Calais the bomber boys cracked at the docks and there was a lively bit of 'archie' for a time. There was never any indication of Jerry fighters around and all went well save for one unlucky Hurricane pilot who was winged by shrapnel and had to jump. We were back at base after 1:30 and our first show was over.

March 2, 1941

We did a fighter sweep again today and about six squadrons swept from Le Touquet to Dunkirk. We were second from the top and though there were some 109s above, we did not engage. 74 Sqn. behind us had a brief dust up and I believe knocked down a couple, but on the whole it was almost without incident.

These 'sweeps' were a response to the declining pace of German raids and the increasing strength of the RAF. The plan was to start taking the war to the Germans, in the form of large forays across the Channel and over occupied Europe. The first time Skeets went on one of these multi-squadroned operations, he described it as a different kind of experience to the combat he had become accustomed to over his home territory:

> It was scary in another way, with all that water behind you, and you were over enemy territory. The German flak guns would all open up and there were black puffs all over the sky. But it never seemed to be a problem, I never saw anyone get hit by that. So we flew around, there were something like 275 Spitfires and Hurricanes on that first sweep. It was an incredible sight, to be climbing, climbing all the time and see all these other guys, some below you, some behind you. We were just looking for trouble, but on this sweep we didn't find it. The Jerries just wouldn't bite, they weren't too keen to engage unless we had bombers with us. So they'd send over a squadron of Blenheim bombers or something with an escort of 250 fighters. First of all we just crossed the coast and looked for their aerodromes along the coast. Gradually the 'thin red line' kept going farther and farther inland. About the farthest we could handle was Lille, in France.

It was a place he would become more familiar with as time went on.

Mar. 5, 1941
Fighter sweeps again: we were top guard and lost the squadrons below in cloud. It was uneventful for us but I gather the squadrons below had some slight opposition. We also had a couple of patrols which were monotonous and damn cold as we stayed around 30,000'.

At some point early in his time at Biggin Hill, Skeets had the opportunity to fly as number two to 'Sailor' Malan. The wing commander flying came down to take to the air, with 609 Squadron leading the wing. But what should have been a high point for Skeets turned out to be one of his worst days, and at the same time perhaps one of his luckiest. He recalled the day's events during an informal interview long after the war:

> Sailor Malan asked me to be his number 2, which shook me good. I was really very proud to do this. Anyway, we were briefed for our

mission which I think was a fighter sweep over Lille, France. We took off as a wing and we were climbing away to get our altitude. I was looking around and noticed the Spit on my left whose wheels were half down. It wouldn't take long for his engine to overheat if he didn't get his wheels up, so I rocked my wings to get his attention. He looked over and I lowered my wheels and put them up again, and he got the message and put his wheels up. I looked up and there was my prop, almost tickling the rudder of old Sailor's machine. If I had pulled up I would have whacked his rudder. Anyway, this chilled me in a big hurry and I paid a lot more attention. I thought, if I ever hit Sailor Malan's aircraft, he would have chased me all the way back to South Africa.

We got over France and didn't run into anyone on the way in, then turned to come back and some 109s started to come down and we broke up a bit. Sailor said, 'Two 109s below around 5,000 feet . . . let's get them!' and he peeled over and went straight down. I turned over to follow and we went down, screaming at these two 109s, got down to their level and behind them and Sailor knocked his off straight away.

When I levelled off I blacked out from the 'g' force, happens all the time, and by the time my eyesight came back again, I couldn't find Sailor or anyone else. There wasn't any point climbing back up again, it would have used too much gas, so I headed right back for the coast. We were pretty much right on the deck by then, so I came out somewhere over the Channel and the flak opened up. I was on my own by then.

I settled down to fly back across the Channel and headed back for England when all of a sudden saw something out of the corner of my eye on my left. It was tracers going by across my left wing. I pulled around to the right, looked back and there were three 109s on my tail. No matter which way I pulled, one of these guys would be shooting at me. If I turned left one guy would fire, turned right, another would fire. I used everything I had ever learned and lots I didn't know. I ended up climbing straight up into the sun and rolling and twisting until the aircraft was near the stall, and when I came out it was nice and quiet again. I had somehow lost them for whatever reason . . . they obviously weren't too darned good or too darned keen, or maybe they figured I was a trap, trying to lure them in so some other Spitfires could take them down.

Anyway, big sigh of relief. I levelled off again and set my compass and headed back across the water, and in about 5 minutes I came out over land again. The flak started popping. I had made the basic, stupid mistake of doing what they called putting your ring on back, setting the compass 180 degrees the wrong way.

So I turned around and started to get the hell out of there and all of a sudden the old tracer started coming by my wingtip from behind me again. There were these same three 109s after me again. We went through all the same damned thing over again, going straight up and diving straight down, and I finally lost them . . . again. I set the compass and headed for home, finally did get there. I think I had to land at Manston, to get some fuel.

It wasn't my best day. I never heard anything from my CO, and I never heard anything from Sailor, so he must have just thought he lost me. He got his 109, so I guess he was happy.

It was one of the days I wasn't proud of. The mere fact I didn't clobber old Sailor was something.

When he was asked how close behind him the 109s had come, the answer was classic Skeets: 'Well, they seemed close, but they couldn't have been too close. Either that, or they were the worst shots the Luftwaffe had. I was a sitting duck, thinking of nothing in particular when the tracer started drifting by my wingtip. They could have come right up behind me. Maybe they got in each other's road. Big yellow noses . . .'

13

BOMBS ON LONDON

On the evening of 8 March, Irene wore her special red dress to Hatchet's Restaurant, accompanied by her fiancé, Chili. They were listening to Stéphane Grappelli and George Shearing (who were playing at the time with Hatchet's Swingtette house band), two or three blocks away from the Café de Paris on Coventry Street in Westminster. They were with friends of Chili's: Richard Long, later Earl of Wiltshire, and his wife, Gwen. Not Irene's favourite companions, as it turned out. At some point early after meeting Irene, who always prided herself on her civilized behaviour, Gwen made the egregious error of offering to teach the young woman from the colonies some 'English manners.' Irene was outraged and emphatically declined the offer, but of course did it through Chili, not directly. Her response must have blistered Chili's ears—it was the kind of slight that would take Irene several lifetimes to forgive, if ever. In any case, that evening the music and dancing, if not the company, returned the outing to being a pleasure, at least until the air-raid sirens went off.

The *Times* coverage of the evening's events describes 'the bright moonlight of Saturday night' being disrupted by the terrible noise of bombs and anti-aircraft guns. Irene talked about what it was like for them, directly in the pathway of the bombing: 'You heard a bomb and waited to hear the next one so you'd know whether they were coming towards you. We could feel everything shake but nothing fell off the tables where we were. We went outside and could see all the damage, but didn't know at the time that the Café de Paris had been hit.' Going outside was an odd thing to have done under the circumstances; Hatchet's, like the Café de Paris, was a basement club that was reached by a long, steep staircase. Being underground, and thus relatively protected, club goers usually weren't too worried unless the bombing got uncomfortably close. This night, however, Irene and Chili could see the flashes and hear the loud roar of explosions as the bombs fell across their part of London.

Guyanese dancer and swingband leader Ken 'Snakehips' Johnson and his West Indian Orchestra were the house band at the Café. Not long after it began to play, the band had started into 'Oh Johnny,' one of its signature tunes. That's when the bombs began to fall in the West End, between Piccadilly Circus and Leicester Square. A single high-explosive bomb found its way down an air shaft into the club and went off, shattering the club's glass ceiling. All but one of the lights went out and couples who had been dancing together were blown apart. As of 6:00 the following morning, the London Civil Defence Situation Report tallied 34 dead and 82 seriously injured. Sadly, 'Snakehips' Johnson and saxophonist Dave 'Baba' Williams were among the more than 150 people killed that evening in London. An eyewitness recalled how Johnson was found lying dead but unmarked by any outward signs of injury, a flower still in his lapel. He was twenty-six years old.

There was no avoiding the Blitz—the bombs caught everyone, one way or another. Irene was at Dora's (Chili's sister's) home one night outside London when the explosions were particularly bad. Irene's mother, Jean, was actually blown out of her bed. Irene remembered looking at London and watching the flames, wondering about her mother and worrying for some time after until Jean was finally able to get to a working phone and call her daughter to reassure her. It was a close call, though. One bomb took part of the roof off and left Jean in her bedroom watching nearby parts of London burn through the hole it had made.

14

A NEW ROLE

T he 609 Squadron operations log for early March 1940 makes
reference to the introduction of a new and more challenging role
for the Spitfires, recording that on March 10 'Officers Forshaw,
Bisdee, Ogilvie and Atkinson practiced [*sic*] dusk landings.' There were few
night-qualified pilots at this time. In any case, the Spitfire was not considered to be a good night aircraft, mainly because of the bright flames from
its exhaust that virtually blinded the pilot on take-off and landing. Further,
it had no radar or other means of locating enemy aircraft in the darkness.
Nonetheless, the log notes: 'The Squadron is liable here to be called on to
supply dusk patrols or "forward layers." These operations are unpopular and
are seldom performed owing to a dearth of night operational pilots.' But
the squadron had to be ready for whatever role they were handed. Even so,
in his diary Skeets reported a definite lack of operational action during the
middle part of March:

> *March 15, 1941*
> Nothing much exciting. We are getting in lots of flying hours
> mostly on stooge patrols. We have moved from the mess to a coun-
> try house some five miles from the aerodrome as the GC[54] believes
> in dispersing the pilots. It is a large home, a bit beaten about by
> bomb splinters, but we should have good fun out here.

Indeed they would. Biggin Hill had been a constant target for German
bombers. Parts of the aerodrome had been flattened and the mess was . . .
just that. So while they ate at the station, the squadron lived on a private
estate. This was Southwood Manor, a large and imposing property about

three miles from Biggin Hill aerodrome. The 609 Squadron operations log describes life on the estate thus: 'There, on "off" afternoons, such squire-archal [*sic*] pursuits as tree-felling, vegetable-growing, rabbit shooting and beer-drinking take place, punctuated by nocturnal raids on the taverns and clubs of London and Bromley. Problem: to organize the lords in time for dinner at the Mess; and get them back to sleep.'

Ogilvie took advantage of the lack of (flying) activity around this time to write to the Patterson Avenue Red Cross branch, for which his stepmother, Margaret, continued to serve as secretary and bookkeeper. They had sent a personalized 'care' parcel of some kind to Skeets that elicited the following sincere and polite note by way of response:

Dear Ladies,
This will be just a few lines to thank you all for the marvellous parcel which I have just received from you.

It was a most welcome surprise and had all the elements of opening a Christmas parcel besides containing a great variety of things which are a real treat now.

At the moment I am living in a country home a few miles from our aerodrome, along with the other boys of the Squadron so you can readily see that your magnificent parcel was enjoyed by more than just one person.

It is indeed a most cheering thought to know that we are so much in the thoughts of you all at home and it does make it so much easier to wait the day when we will all be home again.

Once again, sincere thanks for your very kind remembrance, it was warmly appreciated, I can assure you.

Sincerely yours,
Keith Ogilvie

March 20, 1941
A bit of action today. We were patrolling a convoy by sections and mine was first off. I had Zura and Olenski along. We were warned that there were 'snappers' [enemy fighters] about and kept our eyes open. Even so, I did not see a thing until I heard Zura shouting, 'Ogie! Ogie!' and in my mirror I caught sight of a coloured snout of a 109. I lost no time getting out of there but even so caught

three machine gun bullets in my port wing, one going through to puncture the tire, but I was lucky to pull off a decent landing. In fact I was just plain lucky.

The other three sections went off in their turn and never saw a thing; our turn came again and we resumed patrol. We were just turning into sun when I saw the last of three Hurricanes below us roll over and go down streaming smoke into the drink.[55] Almost at the same time, I saw a 109 streak down beside me. We dove after it and it was joined by a second one. I got one squirt before they saw us and I think I got his glycol as he immediately poured white smoke and streaked for home. We chased them for a long way across the channel but were unable to gain a fraction of the distance. At that range—250 yards—I gave him repeated bursts but doubt if they did any good. These must have been the new 109F, as no ordinary 109 could travel away from a Spit at that height—9,000'. This is the first our squadron has engaged since we arrived here and I'm only sorry we did not have a scalp to hang up.

That night I had a big thrill when I had a dance with Vivien Leigh—'Scarlett O'Hara'—at a mess party. Off on leave in a few days. I shan't be sorry. I have had more flying this month than the past three put together so far. With Teeny [Overton], Bick and Bish away on leave, I had the flight to look after and it all makes for work.

Skeets continued to fly for the next two days, when it was his turn for four days of leave.

It is worth taking a moment from the combat action to explain the odd entry in Skeets's flying log book describing (usually) short trips in a Puss Moth, designated PR in his log, PR being the squadron's first two call letters for all its aircraft. The unit was, according to Ziegler, 'unusually rich' in non-combat aircraft. It had a Miles Magister at its disposal for picking up marooned pilots or taking them on leave. Michael Robinson, the CO of 609, was either owner or beneficiary of the Puss Moth, the favoured aircraft of the two because of its enclosed cockpit and greater comfort. Robinson also owned two copies of a fragile and strange aircraft called a 'Drone' that he brought with him when he joined the squadron.

The Drone was, according to Ziegler, 'a sort of glider powered by a Ford 10 engine, with the pilot sitting in the extreme prow.' Its top speed was about 40mph and it sounded like 'the buzzing of a million bees' as it drifted by, often with the CO of the squadron sitting in the pilot's seat and smoking a cigarette. The Drones were promptly designated PR! and PR?,[56] even though they were patently a far cry from the unit's usual flying machines.

When the squadron moved on, the former had been left in a Middle Wallop hangar in a damaged condition. Ziegler hypothesizes that 'it may have been this one (powered only by a motorcycle engine) that airman Hubert Fovargue recalls being so indifferently landed by Keith Ogilvie that "his feet finished through the floor of the cockpit on the runway"—perhaps the only occasion on which an aeroplane has been taxied in with the help of human legs.' Somewhat understandably, there are no entries in Ogilvie's log book describing his flights in the Drone—just the Magister and the Puss Moth.

March 27, 1941
Came back from leave to find the squadron a bit knocked about; Terry Forshaw posted to a ferrying job, and Teeny (Overton) is definitely finished operational flying and will go to an O.T.U. Olenski left and he was the last of our gallant Poles to go. They will be a great loss to the squadron, in many ways. Finally on a flight scramble 'B' flight got jumped by some 109s and lost Serg. MacSherry which was tough luck.

The end of March had also seen the departure of Skeets's trusted wingman, Jan Zurakowski, 'Zura,' posted to become an instructor. In their short, intensive experience together Skeets had come to rely on Zurakowski and they made a formidable team. The wingman's job was to guard the flank and rear while the flight leader kept an eye ahead. He would miss Zura's consistent and careful oversight.

About this time the Luftwaffe resumed its large night-time raids. Ogilvie's flying log shows the occasional dusk patrol or landing in April and May 1941. Ziegler also notes that one night when some 500 aircraft attacked London, Ogilvie and three others, including the CO and Bisdee, were ready to take off when bombs cut off all radio communications and continued to land around the station as the night went on. Perhaps fortunately for them, they never did get off the ground.

April 3, 1941

Teeny (Overton) left today for an O.T.U. and John Curchin takes over 'B' flight—good show. Paul Richey is joining the squadron and takes over 'A' flight which should work out alright. I find that last month I put in more time in the squadron than any other month since I joined—37 hours, bringing my time up to 415 hours. I may soon learn a bit about flying if I'm not careful. I picked up an infected throat somewhere which I fear may put me off flying a few days. I hate being around and not flying!

April 5, 1941

Our international tinge was preserved by the sudden appearance of five Belgian pilots, later followed by two more. They are all very nice chaps and we should have no trouble filling them in. They are all experienced pilots with one exception, and nearly all came from other squadrons. They are party men as well, as we found to our sorrow; we had an absolute screeching party and ended up by nearly demolishing the mess. Fun, fun!

This day seems to have been noteworthy for Skeets on another count. First, the squadron wasn't flying because of heavy rain, but it had received a visit during the day from Secretary of State for Air, Sir Archibald Sinclair. The visitor observed that the new Spitfire IIs were supposed to do 360 miles per hour, but was promptly corrected by Ogilvie, who estimated a more modest 300–330mph, to the chagrin of the Secretary of State.

The arrival of the Belgians was eased by Michael Robinson, who organized a dinner party at which Belgians and 609 veterans were interspersed. Ziegler devotes nearly two full pages in his squadron history to this event, so it clearly ranked as one of the unit's most memorable gatherings. He reports that while things began in silence, with wine came gradually loosening conversation, despite the language barriers. With port came some stories of the Belgians' varied flying experiences. With brandy came the discovery that one of the Belgians, Bob Wilmet, could play the piano, and that another, the charismatic Vickey Ortmans, could tap dance on top of that same, long-suffering instrument. Ziegler recalls the evening 'culminating in a war dance round a bonfire in the dining room. When a table laden with glass and crockery also began to dance, and Sidney Hill was found beneath it, Michael (the CO) decided it was time to stop, and at his orders his international squadron's first operation was sweeping and tidying everything up. To cement the new alliance, a landmine that night blew in the windows of Southwood Manor.'[57]

By this point, Curchin and Ogilvie were among the most experienced of the squadron's pilots. On April 6 they flew together to 'beat up' the Home Guard, according to the squadron's Operations Records Book (ORB),[58] and two days later were on dusk patrol over Dungeness. Curchin's inseparable companion, however, was Sidney Hill. The evening of April 6, Southwood Manor was awakened by some shattering explosions. Pilot Officer Hill was seen emerging from Curchin's room after a lengthy celebration of Curchin's promotion to flight commander, with a smoking revolver in his hand. Hill had apparently tired of the sight of his own haggard face, and the squadron's ORB somewhat languidly reports the consequences as 'Result—1 mirror Cat. 3, P/O Hill shot in effigy.' It can't have done Curchin's beauty rest much good.

April 15, 1941

A long spell of practice and 'stooge' flying was broken today by a three squadron sweep across the pond. Together with 74 and 92 squadrons, we patrolled the Boulogne–Calais area but met with no opposition save for a few rounds of 'archie.' One odd burst was a bright red and was taken as a signal to enemy fighters which never did appear. I have been moved to 'B' flight as deputy C/O to Johnny (Curchin).

At some point in this new phase of the adventure, Skeets became the butt of some good-humoured ribbing from his colleagues. He and his fellow pilots were 'just hanging around the Readiness [hut] one day when a party of visitors showed up with a photographer, Cecil Beaton, actually, the Queen's photographer.' Beaton took a picture of Skeets in his Mae West, gazing into the sky—a classic dashing fighter pilot photo. But Skeets paid the price: 'The squadron gave me a hard time, because the picture came out in the London weekly photographic magazine, describing the pilot as "tough, confident, aggressive." It was good for a laugh . . . we were just waiting around for the Jerries to show their faces.'

It wasn't always such a seemingly easy time. As Skeets remarked:

The busy days, all the squadrons were on the ready. We'd get a bell, like a ship's bell. It would start clanging and a little guy would run out of the hut yelling, "Scramble!" They'd get orders from Fighter Command to scramble one flight, two flights, the squadron. We'd often get one flight scrambled, if there was just one Jerry intruder, but during those busy days, it was always a squadron scramble, the whole caboose. Your parachute was on the wingtip of your plane and you'd run like mad to your plane, get your parachute on and climb in while the boys would plug in your oxygen and radio and get the cart wound up to get the engine going.

The night of April 16 marked an especially intensive bombing effort by the Luftwaffe. At 1:20 a.m., the phone rang at Southwood Manor calling four pilots—the CO, Bish, Curchin and Ogilvie—to readiness, with orders to take off at 03:00 hours for a patrol over London. The controllers' radio failed due to bomb damage, however, so the pilots waited the night out until the following morning when the remainder of the squadron were called to readiness. Skeets described the action, observed from the scramble hut.

April 16, 1941

Only one stooge patrol today which produced many smoke trails but no Jerrys [*sic*]. Shortly after dark, however, Jerry began roaring in in absolute droves bound for London. It very soon became evident that it was to be no ordinary Blitz as they came in steady streams and literally showered down incendiaries, HEs, flares of all sorts. There was nothing more than incendiaries in the camp but several HEs fell in the neighbourhood and altogether it was the most appalling yet fascinating sight I've ever seen. The greenish glow of incendiaries constantly burning somewhere around, occasionally turning to red as they connected; the steady roar of many aircraft; the frenzied outbursts of 'archie' and the boom of bombs. All blended to make the most devastating air raid ever attempted. I'm very glad I was not in London last night. As it was, five of us were at 'readiness' all night and would have been sent off had the wireless station not been clobbered by the bombs. The idea was to patrol over London in stepped up layers and [it] might have worked if we could have found the aerodrome to land again.

The destruction of this day wasn't limited to the Blitz on London. Sidney Hill had a particularly memorable time, starting with the collapse of his undercarriage on landing, followed by a forced landing on his next flight due to erroneous fuel gauge readings. Finally, after a bit of recreational flying he somehow landed the unfortunate remaining Drone in a strawberry patch, causing some damage. Curchin finished the job on the ill-fated aircraft, attempting to take off again through a hedge. A piece of the tailplane, salvaged from the wreckage and inscribed PR?, quickly became one of the squadron's most prized possessions.

April 20, 1941
The monotony of day patrols was varied today and I took a section to Gravesend to do a dusk patrol. Joe Atkinson and I did the patrol and though it was quite uneventful it was my first night effort in a Spitfire. It was a bit eerie to watch everything gradually darken up into blackness and see the searchlights light up the clouds beneath us. We had no trouble picking up the aerodrome in the dark and pulled off a successful landing. Personally, I think the whole thing is a waste of time, because visibility from a Spit is bad enough anytime and it is hopeless at night.

The squadron's Operations Records Book describes a typical evening's response to the 'monotony of day patrols.' The evening in question was that of April 22, a day in which no flying is recorded in Ogilvie's log book. Notably, none is recorded on the 23rd, either.

A Squadron 'Night Attack' on London was pressed home after a 'Defensive Circle' had been formed at Prunier,[59] in the centre of which the C.O. and P/O Ogilvie competed to see which could remain inverted the longer. Party then adjourned to the Suivi, but there is no coherent record of what transpired there. Later P/O Hill, 'sans coulotte' in a canary-coloured sweater and hair awry, was observed entering Lyons Corner House shouting impossible demands in a loud murkey [*sic*] voice, and being gently eased to a seat by two loyal drivers. Return to base was accomplished in 30 minutes.

Ziegler marvelled at how the squadron's pilots could return home at 4:00 in the morning in such thoroughly doubtful shape and still perform their wonders in the air, starting early the next day. This wasn't always required, fortunately:

'One morning it was not necessary to get up. "There's a knife outside you could cut with a mist," drawled Keith Ogilvie sleepily as he returned to bed.' Ziegler goes on to say, 'When he did have to go on patrol with a hangover, he referred to the hammerings in his head as "The MacGillicuddy Boys."'[60]

April 28, 1941

One of those days again. For weeks we go along on ordinary routine work, then for no apparent reason the lid blows off. As I was on night patrol from Gravesend last night I was spare this a.m. and the squadron was sent to escort Blenheims who were to bomb four ships off Dunkirk. It was rather sad as 74 Sqn. missed the rendezvous; the Blenheims missed with their bombs; and finally 109s dropped on the boys and Sgt. Bennett has failed to return. Poor old Bennett was the longest surviving member of the squadron[61] and had previously been shot down over Dunkirk. Later on 'B' flight were patrolling over Dungeness and four 109s got above and came down for a fast crack. Two got behind Hill, whose R/T had packed up and was unaware of their company. I had a crack at the first one and he promptly broke away; I got a second squirt at the second Johnny and someone dove at me from the sun. I pulled my nose up and gave him a short burst before I recognized it as another Spit. Luckily I missed and it turned out to be Sid still wondering if there were any 109s about.[62] On a later patrol 'A' flight also had a couple of cracks but nothing was claimed or lost, save on the morning's sad affair. A week's leave looms up and I'm very glad I think for the first time. We have been flying a great deal and a cold has not made me feel any better. Flying hours are now over 450. I'm getting on!

Ogilvie's flying log book is terse on this encounter: 'Engaged two 109s. No result.' Naturally enough, it also says nothing about the later events that took place to celebrate the visit of the Belgian air attaché and his staff. In typically robust fashion, the Operations Records Book notes the squadron as having hosted another entirely satisfactory event in honour of the occasion:

Evening saw a concert by Noel Coward, Beatrice Lillie, Caroll Gibbons and his wife, followed by an excellent cold table in the Mess which was impossible to get near. Dancing ensued, and by 03.30, 3 Squadron Leaders were serving waiters from behind the bar.

15

OTHER PURSUITS

S omewhere in this period another momentous event took place—the first meeting between Skeets and Irene. Irene had not long before broken off with her long-standing beau, Chili. He had admitted one evening that he wasn't quite ready for a long-term relationship and wanted to play the field a bit. Either his judgement was temporarily clouded or he didn't know her as well as he thought he did; in any case, she took great umbrage and gave him his marching orders. When he called her the next morning in the clear light of dawn, apologetic and asking his way back into her life, she simply told him to get lost and hung up. And that was that.

Not long afterward, Jean confided in her daughter that it was her twenty-fifth wedding anniversary. Not much of an occasion to mark, perhaps, given the family history, but Irene read a certain regret and sense of loss into her mother's confidence and proposed a 'celebratory' trip to a nightclub. On hearing the offer, Jean further admitted that she had never been to a nightclub. Well, that cemented the plans. Irene called her friend Chris who was a waiter at the Wellington Club, and who had been particularly good to Irene and Chili when they were on the town. With Chris's help, Irene arranged a private, sheltered table on the balcony overlooking the dance-floor band, and off the two women went.

It was a memorable evening altogether. Among the gathering at the club was Clare Boothe Luce, the American author, journalist, politician and, later, ambassador. Boothe Luce was travelling in England at the time and partying with friends at the Wellington. In their corner of the room, the two Lockwood women were enjoying themselves, watching the other partygoers when John Bisdee, Skeets's frequent flying companion, came over to say hello.

The Wellington was another favourite haunt of the 609 pilots and Irene had somehow met Bisdee before, when she had come with Chili. Bisdee seems to have been aware of the recent break-up because he announced, 'There's a Canadian who has just arrived—I want you to meet him.' This was Skeets, who spent the rest of the evening trading small talk with his fellow expatriate Canadians.

Sometime later one of Skeets's gang came up and said, 'We're going nightclubbing, do you want to come along?'

Irene felt obliged to say no as she needed to see her mother home, but Skeets asked, 'Do you think your mother would mind if we saw her home together and then you could come on with me?'

'I don't know, ask her!' was the reply.

He must have charmed the two women, because when he did ask, Jean agreed. Skeets took her down and put her in a cab, paid the driver and saw her safely off home. Keith and Irene headed off to the Suivi Club, a place with a big dance floor and a 'marvellous' band. After a long, late evening of conversation and dancing, he finally took Irene home. Irene remembered that at that time, everybody, including at least some of the Canadians she knew, were coming over to England go to war and often misbehaved badly. Many hadn't been out of their own back yards, in her opinion, and were thinking, 'As long as I'm here, I may as well try everything, live for today' . . . and that's what they did.

So she was somewhat wary as the two made their way to her house, having for much of the time been thinking to herself, 'I hope I won't have any trouble with this guy.' Yet the evening had been so pleasant and she found him so nice that she contemplated inviting him in for a coffee. When they arrived at Irene's apartment, Keith helped her out of the taxi and held her hand to the door. She thought, 'Here comes trouble,' but Skeets simply turned to her and said, 'Thank you for a wonderful time' . . . and offered Irene his hand to shake in parting. After all her trepidation, she was utterly dismayed, having decided by now that she quite liked this quiet, unassuming but obviously dashing fellow. But her new acquaintance was either too shy, too afraid of frightening her off, or too much the gentleman even to offer that modest sign of affection. Whatever the reason, off he went into the night leaving the frustrated Irene to make her way into her apartment. It would eventually turn out to have been an excellent strategy!

Lockheed Sirius piloted by Charles and Anne Morrow Lindbergh, on the Ottawa River, August 1931. COLLECTION OF A.K. OGILVIE

No. 15 Course, Hullavington, No. 9 Flying Training School, November 1939 to March 1940. Halos drawn above those lost in wartime action; black hats on those who did not complete the course. Skeets in fourth row at far right. COLLECTION OF A.K. OGILVIE

Skeets and mates at Hatfield, 1939. Skeets at far right. COLLECTION OF A.K. OGILVIE

Skeets 'shoots a line' with Tom Rigler and Ken Laing, early summer 1941. COLLECTION OF A.K. OGILVIE

No. 609 Squadron on standby, fall 1940.
Skeets seated on the wing of the Spitfire.
COLLECTION OF A.K. OGILVIE

Skeets and Spitfire, September 1940.
COLLECTION OF A.K. OGILVIE

No. 609 Squadron pilots horsing about
while they wait on standby, 1940. Skeets
on right. COLLECTION OF A.K. OGILVIE

No. 609 Squadron publicity photo, fall 1940.
Skeets on left.
WESTMINSTER PRESS PROVINCIAL NEWSPAPERS LIMITED

above—No. 609 pilots on standby, 1941.
Standing: John Curchin, W. Van Lierde.
Seated: Skeets, F.H.R. Baraldi, François de Spirlet,
'Vickey' Ortmans. COLLECTION OF A.K. OGILVIE

below—Pilot Officer A.K. Ogilvie, RAF,
August 1940. COLLECTION OF A.K. OGILVIE

above—Skeets and 'Red' Tobin at dispersal,
on standby, September 1940.
COLLECTION OF A.K. OGILVIE

below—Skeets on standby at Biggin Hill,
April 1941. PUBLICITY PHOTO TAKEN BY SIR CECIL
BEATON. COLLECTION OF A.K. OGILVIE

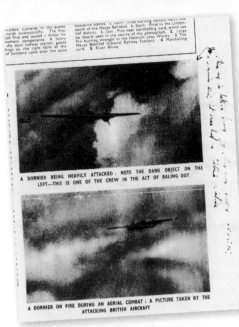

above—Newspaper clipping showing camera
gun shots from Skeets's Spitfire during action
of September 15, 1940. NEWSPAPER UNKNOWN.
COLLECTION OF A.K. OGILVIE

bottom left—Main body of Do. 215 wreckage
near Victoria Station, September 15, 1940.
LONDON *DAILY MIRROR* PHOTO, COLLECTION OF A.K. OGILVIE

bottom right—Do. 215 shot down over London,
September 15, 1940. LONDON *DAILY MIRROR* PHOTO,
COLLECTION OF A.K. OGILVIE

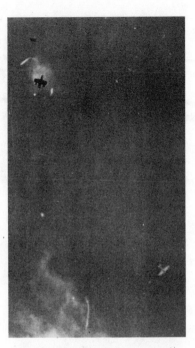

above—Do. 215 shot down over London,
September 15, 1940. Note unidentified
fighter visible at bottom right. LONDON
DAILY MIRROR PHOTO, COLLECTION OF A.K. OGILVIE

above left—Do. 215 wreckage near Victoria Station, September 15, 1940. This is now the entry to a pub, with the marks from the crash still visible in the stone foundations. LONDON *DAILY MIRROR* PHOTO. COLLECTION OF A.K. OGILVIE above right—Do. 215 tail section on a rooftop in Vauxhall Bridge Road, September 15, 1940. COLLECTION OF A.K. OGILVIE

left—Portrait of Pilot Officer A.K. Ogilvie by Capt. Cuthbert Orde, dated June 10, 1941.
COLLECTION OF A.K. OGILVIE

below—No. 609 Squadron pilots making hay, June 28, 1941. *On hay wagon:* Sergeant R.J. Boyd, Pilot Officer Peter MacKenzie, Sergeant Tom Rigler. On ground, Pilot Officer 'Vickey' Ortmans, Flight Lieutenant John Bisdee, Skeets Ogilvie, Flying Officer B. De Hemptinne.
EVENING STANDARD PHOTO. COLLECTION OF A.K. OGILVIE

above—The young William 'Billy' de Goat and No. 609 Squadron friends at Biggin Hill. *Bottom:* 'Vickey' Ortmans, Tom Rigler, Skeets, John Bisdee, Robert Wilmet. Rigler is holding Spitfire, a squadron mascot. Wilmet is holding Sailor Malan's dog Petie, who had the reputation of infallibly greeting the returning aircraft containing his master. Photo taken June 28, 1941, about one week before Skeets was shot down.
EVENING STANDARD PHOTO. COLLECTION OF A.K. OGILVIE

below—Skeets on standby at Middle Wallop, September 1940. COLLECTION OF A.K. OGILVIE

Spitfire, probably a Mark V, flown by 609 Squadron from Biggin Hill (undated).

above—Hospital in Belgium, late summer 1941. Skeets is standing in the middle, arm in a cast. COLLECTION OF A.K. OGILVIE

Audrey Locksley and Irene Lockwood feeding the pigeons in Trafalgar Square, 1945. COLLECTION OF I.M. OGILVIE

RCAF photographers Pat Collins, Helen Baker and Irene Lockwood, London, 1943. COLLECTION OF I.M. OGILVIE

Irene and friends during 'Carnival' (RCAF Europe), December 1945. Not all eyes are on the gaming table! COLLECTION OF I.M. OGILVIE

LAW Irene Ogilvie, 1944.

above—Henri Picard caricature of Skeets, dated
November 2, 1943. COLLECTION OF A.K. OGILVIE

left—Henri Picard drawing of Skeets, dated
January 5, 1943. COLLECTION OF A.K. OGILVIE

Residents of the 'Rackets Room,' Stalag Luft III, undated. *Top row:* Marcus Marsh, Peter Coleson, Ken Jones, Skeets, Ernie Abbott, Peter Walker. *Seated:* Group Captain Herbert Massey, Squadron Leader Bill Jennens.

Stalag Luft III theatre party. Skeets in centre with 'female' actor's arm on his shoulder.

Sam and Og at Stalag Luft III. Skeets on left and Samuel Pepys in a hockey sweater, holding the tray. COLLECTION OF A.K. OGILVIE

A sunny window in Stalag Luft III. *From left:* Flight Lieutenants Barrett, Snow, Ogilvie and Carter. COLLECTION OF A.K. OGILVIE

Stalag Luft III hockey game on the fire pond. Skeets seated middle row right.

Skeets and Irene on the porch of the Ogilvie family home in Ottawa, July 1946.

Skeets after his first T-33 solo, June 1953. COLLECTION OF A.K. OGILVIE

16

BACK TO WORK

Skeets continued to note events in his diary:

May 10, 1941

Have just finished seven days' leave and enjoyed a complete rest at Heytesbury which I figure I needed about now. Came back as usual to find the squadron had done big things. Unfortunately we lost Sgt. Bennett, the longest surviving member of the squadron, one day when they were accompanying Blenheims to bomb shipping off Dunkirk. Several of the boys had a rough time, particularly Curchin when they were jumped on by 109s; all returned except Bennett.[63] On the eighth a dinghy was reported in mid-channel and the squadron went along for a look-see. They found two 109s circling it and sent a section down. From then on it rained alternate layers of 109s and Spitfires and when the smoke had cleared there was an additional six 109s in the channel, along with two probables with no loss to ourselves. Amongst the scorers ranked Sgt. ('I've got one') Rigler who clobbered two; the C/O got two; Church and Rees divided one, besides getting one each; with Sgts. Palmer and Mercer dividing two probables. Mercer, flying my machine, got shot to ribbons but arrived back OK.

This action became known as 'The Battle of the Dinghy' and was celebrated in an oil painting by renowned aviation artist Frank Wootton. It is now part of the Royal Air Force Museum collection, after having hung for several years in the officers' mess at Biggin Hill, and subsequently in the mess at Church Fenton. The action remains a legendary part of the squadron's history.

Skeets's diary entry carried on:

Next day on a sharp encounter, old Mercer got shot up again and for some obscure reason crashed into the Dover cliffs.[64] Rough luck. I arrived back on the tenth and we had three soft days when we were on night flying from West Malling. Not only did we not fly, but we had the following days off and wandered up to London. On Saturday night, London was blitzed badly, Westminster Abbey, Houses of Parliament and British Museum all being hit.

The night of May 10–11 was arguably the worst night of the Blitz and saw the deaths of 1,486 Londoners who perished in the destruction of more than 11,000 homes. Over 2,000 fires raged throughout the capital. The concentrated night-time bombing tactics were brought to an end on May 15, partly because of the resistance of the RAF and partly to divert German resources to Hitler's invasion of its former ally, Russia. London continued to suffer aerial attacks, but at a reduced level for much of the balance of the war.

May 16, 1941
Bright sunny weather, unhappily reminiscent of last summer's Blitz days, seems to have arrived again, and with it occasional skirmishes with Jerry fighters.

Yesterday De Spirlet had a narrow escape when his machine was shot to ribbons but he force-landed safely at Eastchurch.

Today we were patrolling about ten miles inland from Dover when someone shouted that our weaver had been shot down. It was Palmer, but he force landed safely at Detling. We turned sharply and saw four 109s below. My section was nearest so I led in. Got a good burst in at close range and the leader rolled over and down steeply, pouring black smoke. I followed him at a hell of a rate— over 450 mph—and we passed over Dover at 1,000' still diving and me about 250 yds behind giving him short bursts. About half way across the channel I ran out of ammo and came back, figuring that he had gotten away with it, but luckily the Dover guns saw him crash into the sea about three miles off the French Coast. This is my fourth confirmed. Sid Hill also had one confirmed and Vickey one damaged.

May 17, 1941

We continue to do a great deal of flying these days. 'A' flight had a brief skirmish with the Hun and Joe Atkinson piled into a field, escaping with a slight cut over one eye. I did a dusk patrol with the C/O and managed to land again safely after making one rather savage dart at the Chance light, frightening everyone there, and certainly myself, before finally getting it down. All good clean fun.[65]

Flight Lieutenant Atkinson, known later more formally as Sir John Atkinson, KCB, DFC, was in fact not named 'Joe.' He got this appellation from Ogilvie on being made responsible at Warmwell for the squadron's defence against gas attack. Ogilvie immediately labelled him 'Joe the Gas Man,' all 'gas men' in Canada of course being called 'Joe' after a popular cartoon strip. The name stuck for the duration of the war, and for friends and even Atkinson's wife Peggy, for the rest of his life.

The date of May 17 was also the day Pilot Officer Ogilvie became Flying Officer Ogilvie, a well-deserved promotion, according to the squadron log, which went on to note that with the large number of patrols being flown, 'he can't find the time to put up the wider stripe.'

May 20, 1941

For the past three days some of us have known about a couple of daylight raids to come off today. They were on a large scale involving nearly all fighter aircraft of 11 Group. The first one came off but the second did not, due to the weather. The first 18 Blenheims were to bomb an oil plant at Bethune, about 30 miles into France. Our squadron's job was considered soft, namely flying a position to engage any fighters pursuing our boys home. It was an imposing sight as squadron after squadron roared over forming up. We proceeded to our positions about twenty miles off North Foreland and stooged around for some time. We broke into four—one led by W/C Malan, DSO, DFC & bar. I was No. 2 on our C/O. We were attacked head-on by a 109, which I must confess I never even saw save only for the tracer which floated over the top. Several of the boys had bursts, but I never had a squirt. For some weird reason [Belgian] De Grunne's plane blew up and he baled out, but was not picked up by rescue craft. What an end for a Johnny who had fought all through the Spanish war and had shot down seventeen planes. Sgts. Palmer and Boyd both ran short of petrol and piled up in fields. We claim one 109 destroyed by various members. Altogether the raid was a success. The bombers pasted their target and lost only one. We destroyed five fighters and lost six. The second raid would have been more fun for us as we were to precede the bombers into German Fighter H.Q. and beat the aerodrome up at St. Omer, but it did not come off.

May 21, 1941
Put in three hours over convoys in dirty weather. A monotonous job, this one, as one just stooges around and nothing ever happens.

In a letter to Irene after the war, 'Bish' Bisdee recalled one of these operations:

One day at Biggin Hill, Keith & I were due to escort some Blenheims on an anti-shipping sortie. The whole op was badly thought out—the weather was appalling, & we had no radio contact with the bombers. Instead, Keith & I volunteered to go into France in cloud cover & hoped to break out & attack a train or convoy on the road. We duly did this, but in France the cloud was right down to the ground. We decided to return & I hoped to fly back to Biggin on instruments, with Keith beside me. We got back & when we'd landed, he came up to me and said, 'Gee, Bish, I kept beside you like a brother.' You can say we were real close!

May 23, 1941
Sitting around dispersal in the rain waiting to see if we are to carry out low flying attacks over occupied France in pairs.[66] I'm billed to go with the C/O, and he has a big scheme to go a hell of a way into France. This patrol got no further than mid-channel when we ran out into clear weather. It is just possible that I was a bit relieved; still, it might have been good fun.

Sometime around this period, Skeets wrote home with a story illustrating some wishful thinking on the part of the German propagandists. He told his family,

We heard the most distressing news tonight on the German propaganda station. It seems they have wiped out our whole airdrome [*sic*] here. Funny, because it was there five minutes ago. The stuff they send out from that station is pathetic—I don't know who could be stupid enough to swallow any of it. It certainly provides us with several good laughs.

May 28, 1941
Led by W/C Malan and with 92 Sqn as high guard we did an inspired sweep about 35 miles inland of France, turning at Foret Nieppe and skirting St. Omer on the way out. It was quiet, an uneventful jaunt entirely devoid of incident though 92 had a brush on the way back and had one shot up. Wilmet made a forced landing due to lack of petrol.

May 29, 1941
Fog-bound for three days, our sweeps got no further than the haunts of London night life. We successfully swept the Wellington; Berkley; the Suivi; and other spots and suffered no casualties, though the boys were considerably messed about and we left our Humber dejectedly draped over a lamp post. If the weather doesn't clear soon, the squadron will probably need a short session in the rest homes. A ray of sunshine on the horizon when we received delivery of the first of our new Spitfire Vs—cannon jobs.

The fog offered a welcome respite to a busy flying schedule. On hearing the news, Skeets rolled over in bed thankfully and went to sleep again. The rest didn't last long, however, as he was soon dragooned into 'shooting a line' on behalf of the squadron to a visiting Canadian journalist seeking an inside look at the boys on the front lines. He then headed off to unknown parts for another well-deserved rest.

June 8, 1941
Returned from seven days leave in a rather shaken state due to a session at the 'Suivi,' to hear the worst news I have heard yet. They got little Curchin.[67] Anyone else in the squadron, I could believe it, but not Johnny; I never thought they could ever get him. But he

is gone, on a simple party with three 109Fs. The boys got two and damaged the third. Rigler got one and the second got into a terrific dive after Vickey and the thing came apart in the air. The squadron will be a sadder gang without that little bundle of dynamite around, God rest his happy-go-lucky soul!

Curchin, one of the squadron's 'heavenly twins' with Sidney Hill, had been posted to 609 in the middle of June 1940, some two months before Skeets, and was a frequent companion on operations. Skeets's tribute is short, poignant and heartfelt—he was obviously unsettled by the news.

Around this time, Captain Cuthbert Orde, a talented artist, was commissioned by Air Commodore Sir Harald Peake of the Air Ministry to draw the heroes of Fighter Command. He visited 609 several times and drew a number of portraits of the squadron's pilots. The one he completed of Flying Officer A.K. Ogilvie is signed by Orde and dated June 10, 1941. In his portrait, Skeets looks pensive and slightly sad, perhaps because of the recent loss of Curchin.

June 11, 1941

Party today consisted of three squadrons escorting five Blenheims, bombing an oil tanker. We went nearly to Zeebrugge before we found the damn thing and the Blenheims put on a big show, getting seven direct hits in ten efforts. The trip home seemed endless over that water. The C/O pulled up suddenly and I found cannon tracer floating past my port wing and looked up to see two 109s doing a head on attack. I got a one-second squirt at the second one, but could not pull around tight enough to get him. 'Bish' knocked pieces off but they got away. Unfortunately poor old Chestnut, my number two, stopped one in the glycol and nursed his machine all the way back, only to crash into the cliffs at Ramsgate. One of our two new Canadian pilots, he was doing nicely until now.

June 12, 1941

On fighter nights these two nights, we did not fly but during the days I managed to catch up on some visits. Went to Ilsley to see Frankie Howell; Farnborough to see Butch MacArthur; and finally up to Upwood and saw Frank Orme, my first close friend since I left Canada. He is on Blenheims and I wish him luck; he'll need it.

This was the first opportunity Ogilvie had to fly the new cannon-equipped Spitfire V. It was considered by many to be the best version of that esteemed aircraft, a perfect balance of strong armament, power and weight that made it an incomparable fighting machine. One of the things that increased its weight was improved armour plating, something the pilot would be especially thankful for in a few short weeks. Later asked about 'his' aircraft, Skeets set the record straight in his typically modest fashion. He always considered himself to be simply a reliable line pilot, one of the workhorses who supported the big-scoring aces:

> The S/L and the Flight Commanders had their own aircraft, but the rest of us took whatever we could get, back from inspection or over-haul or whatever. We used to have a couple of old clunkers that we would try to avoid flying, that were pretty time expired, but other than that it was just a question of fate. The aircraft were maintained well. The mechanics would jump all over them when they came in, get them ready for the next flight. They had a daily inspection. If you reported anything peculiar they'd investigate it carefully. They were just trying to keep the aircraft in the air—we were short of aircraft all the time.

June 16, 1941
Released this p.m., I flew down to Hullavington, my old training school, and hardly recognized the place let alone the people there. Spent a quiet afternoon in the sun at the CO's home nearby and came home with him at dusk.

Ogilvie's log book shows a morning convoy patrol, then a forty-minute flight to Hullavington followed by a return flight to Biggin Hill the same day. It must have been a great pleasure to be invited to Robinson's home for a relaxing afternoon, followed by a leisurely flight back in the waning light of a calm summer evening.

On June 17 the RAF opened its first daylight offensive, the beginning of a six-week period of continuous strikes into the mainland, sometimes involving as many as three sorties a day for 609 Squadron. These operations usually consisted of a few bombers with a specific target in mind, escorted by a large number of fighters. The purpose of these 'circuses' was to draw German fighters into engagement. There was a significant downside, however; they reversed the advantage previously held by the RAF in action over England, when damaged aircraft and their pilots could be recovered easily. RAF losses increased as a result of these actions over mainland Europe.

June 17, 1941
Damned bright and too clear. Escorted a Blenheim on a calibration job which was quite uneventful. Later in the day the big job came off. At 7 p.m. some 20 fighter squadrons escorted 24 Blenheims about thirty miles inland of France to bomb targets at Bethune. Our job was high escort for the bombers at 20,000'. We crossed the coast and went miles into France, passing over several aerodromes on the way, so far without incident. The bombers reached their target and plastered it plenty as later reports show, and from then on the close escort was heavily engaged. Just inside the French coast Bish was leading and saw two 109s below us, so we rocketed down to attack. I got a two second burst at one and lost sight of him. Bish got his and sent it down in flames. A minute or two later I saw mine below again and got in close before I gave him a smart burst with cannon and MG. He must have been hit in the petrol because he simply blew up and went into the channel [off Cap Griz Nez] blazing like a torch. Our squadron got those two confirmed and another probable (De Spirlet).

All in all, we destroyed thirteen Boche and lost ten fighters, but no bombers. The close escorting Hurricanes suffered most, one squadron (58) losing four and 242 losing three.

Skeets later recalled a humorous end to the day's combat. After his successful engagement, he said: 'I saw someone behind me. I swerved like crazy to try to get out of the way, but it was one of my Squadron boys who was trying to catch up with me. One of the Belgian pilots.'

June 18, 1941
Another brilliant sunlit day and another raid on France. Our job was to patrol the Channel in fours. Our four saw nothing except

someone go splash into the channel and explode viciously. One hopes it was a Boche. Somehow Sid Hills' section became engaged and he was hit. He attempted a forced landing inland but had the incredibly bad luck to turn over and immediately burst into flames. Poor old Sid, what a bloody awful way to cash in. The squadron is starting to look a bit tattered now. We got two new Belgians who are supposed to be hot stuff. We can use them.

The loss of Sidney Hill was another blow to the squadron. When Curchin, his great friend, was shot down earlier in the month, Hill's outlook changed. Hill aggressively pursued every opportunity for revenge and was reported this day to have led his section into battle with a much larger group of Me109s. That evening, the CO had his hands full trying to keep the squadron's morale up and responded by laying on a mandatory party, a night-time swim and a full squadron pursuit in the dark of the poor adjutant.

The longest day of the year, June 21, was also the hottest to date. The Operations Records Book noted that some pilots were flying without their tunics, thus rendering them—theoretically at least—subject to being shot as spies should they fall into enemy hands. It turned out to be an especially hot one for Ogilvie. Nothing is on record as to whether or not he was wearing a tunic.

June 21, 1941
Here is a day that Junior will not forget in a hurry. Continued brilliant sunshine means continued grief for the boys. Our job on the first show was a comparative stooge. We were merely to patrol off N. Foreland and protect the returning bombers who were beating up St. Omer Aerodrome. This we did without incident, although I saw two chaps in the sea, one of whom was picked up by a rescue boat and the second out farther did not seem so lucky.

The afternoon's do was more complicated. We were high cover for the bombers, bombing an aerodrome behind Boulogne. We got over 'sans incident' and I saw the target well enveloped in smoke. It occurred to me then that my section had dropped behind so we beat it up a bit. Boulogne AA let go with some accurate shooting and smacked one plane squarely. He pulled up and went down pouring glycol; it turned out to be a 109. Four planes came alongside and started down and I saw they were 109s. We mixed it up a bit and I gave one Boche the benefit of my cannon which did not jam, luckily. He tired of this sport and after a few feeble wiggles he baled out.

The Operations Records Book notes that when he saw the 109s, Ogilvie 'turned head on and fired, this starting a general dog fight. Ogilvie got behind one enemy aircraft and brought it down to Le Touquet aerodrome "in full view of a number of German mechanics and pilots" as the papers added. The pilot baled out.' Skeets's account of that day continues:

Shortly after I was engaged by the toughest 109 I ever hope to meet. I've never worked so hard in my life to get that boy off my tail. He was always there, firing. I dived, rolled, spun, climbed and prayed and finally lost him well out to sea. I set my compass for home and streaked across the water. After a short time I came over land and had a sudden sick feeling which was confirmed a split second later by tracer going by my wing. Like a complete funny man, I had set my compass back to front and had whizzed straight back to France. The ring-around-a-rosy started again and I stopped two MGs in the wing before I lost him by turning back at him, though my ammo was gone. You cannot outrun these 109Fs, but can outturn and out-manoeuvre them . . . thank God. It was a plenty relieved guy who crossed the Dungeness and made for home. Sgt. Boyd also got one and Vicky Ortmans a damaged. For the day the RAF got 28 for a loss of one bomber and four fighters . . . which is not bad.

This seems to have been the second time he made the mistake of misbox-ing his compass and again escaped the potential consequences. It could easily have turned out otherwise, save for the manoeuvrability of his slower Spitfire and the low-level haze over the sea. 'I made a slight error in compass reading,' he admitted on landing, 'and gave those Luftwaffe boys entirely the wrong impression.' He did not make the same mistake again!

June 22, 1941
Getting to be a question of who cracks first, the pilots or the weather. Today the bombers cracked at a marshalling yard, some-

where behind Dunkirk and our job as a wing was to break up 109s behind Dunkirk before they got organized. It went along OK and I was No. 3 on 'Bish' and Rigler. Bish saw some stuff and went down. I did a tight turn and cut down on some types which turned out to be Hurricanes. I lost my suction then and weaved an erratic course for home. The channel seemed full of Hurricanes so I hung around above hoping for a break but instead my engine began running rough so I wheezed for home. I watched the rescue boats pick up a pilot which turned out to be De Spirlet, who was slightly wounded and baled out. Came home to find Bish had got one and old Rigler pulled the hat trick with three after an incredible scrap. Spent the rest of the day in complete disgust for having missed this show. Total for the day is 27 Boche for one of ours. The squadron score stands at 132 destroyed.

The squadron's actions of the past couple of days were featured in *The Times* and on the radio, apparently, with Ogilvie and Sergeant Rigler figuring prominently in the coverage on June 23.

That was also the day the unit acquired a mascot, William de Goat, thanks to Vickey Ortmans, who received the young creature from a local Belgian pub landlady. William spent his days at leisure while the squadron flew, eating fresh grass outside the dispersal hut. He was also the beneficiary of quantities of beer and cigarettes, provided by the pilots, who were clearly not much concerned about healthy eating habits for their new friend. It was also decided that he should be subject to the full depth of service life— discipline and benefits—and, as a consequence, he had a rather full and eventful existence with the squadron. Gradually promoted through the ranks, he nonetheless managed to find himself on the wrong side of service regulations from time to time, including wreaking devastation to the administration officer's papers. It became a common excuse when papers went missing to blame their disappearance on William. He also received censure for misbehaviour with local female goats in France when the squadron was posted to that country later in the war, and at the rank of group captain, received the ultimate punishment—neutering. But for the moment, all this was off in the future as William settled into his new life on the flight line.

June 23–28, 1941

The good, or at least clear, weather has continued to hold and Command has continued to push up offensive sweeps to amuse Jerry. During these five days I have been on nine sweeps well inland of France, and I do mean well inland, the furthest job being in as far as Lille . . . over 100 miles in from Dover. Several of the boys have missed some due to one thing and another, and I find that Vickey Ortmans and myself are the only two pilots in our squadron who have been on every sweep. I must confess that I am feeling plenty tired now as there is considerable strain flying over enemy territory.

A thoroughly understandable sentiment. During the Lille raid, Ogilvie reported being 'lifted in the air' by flak. Pilots were also very concerned about their limited fuel supplies on the runs that were going ever deeper into enemy territory.

Jerry opposition has waned and it is hard to find a scrap over there now. However, W/C Malan manages to find one somehow and during the week has accounted for seven bringing his score up over thirty. On the Lille trip we had the bad luck to lose S/Ldr Mungo Park DFC of 74 Sqn. but on the whole our casualties have been quite low—3 or 4 a day.

June 29, 1941

A big day for Junior. The C/O wakened me from a sleep provoked by a large night in London—the first in many a day as we were released unexpectedly in the afternoon—and presented me with that elusive purple and white ribbon, the D.F.C. Bisdee also came in for one and I think we are both rather proud kids this night.

The squadron Operations Record Book records the emotions of the event: 'Ogilvie, furious at being made to get up, softened somewhat on having a D.F.C. ribbon pinned to his chest by the C.O.' There would have been the inevitable recognition party that evening for Skeets and Bish, but of this, there is no record.

That same day Ogilvie noted in his diary: 'We did a two squadron sweep up the French Coast from Burcke [*sic*] to Gravesline but saw nothing at all. The sweeps seem to be easing for the moment but I'm quite sure it is only a prelude to big stuff.'

June 30, 1941
Might have known. Sweep today was as high escort for 24 Blenheims raiding Lens, south-west of Lille, and too damn far inland. We started [off to] inland France after a long delay which ran through an hour's valuable petrol. We crossed over at Dunkirk and were greeted by exceedingly accurate 'ack-ack' which burst all around us, one bit nicking Offenburg. We went the long way in and reached the target OK. The W/C then dropped on a couple of Jerries and as usual clobbered one. We started back and were shadowed for a long time by four 109s which finally came down. I turned my section and they scattered, two going vertically down, the other two up again. There were several around and scattered fights broke out from St. Omer to the coast. During which Sgt. Hughes-Rees destroyed one. Vickey [Ortmans] saw his fall 'in little pieces' and Paul Richey got one and a probable, the C/O damaging one—a good day for the squadron as we all returned safely. Score is now 135 destroyed. So ends the most hectic month in the squadron for me. I've flown over 48 hours in 18 days and have been on all the offensive patrols—over twenty in all. Comes the ill news that we are moving to Gravesend![68]

On June 27, Skeets took the time to send a letter from Biggin Hill to Irene at the Edgerton Terrace Hotel in Kensington. While the two were going out with a variety of people, he had apparently been seeing her periodically, when time permitted. He opened by writing,

Gee, I'm tired! . . . I can't bear to keep looking at that sun; it can only mean trouble . . . The last two days have been busy as hell and I've added another four 'sweeps' to my log book. They were quite successful from our viewpoint as the boys cracked down five of Hitler's 'fall guys.' Junior as usual managed to get himself on the wrong end of a 109 and all I got out of those parties was the experience.

He went on to explain a lack of contact:

I didn't phone last two nights 'cause I went straight back to the house to bed . . . all except last night when I darn near did . . . so simple! You see, due to an ugly scene over a colossal phone bill which no one knew anything about . . . we are not allowed to phone out from the house but can receive incoming calls . . . get it!

One wonders whether the erstwhile author of the letter is carefully circumventing any possible personal responsibility for this administrative horror. In any case, he continued, confessing:

I nearly got home, except that we stopped in at a remarkable old gal's place to eat some luscious strawberries and a couple of bottles of white wine. Well, I almost got away, but it was so incredibly peaceful lying on my back in the garden, gurgling wine, which I don't like too much but which was so cold . . . well . . . you see. I did think about you once or twice, but sort of lay still until the feeling passed off.

And then came notice of a hoped-for holiday. 'If everything goes well, I have a week's leave coming . . . and will certainly get as far away as fast as I can. Absolutely bury myself in the hills of Wiltshire, lie in the sun all day and drink Kümmel all night.'

July 2, 1941

One day's respite was merely a come-on-gag as today dawned bright and early and found Keithie with a heavy head and lagging steps, having been entrapped into the Suivi last night. However, Fighter Command thought less than nothing of this, and today's show was a crack at Lille. Our squadron as top cover did not see a thing, though there was heavy scrapping all around us. The day's score was 17 Jerries for 9 of ours. Funny how we could be in the thick of things and yet see nothing. Later on in the afternoon, we took three Blenheims over to beat up a ship off Le Touquet. It was also uneventful: the Blenheims missed their target, the ack ack missed us, and none of the Spitfires all roaring around at sea level collided. And so to bed, a plenty tired guy. That leave on Saturday looks plenty good right now.

17

FOR YOU, THE WAR IS OVER

But there was disappointment to come.

July 4, 1941

How the Gods must have laughed. That leave never came off—and this is why.

About noon we heard the roar of engines in a cloudless sky, and 74 Sqn. arrived from Gravesend, signifying yet another sweep in the offing. We were briefed and the 'thin red line' in the ops chart showed our wing acting as close escort to the bombers doing Lille. In absolute silence we took off, Sailor Malan leading the wing, Michael Robinson our squadron, Paul Richey leading one flight, I had the other.

This was Circus 32, whose target was the Kuhlman Works and Power Station at Choques, near Béthune. The attacking force were twelve Blenheims, with 609 Squadron acting as escort cover at the rear of the formation. Skeets was flying as section commander.

Over North Foreland the bombers crawled in beneath us and wings of fighters formed up ahead, behind and on either side. An imposing spectacle and I never lost the thrill of being a part of the show. We started off across the channel and far below we could see the white streaks as the air-sea rescue launches put out from Dover and Manston. Across the channel and we were greeted by 'ack ack' at Dunkirk, again at St. Omer as we progressed inland. Away to the side the tiny specks as the wary Hun climbed to be in position above and behind us when we turned to go home down sun. From here, he could dive, fire and pull up with the minimum risk, as all we could do was turn to keep out of his way. We turned over Lille, the bombers did their job, and Jerry sent up bags of flak which was spectacular but ineffective. Starting for home when about fifteen 109s floated over us, breaking up into fours, then pairs. A pair came down to attack the Blenheims and I turned in to attack them.

There was one hell of a 'pow' and I was smacked into the dashboard, my port aileron floated away and a great rib appeared up my wing. I just could not believe it. I should have been covered by my section or warned, I can only imagine my radio chose this time to pack up.

After watching his instrument panel disintegrate in front of him, Skeets later remarked:

I felt somebody hit me across the back with a baseball bat. It knocked me forward and I got down out of the way, and was feeling pretty funny. I was all by myself at this stage, and knew my kite wasn't in good shape, I wasn't in good shape, and if I got back to the Channel I could bale out and one of the rescue boats could pick me up.

So he turned for home, trying desperately to keep control of the aircraft.

By holding the control column in the right hand corner, I found my kite would fly with a crab-like motion. There was blood all over and I felt sick, so I blew my hood off and turned the oxygen on full to keep awake. If I could reach the channel, I'd bale out, because I could not land the kite as it was.

I must have passed out [for an instant] because suddenly everything was quiet and through a haze I could see my prop sticking straight up, and smoke coming from under my cowling.

Realising he would have to bale out immediately, Skeets still had the presence of mind to try to disconnect his oxygen and radio connections, but quickly discovered that he couldn't. 'I had no left arm, couldn't use my left arm at all, so I tried to hold the stick with my knees.' Even this was impossible. With major damage to the flying controls, the aircraft was completely unstable and did the job for him of getting him free, at 23,000 feet:

Immediately the plane flipped over, shooting me out the top like a jack in the box, snapping my oxygen and telephone connections like string. I hung in the air, groped frantically for my ripcord, gave it a tug and everything went black. Some time later I came to in a field surrounded by sympathetic Frenchies, who tried to get me up and away, but I could not make it. I had been hit twice in the arm and once in the shoulder, and had lost too much blood. A little while later, a sad eyed German 'sanitary' informed me, 'For you, the war is over' and he was not kidding.[69]

(Skeets wrote 'Aboard SS *Stratheden*, July 26/45' following his description of the events of July 4. It was made after the war and he clearly was not in a position to finish it before then! He took the time while he returned to Canada aboard the *Stratheden* to finish writing up his flying experiences.) His later comment on the experience was that he had no idea what it was like to do a parachute jump. 'I just pulled the ripcord and that was it for me.'

This is the final entry in Ogilvie's combat diary. It is followed by a Red Cross sticker with the motto: 'Be nice to me. I gave blood today.' And recorded in the flying log book is a terse entry for one flying hour followed by the comment, 'Pilot Failed to Return.' Below that is taped a card from the Irving Air Chute Co., Inc. certifying Ogilvie as having 'qualified as a member of The Caterpillar Club on July 4, 1941, his life having been saved in an emergency jump by use of parachute equipment.'

Ziegler recorded the event from the squadron's perspective: 'On 4 July Paul [Richey, Michael Robinson's brother-in-law and leader of 'A' Flight] reported having seen a parachute, and that the parachutist seemed to be wearing black overalls. The only pilot we could think of who wore black overalls was the Station Commander, and for a moment it seemed slightly hilarious to think of a Group Captain baling out. In fact it was Keith Ogilvie.'[70] The black overalls were probably red, darkened by the large amount of blood loss from his wounds. The parachute seat pack would probably also have been similarly discoloured.

The squadron's Operations Records Book also describes the frantic action in the dogfight, then reports ominously:

When they returned, F/O Ogilvie was missing. A Spitfire had been seen going down near the target area emitting glycol and flames; also a parachutist, not necessarily from the same aircraft. F/Lt. Richey, who flew alongside him, reported that he was wearing black overalls, and that the parachute did not resemble a British one . . . Blue 2 reported that several 109s dived on them from behind, and that he saw F/O Ogilvie half-roll to the left, but after that he blacked out.

Skeets later rued the absence of his old and trusted wingman Zurakowski, as somehow his wingman on this day must have either missed the threat of the 109s or lost the flight leader in the intensity of combat. Whatever the circumstances, a yellow-nosed Me109 ended up right behind Ogilvie and the onslaught was sudden and catastrophic—a horrendous noise and pieces of the cockpit flying all over the place. All he could do, Keith said, was to huddle as much as he could behind the armour plating in the back of the seat and try to get out of there. His left shoulder and part of his back—unluckily sticking up over the armour plating—collected two machine-gun bullets and a cannon shell. (The resulting scars were huge, about 1½ inch by 4 inches, and whenever he went to the beach in later years, were a perpetual source of wonderment to his children and grand-children.) When the chaos (and the engine) had stopped, it was obvious there was only one way out. Fortunately, he was able to open his canopy with his good arm and loosen his straps as he watched blood ooze over the top of a shoe. When he tried to stand up and let go of the stick, the damage to the port wing caused the aircraft to roll violently and threw him out.

In one way he had once again been blessed. Without the improved armour plating behind the pilot's seat in the new Mark V version of the Spitfire, it is likely he would have been ripped to shreds. The plating had, for Keith, done exactly what it was designed to do.

Skeets later wrote to his parents, providing a shorter but sufficiently descriptive account for them to understand the brief and catastrophic action:

It happened quite suddenly and before I knew what had really hap-pened, I was taking a beating. Once again, I have Dad to thank for a heritage of courage, or something of that sort, because I did stay to fight it out. There was a crowd of them and they weren't following. Finally my magazine was badly hit, the engine stopped and took fire. I wasn't doing too good myself having an arm broken, two machine gun [bullets] and a cannon shell in me. Somehow I got out and I dimly remember my chute banging open, then nothing but dim patches for hours.

Ogilvie was the squadron's only casualty of that day's action. The French farmers who had tried to get him to his feet realized he was too badly wounded to make any effort to escape. They bound his wounds as best they could and left. A few moments later German soldiers and an ambulance arrived to take him to a hospital in Lille.

As Skeets was starting the strange and unfamiliar process of dealing with his injuries and adapting to his new status as a prisoner of war, Irene was simply . . . furious. Captivated by her new and dashing friend, in the days before she had somehow secured a new pair of nylons and scored some prized tickets for the opening party of the American Eagle Club in London on that July 4 evening. They were 'hot tickets'—in rare supply—and she had been very lucky to secure them through a friend who worked at the Beaver Club, Canada's home away from home in London. Among the VIPs who would be there were Sir Laurence Olivier, Carol Channing and Vivien Leigh, no small slate of well-known personalities! Irene happily consigned her tickets to Skeets and got on with her preparations for the event. She collected all her clothing coupons, got a completely new outfit and, she said, 'Felt like a million dollars.'

On the big day, Irene spent extra time getting ready for the main event and waited for her date to show up—but he never arrived. Here she was, stood up for one of the season's premier social events and she was livid, thinking he had forgotten all about it or, worse, that he had decided to take someone else with her hard-won tickets. It wasn't until 609 Squadron's CO, Michael Robinson, called her the next day that she understood the reason for the missed date. Robinson's personal call was an indication of the esteem in which they held their Canadian squadron mate, and Irene as well. He didn't pull any punches, simply telling her that he was missing and presumed dead since his plane had last been seen going down in flames before it crashed, and that no one had seen him leave the aircraft.

In fact, her precious tickets had gone unused. She wouldn't see Keith again for another four years.

In another sad and ironic footnote to the whole episode, Keith's two brothers, Emerson and Jim, had just arrived in England with their Canadian army unit on July 3 and were looking forward to a long-awaited reunion. But the fates always had the last laugh. Shortly before being shot down Skeets had written home and informed his parents that he had been offered a chance to join 401 Canadian Squadron on Kittyhawks, but had turned it down to stay with 609 Squadron because he felt 'there's a job to be done here and I'm trained for it. It's my duty.' When he got the posting, he had asked Squadron Leader Robinson if there was any way he could get out of it, and stay with 609. Robinson was able to arrange the cancellation. Skeets's later wry comment was, 'Probably one of the dumber things I did.'

FOUR LINGERING YEARS

The Camp, Escape and
the Long March

18

RECUPERATION

Skeets's family in Ottawa were notified by the usual telegram, dated July 5, 1941, and addressed to C.E. Ogilvie Esq.: 'Immediate from the Air Ministry. Regret to inform you that your son Flying Officer Alfred Keith Ogilvie, DFC, is reported missing as the result of air operations on July 4, 1941. Any further information received will be communicated to you immediately.'

A letter that followed, dated July 7, didn't offer much more hope:

> The only information available is that your son was the sole occupant of a Spitfire which was engaged with enemy aircraft over Northern France on that day. This does not necessarily mean that he is killed or wounded, and if he is a prisoner of war he should be able to communicate with you in due course. Meanwhile enquiries will be made through the International Red Cross Society, and as soon as any definite news is received, you will be at once informed.

Coincidentally, the July 5 telegram was also when the family learned that Skeets had been awarded the DFC. It would be another six weeks before they would find out he was still alive, but in enemy hands. The uncertainty must have been terrible for the family. His father, Charlie, later said he had always had a deep faith that his son was still alive. And although she never talked about it, Margaret must have been inspired by this, as she kept on with her local Red Cross activities.

Finally, after what must have seemed an interminable wait, a second telegram arrived on August 27 telling them that 'Further information through International Red Cross Society states your son Flying Officer

Alfred Keith Ogilvie DFC previously reported missing is now reported a prisoner of war badly wounded. Any further information will be immediately communicated to you.' What a mixed blessing, to finally read the words 'alive' and 'badly wounded' at the same time.

The 609 Squadron record also reveals that following the loss of Skeets, they too had no idea what had happened to him:

> Six weeks later Lord Haw-Haw broadcast over the German radio that F/O Ogilvie was a prisoner of war. He, W/C Malan and P/O Ortmans had not missed a single Circus since they began on an intensive scale. Hard as he had worked, in the air and on the ground, he had always remained cheery. Many a time and oft had a Canadian wisecrack from him ended a period of tension. Ironically, he was just about to depart on a well-earned period of leave, and he has probably laughed quite a lot since about that.

He wasn't laughing much in the beginning of his extended stay as a guest of the Luftwaffe, however. His wounds were grievous.

Retired General Dave Adamson, a post-war RCAF colleague, recalled:

> I remember flying with Skeets one time, and asking him what it was like being shot down. He said that he'd had the good sense to get out of the aircraft when he realized it was finished and before it burst into flames. He remembered coming to on the grass, and feeling around for all his parts. He was all there, but he couldn't find his left arm. He said he remembered saying, ‚Where's my left hand?' again and again, and reaching around behind him with his right arm and discovering his left arm back there. The whole shoulder had collapsed due to the damage from the bullets which had hit him. He pushed the arm around the front, and was holding the left hand in his right, stroking it and saying, 'Here's my good left hand!' He looked up to see a German soldier pointing his rifle at him, and realized that the flying war was over for him.

Although Keith's memories of subsequent events were hazy, the French farmers who first found him, and his immediate captors, gave him competent enough first aid to keep him from bleeding to death. He was transferred to a hospital in Lille for badly needed, more comprehensive treatment. It was ironic—after all, Lille, in French Flanders near the Belgian border, had been the target of many of the fighter sweeps and bombing raids he had participated in over the past month, including the one in which he was shot down. As a major industrial and logistics centre, it attracted bombing by the Germans at the beginning of the war and was a major target for the Allies during German occupation.

On his way to the hospital, Skeets recalled looking up at the sky. 'Just minutes before it had been filled with noise, fire, smoke and violence,' he said, 'and now it was serene, timeless and as inscrutable as ever.' Once again fortune smiled on him, or at least as much as it could under the circumstances.

> I always felt that even when I had bad luck, I had good luck . . . they took me to a troop hospital where they specialized in gunshot wounds, where they put all the German guys who had come back from the Eastern Front. They put me in a room by myself, in a hospital that was so full they had Germans out in the hallways in beds. They patched me up, did a good job. I was there for about three months, then they sent me to Brussels. After I had been in hospital for a couple of months a German Air Force officer came in to interview me and asked me where the rest of the crew was. I told him they were in England—he thought I was part of a bomber crew.

The transfer to Brussels was for longer-term recuperation, once his wounds were finally stabilized. The new facility was one where mainly senior German officers were treated. Skeets was always grateful for the high quality of medical attention he received from the 'little Belgian doctor' who oversaw his recovery, and from the German doctors in Lille, to whom he accepted he owed his life. Ogilvie wrote to Ziegler after the war, expressing in his inimitable way how privileged he felt: 'The Jerry docs fixed my arm up really well,' he said, 'though I can still tell when rain is in the offing.'

For a good part of the nine months he was to spend in hospital, his left arm was held at head height in a hip-to-shoulder cast, in a posture like a sea captain about to shade his eyes and scan the horizon. While the wounds received regular attention, he was bothered by the feeling there was more than just him in his cast, and indeed there was. A doctor told him the sensation was maggots, but admonished him not to worry—the medical staff were monitoring carefully for any infection and the lodgers were keeping the wound clean. It might have been better not to know—with this knowledge in hand, it must have been even more of a challenge to fall asleep at night.

Skeets spent four or five months in the Brussels hospital, initially sharing a room with a German air force (Luftwaffe) officer and later with some badly wounded British officers. The days must have been long and boring, excellent care notwithstanding. At least he was able, under the rules of his incarceration, eventually to establish letter contact with his family and from time to time with Irene. She had written to him several times care of the Red Cross, without any specific information of where he was being held. His first letter to get through to her in November 1941 had an unusual return address and gave some insights into the ordeal he had gone through, even written in his usual cavalier style.

Flying Officer A. Keith Ogilvie (42872)
British Prisoner of War
Chirurg Sonder Lazarett
d.o.K.H. Brussels, Belgium

Dear 'Aunty,'
Surprise! Surprise! I have just received a letter from you dated Oct. 1 and am slowly recovering from the shock. Such sense as it does make leads me to believe that you have written before but so far that mail must be still wandering over the wilds of Europe. Yours was the first letter that I have received from England but I suppose I must be grateful for even these small mercies. I can't imagine where you got this address from, regular little detective, aren't you? You must excuse my exhilarated spirits but I have just had a cup of straight Ovaltine and it really has hit me.

Now that we know each other so well, I suppose I had better tell you the story of my life. I did write you before but it may have gone astray. Anyhooo, ages and ages ago I went looking for a scrap with some laddies, and as happens to people who go looking for trouble I found it. After a brief exchange of pleasantries, I found myself in a blazing kite with two bullets in my arm, one in my back and my arm broken. I was getting bored anyway so I bailed out. The docs did a really marvellous job on my arm and so here I am after nearly five months in good enough shape to lick you, if need be. The old wing is doing alright, though progress is slow. The break has healed nicely and the wounds are nearly closed so soon all I shall have to show for the party is a couple of healthy scars. As I was in a cast for three months, my arm shrank and it is only lately that I finally got it to straighten out. I exercise daily in the gym under the eye of a young 'fraulein' who is quite immune to my charms, and gradually the strength is coming back into it . . .

I was moved from Lille to this address a couple of months ago, and it was nice to come from solitary to a room with other RAF unfortunates. We have a small colony here which ebbs and flows as new chaps come in and old ones leave to go to prison camp. Most of the time not spent eating or sleeping is spent on reading or some nonsense. Even at the risk of your obvious retort I'll mention that I am thus improving my mind. I've got energetic enough to study French for some time each day. All in all the time goes smoothly enough during the day, but I hate the nights. They are too long and full of bogey men.

. . . I apologize for standing you up for the party,[71] but . . . I'm certainly going on a rampage when I get back. The mere prospect is all that keeps me going. Does the 'W' Club still draw the boys? Does the Suivi still struggle along without me? Here, I'll do a big thing and bequeath two bottles that I have there to you, provided you can convince the management . . . or, a bigger threat, provided the boys have not lapped them up.

I have had no news from any of the close friends in the RAF and often wonder how they are doing. In case you ever see Joe [Atkinson] or Mac you might pass along my best and at the same time, stir them up to do a big thing with a pen. My stay here is a bit vague. I may leave in a week or six months, it depends on many things. At any rate letters are always forwarded on . . .

As ever, Keith.

They continued to correspond, Skeets more or less on a monthly basis (inmates were allowed only a small number of letters each month to family and friends), and Irene more frequently. Some of Irene's earlier letters, sent to Geneva for forwarding, finally arrived after this first one, giving Skeets lots of welcome reading material. Among Irene's suggestions for ways to make life more palatable, it seems, was the idea of sending on Skeets's diary and snapshots. He felt obliged to gently chide her about this, for the obvious reason that they would have been a treasure trove of intelligence for his captors! He was diplomatic about this, though, for her descriptions of her social life received similar 'kibitzing' responses.

Somehow, despite all the formality and 'fog of war,' some souvenir photos have survived from this period. There are several pictures of British patients hanging around in pyjamas, playing cards or reading, or posing as a group for the camera. One shows what appears to be a bottle of wine on a bedside table. Among others, there is a wonderful photo of several nurses, in formal uniforms with starched white hats, that seems to come from the same time, nearly all looking either dour or a bit uncomfortable, with a uniformed man winking slyly in the background.

On September 26, 1941, while Skeets was still in hospital in Lille, his long-time and close friend Eric Dewar, then a member of Coastal Command's 48 Squadron, lost his life when his Hudson aircraft crashed on landing at RAF Odiham in Hampshire. Skeets never mentioned the loss, nor is it clear when he learned of Eric's fate—whether it was while he was in hospital, or some time later. Given how close they were and how much they had shared, it would have been a saddening moment, even for someone inured by then, through bitter experience, to the enormous human cost of war.

Still, Skeets valued any contact he could get. In a letter to Irene on January 19, 1942, he expresses his pleasure at hearing at last from Joe (Atkinson, no doubt), in what he refers to as 'a nice letter containing NEWS.' He goes on to say that 'I have heard of nearly all the chaps and so I'm content on that score. One of my best pals is in the Air Force prison camp, awaiting my arrival patiently.' (He doesn't mention the name of this pal, or in which camp he was supposed to be incarcerated.)

In the same letter, obviously written over a period of days, Skeets describes the healing progress he had made as having slowed down, and his wounds having opened up again. Eight of 'the fit boys tottered off to [prison] camp' while he and four others remained, 'not all that sorry not to be going, as it is somewhat chilly these days.' Then almost immediately came the shock, described in the same missive, of having been informed that 'tomorrow we four are off to our "Oflag" [officers' prison camp]. A big surprise that, as I felt I'd never get away. Our medical history has been sent on and we shall continue treatment there.'

So off he went, from the relatively pleasant (and warm) confines of the medical centre to what was no doubt a considerably less hospitable army camp at Spangenberg, near Kassel, in the centre of Germany. The camp held senior Allied officers captured at Dunkirk. Led by Major General Fortune, one of the most senior British officers captured during the Second World War, they were mainly from the 51st Highland Division. They had been left in France and forced to surrender when further naval evacuation proved impossible.

It was unusual for an air force prisoner of war to be sent to what was now essentially an army prison camp. Oflag IX A/H had housed RAF and French Armée de l'air POWs until it closed in October 1941, before being reopened in January 1942 to take British and Commonwealth army officers. In retrospect, Skeets figured wryly that the German administration wasn't much better than the British and had been unaware of the transition when they sent him there. He was not long the sole airman, however, as he was soon joined by a Polish squadron leader from the RAF. For the rest of their brief stay they remained the only two air force officers in the camp. In any case, their army 'hosts' treated them very well, sharing whatever they had to share.

Two months later, judged to be better housed with air force colleagues, Skeets and his Polish companion were put on a train and sent to the new 'escape proof' North Compound of Stalag Luft III, his home-to-be for the next three years.

19

THE CAMP: STALAG LUFT III

Situated in Silesia, German-occupied Poland, on the edge of the village of Sagan (now Zagan), Stalag Luft III was opened in 1942 to accommodate the growing number of captured Allied airmen. It was meant to be escape proof, with enough ground cleared outside the fence to require at least 100 yards of tunnelling through the unstable, sandy soil. Microphones and seismographs were buried in the ground to detect any digging noises, and frequent checks were made of the inmates and their lodgings. A warning wire was strung a foot off the ground, 30 feet inside the 9 feet high double-barbed-wire outer fence. Any move over the warning wire was guaranteed to attract a bullet from one of the many lookout posts. From these 'goon boxes,' 15 feet in the air, the sentries could keep a close eye on the goings-on anywhere in the camp.

Many of the guards were themselves veterans of other campaigns, some having suffered their own grievous injuries that had made them unfit for fighting but still allowed them to do guard duty. They were generically named 'goons,' an insulting reference to comic-strip characters of the day.[72] The beneficiaries of the insult didn't object, however, as the term was always explained away as an acronym for 'German Officers or NCOs.'

Stalag Luft III was operated by the German air force, the Luftwaffe, and although there were plenty of individual instances to the contrary, the overall treatment by the guards was better than that in many other camps. The Luftwaffe under Hermann Göring, himself a First World War air ace, still hewed to a kind of old-school gallantry, grudgingly acknowledging their foes as honourable warriors, 'gentlemen of the air,' and treating them with a measure of respect that was rare or non-existent in other branches of the German military. The camp Kommandant, Friedrich Wilhelm von Lindeiner-Wildau, was one of this ilk, a professional soldier who had seen action and been wounded in the First World War. He had joined the personal staff of Luftwaffe chief Hermann Göring in 1937 and was given the post of Kommandant when he refused retirement at the age of fifty-seven.

But this was all relative, and despite its tongue-in-cheek label as 'Goering's luxury camp,' life was by no means easy for the 'Kriegies'— the name the English prisoners gave themselves, from the German Kriegsgefangener: prisoner of war.

There were about 300 inmates in the camp when Skeets arrived and every prisoner in the camp, by the very fact he was there, had a story to relate.[73] Skeets remembered one of the first prisoners, a British pilot who was flying an Anson up the English Channel doing reconnaissance work on the day war was declared, and was shot down half an hour after hostilities opened. He was picked up by the Germans and spent the rest of the war in the camp. Skeets claimed there were prisoners in there from every raid of any note in the war—Dambusters, the bombing of the bridges in France when France fell, any raid at all. Each and every one of them, he claimed, had a tale worth telling.

At first, it was only RAF prisoners, and then Americans began to come in a few at a time when that country joined the war. When the US forces' daylight raids began, the Americans started coming in 'a hundred at a time,' to the point where the Germans built a second camp adjacent to the North Compound and moved the Americans in there. The North Compound reverted to mostly RAF and Commonwealth aircrew, which no doubt suited at least some of the British inmates. In the records held by the museum at Zagan that now preserves the site and relics from the camp, is a letter from the senior British officer to the Kommandant, suggesting that von Lindeiner separate the Americans from the British prisoners because of the former's 'lack of formality' over rank, something carefully preserved by the British.

Skeets was assigned to Hut 110 and given prisoner number 1409. Like the other inmates, he quickly discovered the monotony of prison camp life: 'We were all young fellas, full of beans, living an exciting life. And all of a sudden, crunch, you're in the bag. You're in your own wire-bound world. That's all we saw—wire, sand and trees.' Daily life quickly became routine in many respects. Andy Wiseman, a 1944 arrival at the camp, offered his ironic agreement: 'That's what it was all about, learning to live with each other. Because you couldn't get out . . . Those who went to English public schools found it more acceptable, because it was cold, the food was lousy and there were no women.'[74]

The camp functioned under the same strict military hierarchy that kept officers separate from NCOs in the South Compound. Daily routine started off with morning 'appell' or roll call. There were two regular and sometimes unscheduled appells where inmates lined up in rows and groups of five to be counted and recounted by their German warders. The camp adjutant reported anyone not on parade, who were in hospital or sick in their rooms. After the evening appell they would return to their huts and the guards would lock the prisoners in, as being outside after dark was strictly forbidden.

Prisoners were required to sign an 'undertaking' that would allow them certain privileges in return for their promise as gentlemen not to attempt to escape. Skeets's memorabilia includes his own signed agreement that reads: 'I promise not to try to escape or prepare an escape while gardening, practising sports or taking walks under escort outside the camp. Any abuse of this permit will entail severe punishment for me and cancellation of the above reliefs for all. Name: A. Keith Ogilvie, Rank Flying Officer, No. 1409.'

Not long after his arrival, on May 25, 1942, Skeets was promoted to flight lieutenant. Not that it made much difference in the camp, but it was not uncommon for prisoners of war to be promoted in recognition of their length or circumstances of service.

Skeets described the conditions in the huts:

They were long narrow wooden huts, maybe twenty rooms. We started off with four in a room, and toward the end of the war we were ending up with twelve in a room. We had bunk beds, one tier, two tiers, three tiers, they kept climbing, basically with a straw mattress and a certain number of boards to hold the straw mattress. As time went on, most of these [boards] went into the tunnel building and instead of sleeping on twelve, you'd end up sleeping on three, string and stuff holding it together so you wouldn't fall through on the chap underneath.

Each of the huts had a stove, coal or wood, and each room was allowed so much time on the stove, about 15 or 20 minutes, so whatever you had to eat [that] you had to heat in any way, was cooked on the stove.

The biggest and most constant preoccupation for prisoners was food. Most new arrivals lost significant body weight in the first few months on the minimal basic ration provided by the Germans. In his definitive book, *The Great Escape*, Paul Brickhill described the 'formal' menu in some detail:

> German rations allowed a very thin slice of bread, margarine and ersatz jam for breakfast, a couple of slices for lunch and a couple for dinner, probably with neither marg nor jam. Usually there were a few potatoes, and once every three weeks a little minced horse-meat. Occasionally there were some vegetables or barley or sauerkraut. If Red Cross parcels were coming in (thank God they mostly did after the first couple of years), there would be an evening meal of bully beef or spam and extra luxuries like chocolate, coffee, cheese and jam.[75]

The Red Cross parcels that the Luftwaffe allowed to be delivered to the inmates were donations from mainly British, Canadian and (after 1941) US Red Cross societies—including the one to which Skeets's stepmother Margaret and her neighbours so assiduously contributed. The parcels were intended to be distributed weekly to each Allied prisoner, but many inevitably went astray before getting to the prison camps. Those that did arrive intact were a vital supplement to the limited rations provided by the Germans and led to some innovative menus created by the inmates. Skeets credited the Red Cross (and, by implication, the Luftwaffe) for ensuring the parcels got into the hands of the prisoners.

> We would have been 'gone pigeons' without those Red Cross parcels. I had the job of looking after them and I know their value. Our prison camp diet was calculated only to sustain us and that was all. I marvelled at what they (the Canadian Red Cross) were able to get through to us. For instance, we had games parcels, even to running shoes, which none of the others were allowed to send.

Depending on where they came from, some of the parcels contained luxuries from powdered milk, to butter, to chocolate, to cigarettes. Skeets claimed the Canadian parcels were much the favourites with the Kriegies, containing the most luxurious selection, things that just didn't appear in the British parcels. These featured more plebeian fare like corned beef or Spam. The Canadian parcels also had porridge and packages of soda biscuits that could be ground up to make cakes for special occasions, along with canned butter.

While not everyone smoked, the cigarettes were probably the most versatile of the parcels' contents, as they formed the basic currency of the camp. All items of food had a price under the 'Foodacco' system, allowing the allocated recipients to exchange for a fixed valuation. John Colwell, prisoner number 973 in the North Compound and a Canadian who had been shot down in 1943, kept a meticulous diary of his camp experience, documenting (among other things) the price list for a range of food items. The most expensive in the open prison market were butter and condensed milk, commanding up to 100 cigarettes each. It was a competition for the cheapest: only 15 cigarettes would buy a can of sardines or anonymous 'meat paste,' American soup or British prunes. Even articles of clothing or things for daily use could be purchased: a shirt for 120, a blanket for 300, a pair of shoes for 600 or a pair of sneakers for the exalted price of 1,000 cigarettes. Other parcels, mainly from home to individual inmates (each inmate was allowed four each year), occasionally made their way into the camp, with ordinary items that would be luxury to the prisoners—hand-knitted scarves, mittens, treats of various descriptions.

Back in Ottawa, Margaret, Keith's stepmother, was continuing her own contribution to the war, fastidiously recording the activities of the neighbourhood ladies' Red Cross group activities:

8 January, 1942
Annual Report
Since the organization of the Patterson Avenue Group of the Red Cross Society on the 28th Nov 1940, we have held 29 meetings, with an average attendance of around 20 members. During the year we have also had a bridge, a demonstration tea at Mrs. Higgerty's and a tea held at Mrs. Edmund's home. Boxes and cigarettes have

been sent to some of our boys overseas, and money donated to the Red Cross for the purchase of blankets and for Russian Relief.

We close the year with a balance on hand of $29.78.

These well-meaning and steady women had no idea how important those small contributions from home were to the recipients. And despite the donations from the Red Cross and from home, hunger remained a constant preoccupation for the prisoners, along with the cold and frequent illness that came from the poor conditions.

Prisoners needing medical treatment had access to one doctor and one dentist. The hospital—whose concrete foundation and floor remain on the site of the camp today—was the largest structure and the only one with a basement, used to store medical supplies. To visit the doctor an inmate first had to be 'triaged' to determine whether he was really sick enough to warrant a visit. A trip to the dentist, a woman, was even more complicated, as her office was outside the camp. It required seeking the permission of the senior British officer and giving one's 'parole,' or word, as an officer that one wouldn't attempt to escape.

20

THE 'RACKETS ROOM'

Once again in the face of challenge, Skeets's luck held out for him. When he arrived at the camp he was assigned to a room containing an 'exceptional' set of inmates. Peter Walker had been the assistant manager at the Savoy Hotel and had taken a three-year cooking course in Switzerland. He, naturally, became the resident chef after volunteering to cook if the rest of his bunkmates would look after the cleaning and other domestic chores. His cooking was superb, under the conditions, but Skeets quickly discovered that if there was something he didn't like he dared not say so, on pain of being immediately and summarily promoted to cook himself.

> We pooled our rations. When we got our Red Cross parcels we kept individual things like bars of chocolate but we pooled all the rest of the parcel and Peter did our cooking, cooked amazing meals out of nothing. The Germans only gave us 700 calories a day. It was calculated to sustain life and half the time it was potatoes that were half rotten and soup they had boiled the potatoes in. The coffee was made out of chimney soot, as far as I can remember. So we didn't rely very heavily on the German rations. They did bring us in their dark rye bread and liver sausage, small portions. Some of the rooms, the chaps got their own parcels and kept them. They would woof their parcels in a couple of days and the rest of the time had nothing to eat, just what the German cookhouse gave us. As I say, we were very lucky with Peter. We seemed to have good meals all the time. Or at least good meals with what you could do with the Red Cross parcels.

Peter also functioned as a camp interpreter, which brought another kind of benefit. Whenever the Germans wanted to have any dealings with the camp's senior officers, they would work through the interpreter, so the inmates of the room were always abreast of everything going on in the camp. And with his connections, Peter somehow managed to put his hands on the occasional onion or something that no one else would have access to, to enhance and supplement their rations. Skeets said: 'They used to call our room the 'Rackets Room,' a kind of disparaging remark but based mostly on jealousy, I think.'

Besides Peter, the room contained the camp's adjutant, Squadron Leader Bill Jennens, 'a real character,' according to Ogilvie. As the war went on, other roommates were added. Skeets described one new arrival:

> One day one of my best friends, Norman Winch, came in with a Group Captain. This unfortunate Group Captain Massey had been shot down by Goering's squadron in the First World War and had a pretty damaged leg that he limped around on. He was a station commander in this war, and went along to see what the form was with the boys. He was Norman's second pilot this night and found out in a hurry when they got clobbered. They all had to bail out and Norm was saying the G/C was sort of poised in the door and Norman just hauled off and gave him a swift kick out the door. The only time in his career he had a chance to kick a G/C! He was a wonderful old guy, G/C Massey.

All the inmates were given a camp role on arrival. Ogilvie's job was in the 'parcel department,' processing the incoming Red Cross parcels to ensure there was even distribution and to prevent pilfering. It was also the responsibility of those assigned parcel duties to keep an eye out for contraband being smuggled into the camp as part of the parcels—vacuum tubes for radios in cans of coffee and the like—although Skeets claimed he never saw anything coming into the camp by that route. All this had to be done with the utmost caution. Skeets recounted:

> All the incoming parcels were placed in a room and, before I could give them to their owners, the Germans inspected them for contraband. This posed quite a problem for me since, in addition to handling

legitimate parcels, I was responsible for smuggling into camp civilian clothing, ink for passports, radio parts, etc. It was a constant battle of wits with the German searchers. We had to have these items in order to keep our hidden radios serviceable and to prepare the prisoners for their escape attempts. Through devious means I managed to keep my supply section well stocked.'[76] Some things could be saved, but this was against camp rules—in fact, the Germans required any tins to be punctured when they were distributed.

Christmas in the camp saw the arrival of special parcels, with Christmas cake and pudding, bacon, salmon and other rarities, accompanied by notes from the president of the Canadian Prisoners of War Relatives Association and once even from the prime minister of Canada, expressing the hope that

> in spite of the difficulties and uncertainties of transportation these [food packages] will arrive at the camps in time for Christmas. Each Canadian will receive a small parcel for his personal use, but the greater part of the gift will be of a collective or communal nature, comprising articles such as gramophone records and cooking utensils, which will be delivered in bulk to the Spokesman at every camp in which Canadians are interned, with the intention that their use might be shared as far as possible with all prisoners in the camp regardless of nationality.

The gramophone records must have been a special treat, if inedible. Somehow, the prisoners contrived to get hold of several gramophones and eventually amassed more than 3,500 records. According to Don Edy, some of the records that came from 'home' were little more than a month old. In a 1995 interview, Andrew Wiseman, one of the Stalag Luft III inmates, acknowledged the importance of this collection: 'We had sets of all the major works, all the concertos, nearly all the symphonies and so on. For me, it was an enormous help, to survival in the prison camp. In fact, without the music, my life would have been very different. And I think, hopefully, for a lot of other people as well. The ability to lose yourself in music was a major asset.'[77]

In addition to the contents of the Christmas packages, special food items would be hoarded in small quantities for weeks ahead in preparation for holidays, with the intention of making the holiday meal as memorable as possible. John Colwell recorded the menu for Christmas 1943, for hut 120, North Compound, as follows:

BREAKFAST—10:00 a.m.
Sausages with Cheese Soufflé
Toast and Jam
Coffee

LUNCH—12:30 p.m.
Toast and Jam
Tea

DINNER—5:30 p.m.
Maccaroni [*sic*] with Cheese and Tomatoes
Roast Beef and Baked Potatoes
Christmas Pudding and Fig Melange with White Sauce
Coffee.

The menu for 1944 was even more elaborate, and Colwell managed to persuade many of his fellow officers to sign his diary in honour of that year's New Year's Eve celebrations, such as they were. They were a motley crew, most from various parts of the United Kingdom, but others from Czechoslovakia, Canada, Australia and New Zealand.

Skeets's room organized similar feasts: 'We did Christmas dinners from what was in our Red Cross parcels. Our pièce de résistance was when Peter ground up some of these hardtack biscuits into flour. We had some raisins from one of the parcels and made a big Christmas cake out of this which we scoffed in short order! I don't know what he used for icing, but we got sugar in our parcels too.'

Improvisation, and not just with food, was a way of life in the camp. Roger Teillet, a former inmate of Stalag Luft III, a cabinet minister in Canada's government under Lester Pearson and a staunch member of Ottawa's POW Association, remembered in a 1994 interview that 'We were really a bunch of crooks, and we could improvise anything.' One of his colleagues, Ed Rae, reminded the same interviewer of how little they had to work with in the beginning. 'Remember, everybody in the compound just dropped out of the sky with the clothes they had on their backs.'

John Colwell was just one example of those inmates who turned out to have a hidden talent. In John's case, it was his ability as a 'metal basher,' fabricating sometimes extraordinarily complex items from the discarded food tins and other 'found' objects. In his diary he documented his production of a huge variety of 'tinware' for daily use, everything from water pails and pots to sinks and stoves.

The Kriegies sought and found innumerable ways to find diversions from the routine. Of course, mail and parcels from home were a highlight. Irene and Skeets continued to correspond more or less monthly during his time in the prison camp. The letters that survive show on his side a cheery bravado, jokingly chiding Irene on her ongoing social life back in England, but with the occasional glimpse of a real wistfulness for experience of something more than the ennui of the camp. But apparently they weren't the only letters Skeets received. There was evidence of a concerted effort to keep his spirits up, as a scrapbook entitled 'Photos Received in Germany from July 4/41' contains pictures of a number of young women, not all of them family—Monica, Bette, Mickey, Gloria, Lilian—but no other record of correspondence or previous contact exists in Skeets's diaries. There was clearly a steady stream of outside news coming to him from many attractive quarters!

21

BACK IN LONDON

L ondoners were experiencing some narrowing of their own world, between the ongoing air raids and the privations imposed by rationing. When Skeets was first shot down, Irene wrote to his family to offer her condolences, and they began their own occasional correspondence. They were obviously sympathetic to the situation in London. From time to time she would receive a small parcel from them, often containing canned corn—one of her favourite foods and a great luxury for Irene. The family of her aunt, Jean's sister Kate, also sent packages. Irene recalls getting clothing that she couldn't find in London, and on one occasion, to her surprise, discovered a cocktail hat in her parcel. It was perfect, Irene claimed, and she wore it to a formal party to which she had been invited, but had not planned to go. She recalled, 'Everyone thought it was fantastic, that I was shopping at the most expensive places!'

While it may not have held much significance for Skeets and his fellow inmates of Stalag Luft III, June 1, 1943, certainly was a big day for Irene, as that was the date she joined the RCAF in England. She had applied five or six months previously to join the navy WRENs,[78] who had been advertising for women volunteers. She had gone so far as to have an initial medical examination, but had not heard anything from them since. Feeling there was more she could do and frustrated with the delay in response from the navy, one Friday lunch hour on a whim she dropped by the Royal Canadian Air Force (RCAF) office at Lincoln's Inn Fields, just behind the MI9 office at High Holborn, and filled out an application to join up. On Monday, she received a letter of acceptance—and, naturally, fate being what it is, got one from the navy the same day. She made up her mind after thinking about the two offers over the course of the morning, finally choosing to join the RCAF. Irene later admitted having made this decision because the RCAF offered to repatriate her to Canada at the end of the war. Although she had no specific plans at the time, she was sure she wanted to return to Canada at some point, and with the limited resources at her disposal, this seemed the best opportunity.

Irene joined the RCAF at the same time as Helen Baker, a Canadian woman who was married to a British serviceman, and Renée Hemingway, another Canadian who later married Freddie Crouch, an RCAF photographer. Older and itching for some independence now, Irene decided after a minor tiff with her mother to move out on her own—or, rather, in with her new friends and working colleagues. The three of them shared a top-floor flat in Challinor Mansions, two underground rides from their work. The name of their new digs was a bit misrepresentative. There were lots of cockroaches, Irene reported, but claimed, 'You learned to live with it.'

The young women went to Gloucester for their initial basic training and were offered the opportunity to work in meteorology or photography. All three chose the latter. They were given cameras and, it turned out, were the first women attached to the photographic section under the tutelage of a sergeant, an 'old bugger' who had lied about his age to join the service. They greatly appreciated the support he gave them. He took his obligations of care seriously, giving them many of the preferred jobs and sending them out in pairs, usually with an experienced man to help in the learning process. On one occasion, Irene was sent to Buckingham Palace to take pictures of people coming to receive medals awarded by the Queen. Cheekily, she asked if she could come in and was told to leave the camera outside. She had a front-row seat for the medal awards.

Photography was not an unregulated activity in wartime. Irene and her colleagues carried special permits issued by the Ministry of Defence along with their cameras, authorizing them to 'be in possession of a camera and to take photographs . . . in any public place and within RAF protected places, excluding photographs of secret and all radar equipment, secret trials or activities or aircraft on the secret list.'

Irene loved her work. The more normal menu of assignments included 'all the weddings, and all the funerals'—the highs and lows of wartime life. She travelled all over the place. 'If a Canadian mucky-muck landed in

Greenwich, I went up and took his picture. When the ships came in, loaded with Canadians, we took their pictures. When they died, we took pictures of their funerals.' She remembered travelling to Greenock in Scotland, near Glasgow, where newly arrived Canadian troops were being landed. The men were happy to be at the end of the long sea voyage and anxious to be going into action. 'You knew in another couple of weeks they wouldn't be so happy. Some would be underground and I would be taking pictures of their funerals.'

The reality of the war on the continent was roughly brought home by some of the photos that came through the office, not to be made available to the public. In an interview late in her life, she recalled that when the Bergen-Belsen concentration camp was taken over, an Allied photographer had documented the grim scene and they were charged with developing the negatives. The photos 'were so awful. They had these bodies lined up like matchsticks. I remember looking at them and thinking it was just terrible. I never dreamed Belsen was as bad as it was.'

Among other tasks, Irene documented the establishment of the burns unit at the Queen Victoria Hospital in East Grinstead, established by Sir Archibald McIndoe to carry out pioneering work on Allied aircrew who had been severely burned or crushed and required reconstructive surgery. The famous 'Guinea Pig Club' was initially established here as a drinking club offering support to patients during their long and painful treatments.

Some efforts were noteworthy for different reasons. On one less than auspicious occasion, Irene was assigned to take wedding photographs for an RCAF officer. When she returned to the lab and developed the pictures, she was horrified to find them all blank. Her boss was a kindly and under-standing sort who handled it well—he sent another photographer to redo the formal pictures and assured her that they had all made a mistake at some point. Not that this allayed any of Irene's chagrin and embarrassment, which remained strong even when she recalled the incident some seventy years later!

Like most Londoners, Irene developed a fatalistic view of the risks of living in London, which continued to be bombed in one way or another almost throughout the war. Residents of the city were continually confronted in some measure with the stench of smouldering fires, fallen plaster and dust, the need to walk around rubble and the remnants of burned-out buildings, and by the sound of broken glass crunching underfoot. The frequent bombing was the source of one of Irene's particularly memorable wartime experiences.

On this occasion, she had been looking forward to her night in a hot bath, always a favourite pastime. She put her tuppence into the slot that activated the gas water heater, filled the bath and sank into the lovely hot water. She was fully relaxed when 'all hell broke loose,' starting with the air-raid warning sirens. Years later, she said, 'I can't describe the feeling, but I can feel it even now.' Helen, her flatmate, said, 'Come on, Irene, you have to get out now.' Irene replied, 'No way am I leaving this lovely tub,' and she sank down deeper into the hot water. Then the bomb blasts started, far away at first but coming closer and closer. Helen and Renée finally both rushed into the bathroom to urge her to get out. Irene finally agreed when they could begin to hear the whistles of the bombs as they fell, thinking they could at least use the water if there was a fire. Helen, who was considerably smaller than Irene, took her arm, yanked her out of the tub and dragged her under the grand piano in the living room—Irene without a stitch of clothing on. They had decided in advance that if they ever needed to shelter, they would do so under the grand piano—perhaps not the best place to be in circumstances like that!

There was a huge explosion, every window in the apartment broke and the lights went out. A bomb had landed near enough to shake the women up, but their sheltering piano, fortunately, proved sturdy enough not to collapse on them. Irene's measure of their proximity to the blasts was that 'all the windows were blown in, but the ceiling stayed up.' As the dust began to settle again, the three women started to laugh, a bit hysterically. After the last bomb fell there was a sort of silence. Suddenly the door was flung open by an elderly air-raid warden who shouted, 'Everything all right in 'ere?' and shone his flashlight on the three of them, still under the piano. It isn't clear whether Irene, still in her birthday suit, or the unannounced visitor was more embarrassed. 'Oh, Gawd,' he said, and quickly withdrew, while the women giggled. It was probably the highlight of the war for him.

Irene always felt Helen had saved her life that night, for when they opened the bathroom door to inspect the damage in that room, the tub was full of large shards of glass.

When they weren't being bombed, the women were scrounging and trading their way through the rationing system, recycling everything possible and trying to find other ways to distract themselves from the constant, grim reality of a wartime existence. Their social life was a redeeming feature. There were lots of parties, and the dates were 'stacked up,' according to Irene.

Helen's husband was away in the 8th Army, but that didn't stop her from (always innocently, she claimed) participating in the hectic social schedule. She remembered one party she had gone to despite not having been invited—a thrash for Buzz Beurling, a fighter pilot of some skill who had after a year of great success with the RAF, transferred to the RCAF. Helen and friends were told to stay away from the big 'do' celebrating this event but peeked in anyway. The party was being well covered by the press, and the interlopers were noticed by more than the invited guests. On September 2, 1943, the *Daily Mirror* featured one and a half columns to an article entitled 'Helen Baker Finally Meets Her Idol!' Helen made sure to send a copy to her husband, with a letter of explanation, before the London papers arrived in the field on their regular delivery schedule.

But there were very sad times as well. They often had to walk to work in the mornings because the trains were out of commission as a result of the bombings—a station or tracks had been hit and people were told to find another way of getting around. Normally they would take two underground rides to work, but on these days the three would walk a couple of hours each way. Irene later recalled one occasion on her way to work:

Our [underground] station had been hit again, and we were told that we couldn't even bus. We started to walk and . . . we passed a church where a lot of people had gone to shelter. They were still trying to get these people free. The church had been so well built it didn't crumble, of course, but it had almost a direct hit. Big chunks of stone [had fallen in] and they had to be very careful because people were still alive underneath and if they came down . . . it happened many times. We were asked not to help, things had to be removed a certain way or it would kill the people trapped. We couldn't stop and help at all. As we passed by, we saw there wasn't much doing in that particular spot. They said, we can't do much because the whole thing would collapse. People were yelling and screaming from inside, it was a terrible thing to hear. We saw long, long tubes of garden hose they were putting all sorts of liquids into the hose with a funnel, pouring hot tea in there and hoping it would get to the people. They were putting something in it, putting them all to sleep [sighs]. It could easily crash down on them, they were anticipating at that point.

When we walked home that day the rubble had all been pretty well cleared away. We asked, 'What happened?' They had done very well. One of the people had died of a heart attack but it must have been someone who had a heart condition. But they got a lot of the others out.

People had been told to go to the church to shelter. On the very first raid that came over, my mother and I were just across the street and went to the church, walked inside and turned right around and came back home. Mother felt the same way. It was too much—babies crying, women crying. Someone outside revved up a motorcycle and it sounded as if things were going to blow up any minute.

The way they went through these things, they're wonderful people, the Brits. A lot of people think they're just 'something or others,' but I think they're wonderful.

22

ZAGAN

In Stalag Luft III, the residents of the camp had their own preoccupations with scrounging and seeking distraction from their own grey environment, but without the liberating celebrations. They remained utterly committed to doing as much as they could under camp conditions to continue participating in the war effort. It was an ongoing challenge to collect, analyse and share intelligence on the war's progress. The POWs were encouraged by their captors to read the German newspapers, but judiciously countered this one-sided view with the latest BBC news, equally one-sided, that they received on an illicit radio. The radio was built from parts procured somehow by the inmates and was hidden in Skeets's hut. Each hut had a toilet at the end for use at night, and the radio was cached in a space beneath this convenience. Skeets claimed the radio saved their sanity, allowing them to discount the German propaganda. The Kriegies became adept at balancing the two sources to maintain an accurate picture of the progress of the war, even keeping up-to-date war maps reflecting the latest action.

And there was always the temptation to rile one's jailers. Understandably, one prisoner described the relations between the prisoners and their captors as 'not great,' despite the supposedly preferential treatment being given by the Luftwaffe to its fellow airmen. Andy Wiseman later said: 'You'd try to annoy them to the point of shooting you, but you'd try to avoid that.' When the prisoners pressed things too far or transgressed the rules of the camp, they were sent to the 'cooler.' The concrete footprint of that building, not far from the camp hospital, still shows the size and configuration of the individual isolation cells, where you got 'a walk twice a day and a room by yourself.' It was a relative luxury for some, and Andy claimed that people who were studying for exams (you could take a course in just about anything in the camp, and some were actually accredited) would sometimes deliberately try to be sent to the cooler, so they could concentrate on their books.

The focus on the war aside, life in the camp did offer opportunities to take advantage of the wide-ranging backgrounds or interests of the growing number of POWs. Lectures, classes and training were given on far-flung topics by professors and other well-educated inmates—who had left their pre-war professions to join the war effort—for those who were interested in furthering their studies. Classes were offered in many languages, often by native speakers who had come to England from other countries on the continent to make their own contribution.

Skeets remembered books supplied by the Red Cross, which gradually grew to a significant library. According to Charles Clarke, a young Lancaster crewman shot down in 1944 (later, Air Commodore Charles Clarke, OBE), the most popular volume was *Sex Life of a Savage*. In addition to books, the Canadian Red Cross sent some winter sports equipment and the Canadians in the camp organized themselves into a couple of hockey teams, playing on the frozen-over fire pond in the camp. In the summer, the inmates played softball and flaunted the rules against swimming in the same fire pond that served as the ice rink in winter.

Arthur Crighton was an RCAF pilot who had had to abandon his Wellington bomber over Nazi-occupied Holland when it caught fire en route to Hamburg in the middle of the night of April 8, 1942. Captured, he always claimed he was intentionally moved to the North Compound of the camp when it was discovered that he was a skilled trumpet player, a talent missing from the camp band. He went on to organize the orchestra and become one of the leading lights in theatrical activities, scrounging supplies and musical instruments, and dedicating himself to the arrangement of the biweekly shows in the camp's theatre. The theatre was built by the inmates with materials supplied by their German captors, based on the theory that if they were busy with such harmless pastimes, it would keep their minds from more troublesome thoughts of escaping. Little did they suspect that the facility would, controversially, later play an important role in escape efforts, first as a repository for the ubiquitous yellow sand removed from the ever-growing tunnels, and eventually as the home of a tunnel of its own, used for storage of contraband and escape materials.

The seats, complete with ashtrays, were constructed for the 300-capacity theatre from Red Cross crates. Lighting dimmers were created from biscuit tins, tar, salt water and pieces of wood. But despite the makeshift surroundings, maintaining a high standard in the productions was important to those involved. 'Prisoners were allowed dress uniforms from home,' Crighton said. 'Most men had no use for them. But I insisted musicians wear them for performances.'[79]

There were no limits on the types of theatrical presentations the inmates were willing to undertake. Some of the men adopted the roles of women, sometimes with memorable results. As Skeets recalled, 'Some of the girls they made up needed a fighter escort to get them in and out of the theatre!'

The singular challenge of having men play in women's roles notwithstanding, the quality of camp productions was high across the board, thanks to the contributions of people like Arthur Crighton and the participation of such luminaries—then ordinary POWs—as Rupert 'Pud' Davies, who later famously played Georges Simenon's detective Maigret, and Denholm Elliott, another post-war staple of BBC television. More than just these big names took their acting talents home. An undated post-war clipping announcing the marriage of Flight Lieutenant Robert Laumans—known as the 'glamour girl' of Stalag Luft III for his roles as leading lady in many theatre productions—goes on to say that 'the Stalag actors recently put on their own show—*Back Home*—in the West End.'

Joe Kayll, a wing commander when he was shot down in July 1941 and eventually becoming an inmate of the East Compound of Stalag Luft III, spoke about the personal impact the theatre had on at least some of the POWs by connecting them with the country and culture they would not see for an indeterminate time. Referring to a production of Our Town, he said, 'I found [it] a very emotional performance; and yet I've seen it since and it has had no effect on me at all.'[80]

Photos of many of the theatre productions (and indeed, of many aspects of camp life) were preserved in a memorial book put together not long after repatriation by Squadron Leader H.P. Clark. In the book, Clark[81] recounts one small and exquisite irony in the experience of a new arrival at the camp, who had been shot down with a ticket in his pocket for a West End presentation of *Arsenic and Old Lace*. He used the ticket at Sagan, for the same production!

The Kriegies also enjoyed the occasional film. John Colwell documents some of the screenings he was able to attend, as frequently as every couple of weeks and ranging from the funny to the racy to the intensely serious: *The Importance of Being Earnest, Messalina, The Corsican Brothers, St Joan*, and more.

And there were other home-made diversions. A small photo Skeets sent home to his family shows what seems to be a makeshift game of skittles, featuring Skeets and a fellow Kriegie in a woman's wig and what seems to be a hockey sweater. It is stamped on the back, 'Stalag Luft 3 Geprüft,' cleared by the censors, along with the pencilled title, 'Sam and Og.' The dressed-up POW is Samuel Pepys, a Blenheim pilot shot down over France a few weeks before Skeets. Pepys was a friend made in the camp who would play a critical role in the final days of the war in preserving Skeets's physical and mental health—and vice-versa—during the Long March. Pepys was also one of the Kriegies who convincingly played women in the plays mounted in the camp theatre. Skeets's scrapbook contains a post-war announcement of Pepys's marriage after he was repatriated to England, but there is no further record of contact between the two, an odd circumstance given their shared experiences.

Sometimes, though, it was enough for POWs simply to walk 'the circuit,' a track around the compound just inside the warning wire, on which Paul Brickhill commented 'You could walk . . . for hours till you were numb and didn't worry about home or the war or even the more important things like sex or liquor.'

Sex was, and still is, a taboo subject in any literature or discussion of life as a prisoner of war. The absence of female company for—in some cases—six years, must have created significant strains in a population of young men in their late teens or early twenties. Whatever distractions the inmates manufactured to divert themselves, however, have remained opaque, lost in the silence of the years since that difficult time.

As for liquor, in fact, they weren't entirely without intoxicants. Some enterprising souls were always creating a generic 'Kriegie brew' from Red Cross parcel raisins, potatoes or any other likely sources. Such 'beverages' played a central role in holiday and other celebrations. One of the key figures in the *Great Escape*, Wally Floody, told a story of one batch that was strong enough to eat into the lining of the pail in which it was being prepared.

He scooped some out and offered a drink to a guard. 'Then I waited to see if he collapsed before sampling it myself,' Floody admitted.

Skeets provided another view of the hazards of 'alcohol' in the camp:

Something to drink? This is another story. Some of the fruit we got in there was used as fruit . . . other chaps used it otherwise. We had a little still going, using a trombone horn. Passed through the water, they boiled this great mash and filtered it through the trombone horn into little containers. We'd save this up for Christmas so each chap had the equivalent of a coke bottle full of this liquid . . . it made the Lemon Hart 130 proof seem tame by comparison. But we kept all this for the Christmas bash. Each hut turned one room into a sort of party room, and decorated it one way or another. After appell, everyone was counted and they brought out this devil's brew they had concocted. I remember one of the boys, Ed Baker, a tough old boy from western Canada, saying 'There's nothing to this stuff!' and after about three drinks, old Ed was just long gone. Completely paralyzed. This was sort of funny, much like most drinking parties, some lasted and some didn't. Unfortunately, some of the boys got out of the hut. One chap tried to go over the wire and got shot, so this brewing was outlawed. We had to use our raisins for legitimate purposes. So much for the alcohol content of the camp . . . there never was any after that. I think that was my first Christmas [1942].

Such distractions aside, life in the camp was by no means easy. Arthur Crighton described 'squatting on an abandoned roadway that ran through the camp, freezing in the winter cold and picking up bits of unburned tar from the macadamized road surface that would be used to cook our evening meal of turnip and barley soup.' The huts, uninsulated, were barely kept habitable by the home-made stoves created by tin bashers like John Colwell, fed by scarce, often scrounged, fuel. And the surroundings themselves were bleak. Inmates felt a chronic and strong sense of isolation that was aggravated by the cloudy skies, the dense and monotonous grey woods surrounding the camp and the dry, sandy earth on which it was built.

23

PREPARATIONS FOR ESCAPE

The Kriegies keenly felt it their duty to contribute however they could to the war effort. It was no wonder that they worked so hard at diversions, including the big one—escaping. For many, it was more than a diversion; it was an obsession that was hard to describe. One prisoner expressed it as carefully and subtly as he could when he said, 'The air outside the wire is entirely different from the air inside. It's the air of freedom. You were outside the wire.'

Escape was always in the air. In fact, Skeets's arrival in the camp in early April 1942 came only shortly after the camp had been opened, but already plotting was taking place among its new inhabitants. For most inmates, despite the miniscule chances of successfully regaining their homes even if they succeeded in leaving the confines of the camp itself, the possibility of being 'outside the wire' was the main source of excitement, a focus offering mental discipline and demanding wits, physical effort and commitment. Joe Kayll put it simply: 'One never stopped digging tunnels or thinking up ways to get out of the gate. It kept one very well occupied.'[82] Not always and not for everyone, though. On rare occasions the stress of incarceration was too much, with sad results. 'We had one spontaneous case of someone trying to escape. An Irish pilot. He had been a prisoner for about three years. He was a keen escaper, and suddenly one night he just went out and tried to climb up the wire. They shot him as he was halfway up. They always said they would and they did. He was one of our very few deaths.'[83]

In any case, the attempts went on in varied and imaginative ways, but always in a semi-organized fashion. If an inmate had an idea, wanted to escape, he went to the escape committee. Skeets recalled:

If they felt there was any chance of succeeding, going out in the garbage wagon or any other way, over the wire or under the wire, and the escape committee thought it was feasible, you got the facilities of the whole camp behind you to put up a digression of some kind while you were cutting the wire. They found that the searchlights from one 'goon box' to another had a dead spot in the centre, so it didn't take long for someone to figure out he could cut his way out through the wire. They made wire cutters from bits of steel someone had stolen. Somebody in that camp could do anything. They had chemists, blacksmiths . . . they could make anything, do anything, really quite an incredible organization.

There were few opportunities for spontaneous escape attempts—most were the subject of intense planning and careful execution. In early 1943, the camp was expanding to hold the growing number of Allied aircrew being taken prisoner, and some 500 or so officers were moved to the newly built North Compound. Watching the construction take place from their current compound, several airmen had (to the pleasure of the camp Kommandant) volunteered to help out preparing the camp. While at this apparently innocent work, they carefully measured and checked out the detailed layout of the new compound, seeking any escape opportunities that the camp's design might offer.

The always-active Roger Bushell—a South African-born former British ski champion and Spitfire pilot shot down in May 1940—was a determined, serious escaper. He had a number of escape attempts under his belt by the time he arrived at Stalag Luft III and was quickly conscripted as 'Big X,' heading the escape committee. It did not take long for him and his small circle on the committee to draw up ambitious plans for three tunnels to be built, with the objective of getting at least 500 men out of the camp in one event. Under the strictest of security, the committee put into place a programme of elaborate preparations involving not just the digging of the tunnels themselves, but working systematically to amass materials to support the digging, collecting and organizing of food and 'civilian' clothing that would be needed to allow escapees to survive and pass muster in the German countryside, and creating the essential passes and identification papers that would allow escapees to avoid detection.

The strict security regime, drawn up under the direction of George Harsh, was vital. Given the sheer scale of the plan, there were a very large number of people involved in escape measures and the German guards were constantly searching for the least evidence of prospective flight attempts. From the time digging of the three tunnels—nicknamed 'Tom,' 'Dick' and 'Harry'—began simultaneously in April 1943, and throughout the preparations for the escape, only about a dozen people ever knew the whole picture. Most of the 600-odd prisoners directly involved were simply engaged in making their own contribution in one way or another, whether digging, disposing of the sand, making tools, sewing clothes or forging false papers. So far as the German guards knew, camp life was going on as usual. Arthur Crighton did his part by keeping the orchestra programme going at full pace. 'We knew the best thing we could do for them would be to ignore what they were doing,' he said, 'to not talk about it, and to keep acting as though everything was normal.'

In his role managing the distribution of the Red Cross parcels' contents, Skeets did his part in foraging for the escape. The carefully inventoried contents included food reserves that were set aside in anticipation of the actual event. More importantly, the job gave him an ideal opportunity to pick out and 'liberate' legitimate materials that could be repurposed to make everyday life a bit easier—evaporated milk (Klim) cans that could be turned into a wide range of metal containers or reused as ventilation tubes in the tunnels; pyjama string for lamp wicks; and a myriad of other package components that found themselves being used in ways never imagined for them.

As digging progressed, one of the biggest challenges became the disposal of tons of bright yellow sand from the 30-foot-deep tunnel. It showed up like a neon light against the dark grey surface earth or winter snow, and the diggers came up with a hundred different and ingenious ways to dispose of it. The most inspired was the work of 'penguins' (of whom John Colwell was one when he was not 'bashing tin'), who would store the sand in bags inside their trousers and surreptitiously deposit it around the compound, shuffling it into the dirty topsoil as they went along. The excavated sand went everywhere, smudged into the ground, buried in vegetable gardens, scuffed into the sports playing fields or distributed by the 'penguins' around the perimeter circuit. In at least one of the huts, it was even stored in the roof, eventually causing a minor collapse when the weight became too much, and precipitating frantic repairs before the Germans could discover the damage.

The 'Dick' excavation eventually became impossible to continue because of the construction of the West Camp, and was turned into a dump for sand and a storage place for papers and other escape supplies. Construction efforts were centred on 'Tom.' Then in the autumn of 1943, to the horror of the inmates, that tunnel was discovered, nearly completed, when a guard accidentally dropped a hammer on the trap door and, as Skeets noted, 'it went "clunk" instead of "bong."' The decision of the German army engineers to dynamite the tunnel after its discovery provided a great entertainment to the camp, when the larger than planned explosion blew the roof off Hut 123, where the trap had been located, and disintegrated the concrete floor.

Thereafter, escape efforts were concentrated on completing the remaining tunnel, 'Harry,' under the noses of the increasingly suspicious German guards. As Skeets remarked, 'As our skill at deception increased, so also did the experience of the German "ferrets" whose job it was to constantly scour the camp for signs of such "Kriegie" enterprises.' Only the day before the eventual escape, the head ferret in Skeets's compound—one widely despised Robert—assured the camp Kommandant at a security meeting that the camp was free of any major escape activity. Skeets later said, 'It was one of our greatest joys, to outwit Robert, who had tripped us up so many times in the past. I can just picture him breaking the news to a livid camp Kommandant. Even now I feel good thinking about that!'

Actual digging of the tunnel was the domain of the most adventurous. A Canadian inmate, Wally Floody, who had worked as a deep-rock miner in Timmins in northern Ontario, was the designer of the tunnelling system eventually adopted to ensure the integrity of the shaft. He never disabused the escape committee of the idea that he was a trained mining engineer, but the truth was simply that he had spent some time working as a mucker, loading ore carts to be hauled to the surface. As important as his actual underground experience, though, was his gift of applying common sense to the problems of digging the escape tunnels.

The system he devised for construction of the tunnels relied on continuous reinforcement of the digging with wooden boards, mostly 'requisitioned' from prisoners' bunk beds, to build a frame around which sand was backfilled to prevent collapse. Skeets wasn't a digger. He made only a single comment on the physical nature of the tunnel, just 2 feet square, with characteristic restraint, saying that 'It wasn't a place for claustrophobics. It was surprising the number of boys who wanted to help but just could not force themselves down that narrow shaft.' There were in fact several collapses that took place as the tunnel progressed, but fortunately the diggers were somehow rescued every time. The sand would make a cracking noise just before it let go, and diggers learned to move like lightning whenever they heard that sound. Even so, there were many narrow escapes, including for Wally Floody, who had to be dug out more than once by his colleagues, on one occasion when he was pinned up to his neck in loose sand.

While construction went on below ground, it was imperative that the movements of the 'goons' in the compound be tracked meticulously. The prisoners became expert at protecting the activity beneath them from the Germans who were constantly on the lookout for evidence of any escape activity. One Kriegie described how guards would come into his room for coffee and a cigarette, practically every day. 'At one point, we had guards in our hut and outside at the other end, with digging going on in between.'

Squads of 'stooges' were organized throughout the camp as part of the POWs' security and intelligence system to feed information back to a coordinator. At the least suspicion of an unusual move or interest on the part of the guards, a tunnel could be closed or preparatory work put away in short order. The trap door giving access to 'Harry' was carved out of cement at the base of a stove that was kept continually burning. It was reported that it could be opened or secured in the event of a warning being given in a matter of twenty seconds, without its existence being evident except under the most careful scrutiny. The diggers also had to get used to responding to occasional announcements of snap appells, which required all prisoners to be present for counting on the parade ground. Those above ground would dally or create confusion in the assembled ranks by changing places as the head count went on, giving time for those underground to come to the surface and join the throng.

As the tunnel progressed, it became more and more sophisticated. Skeets described some of the innovations the tunnellers introduced:

You could barely move in this tunnel, couldn't stand up and had to back out. Some bright guys devised this 'railway' and the tunnellers would lie on this flat board with wooden wheels that had been carved out of something. They would pull up to the [excavation] surface and do their work there, and the sand would be despatched [via the railway] back to the anteroom at the head of the tunnel where it could be stored until you got a chance to get rid of it. So this railway was in 3 stages, about every hundred yards you'd transfer from one to another.

At first we used margarine lamps with wicks made out of pyjama ties, very smoky, sticky things. Our big breakthrough came with one of the chaps, Red Noble, a chap from St. Catherines, I think. He was what they called a goon baiter—he was always getting into trouble with the Jerries. If they said turn left, he'd turn right. One day he was coming out of the solitary where the Germans put anyone they were unhappy with, with his greatcoat on and as he walked by the kitchen, there were some German electricians in there doing some sort of work. There was a pile of electrical wire out there, which Red picked up and put under his coat, and kept going. Shortly after that, our tunnel was equipped with electric lights, courtesy of Red.

The Germans who had lost the wire were too terrified to report it, because there was only one solution for anyone who got caught doing anything there, and that was the Eastern Front, the Russian Front. It was the one place none of those chaps wanted to go. So they just didn't report losing the wire.

All in all, the process of constructing the 365-foot-long, 25-foot-deep tunnel took huge amounts of material, all scrounged from around the camp. Included were some 4,000 bed boards, issued to prisoners to sleep on. Frank Stone, one of the tunnel excavators, said that when digging was at its peak, all the new arrivals to the camp had to give up five bed boards as soon as they walked into the compound. Skeets noted that each incoming prisoner was relieved of half of his bed boards by the camp quartermaster, before he ever saw them, and that prior to the theft of the wire, there was not a pyjama tie to be found in the camp; they all went into the makeshift lamps. Among the other items that went down the tunnels were 1,370 battens; 1,699 blankets; 161 pillow cases; 635 mattresses; 34 chairs; 52 20-man tables; 90 double-tier bunks; 1,219 knives; 478 spoons; 30 shovels; 1,000 feet of electric wire; 600 feet of rope; 192 bed covers; 3,424 towels; 1,212 bed bolsters; 10 single tables; 76 benches; 246 water cans; 582 forks; and 69 lamps.[84] By the time the project was finished, people were sleeping on wire and rags and straps all tied together, and their bed boards were propping up the tunnels.

While the digging progressed, there was plenty of other preparatory activity aimed at putting into place the essentials for a successful escape. The camp tailors were skilled at converting uniforms into passable civilian clothing that would allow escapees to blend in with the local crowds. They converted and dyed RAF uniforms with coffee grounds to remake them as labourers' clothing, business suits and, in at least one case, even a passable copy of a Luftwaffe uniform. Others created compasses from melted phonograph records and magnetized shards of shaving blades. Each was stamped with 'Made in Stalag Luft III. Patent Pending.'

One great challenge lay in preparing the documentation that escapees would need to be able to move through wartime Germany. This was essential—without the necessary papers, escapees would be at great risk of immediate recapture. Joe Kayll recalled the creativity involved in working out the solutions:

> We had a brilliant forgery department [in Stalag Luft III]. Photographs were the most difficult thing to get, to put on the identity cards.
>
> For a period the Germans sent a Nazi welfare officer to the camp whose job it was to extol Nazism. Two or three potential escapers were told to make friends with him and pretend to swallow his propaganda. They were so successful that he thought he had converts; they managed to persuade him to bring in his Leica camera and to take photographs of themselves to send home to relatives. We knew that he was not allowed to bring a camera into the camp but by judicious use of chocolate and other bribes he was persuaded to do so, and he took some photographs. The escape committee decided

that the next time he brought his camera in we would remove it from him and tell him we were going to take photographs, and if he didn't get them developed and bring the prints back, we would go straight to the German Kommandant and inform on him. It was something he might easily be shot for. He went as white as a sheet, and was trembling as he went out of the gate. We took the photographs, it all worked, and when he'd brought the photos in, we gave him his camera back. We had got photos of all the likely escapers. Then of course it was a big job for the forger to make identity cards from them. It took a lot of doing, each identity card took about a week, working four hours a day—it was very close work. You couldn't get a railway ticket without producing an identity card and a letter explaining the reason why you were travelling. We had one officer who could do a typewritten letter, all with brush and Indian ink, and you wouldn't know the difference.

Eventually we got the use of a typewriter, in the foodstore where the parcels arrived. We got the squad who carried the parcels out and did all the work in there to distract the German guards. We had a good typist who could go in and type the letters that were required. We found that I.G. Farben, the huge chemical company with plants all over Germany, who employed thousands of foreign workers, were a good cover. The letter would state that it was necessary for this foreign worker, Frenchman or Pole, to go to wherever it was on the train.[85]

There were other complications to preparing the necessary documentation. The form of passes and identification papers changed from time to time, and the forgers could only hope that the models they had managed to beg, borrow or steal would remain valid as long as they were needed by the potential escapees. At one point, not long before the escape took place, Skeets made an unplanned and important contribution in this regard. One of his favourite camp stories was about spying a wallet sitting loosely in the pants of one of the German camp guards who was overseeing his parcel unpacking activities. Skeets managed to pull it the rest of the way out without the guard noticing and handed it over to one of his fellow inmates while the guard was distracted. The wallet was immediately sent to the escape committee so any relevant documents could be copied and the wallet returned, before the guard noticed it was missing. Skeets always chuckled as he described handing the wallet back to the unsuspecting guard, who nearly fainted at the implications of losing his papers. 'Oh my God, Mr. Ogilvie, if I lost that, Eastern Front!' This was the ultimate punishment for a misdemeanour. Skeets claimed he was treated as a favourite from then on.

Other materials or information were obtained by similarly devious means, as Skeets recollected:

> We had 'tame' goons. Some of them were pretty sympathetic. The Kriegies would invite them in in 20 degree below weather when these guys were supposed to be walking around the camp and offer Hans a cup of hot chocolate. Well, Hans hadn't seen a cup of hot chocolate in some time, and gradually these guys would be won over. They'd say, 'Tell you what we need, is some film, Hans' and Hans would say, 'I can't do that, it would be the Eastern Front.' They'd say, 'Well, suppose we tell your Sergeant you've been coming in here every night for a hot chocolate? Where will you be sent then?' And old Hans would come in with a camera or some film. They just black-mailed some of them. Some were sympathetic, didn't hold with the Nazis. Most of these were older fellows, like our Home Guard, but the one thing they lived in fear of was the Eastern Front. They didn't want any part of that. So one way or another we got things.

Once completed, the forged papers, modified uniforms and other trappings for escape had to be hidden immediately within the camp, in utmost secrecy, behind false walls or cupboards with hidden access panels, down the second tunnel, 'Dick,' or in outside earth latrines. Security and concealment were so good that the German 'goons,' constantly searching, didn't notice that some rooms were smaller than the others and never unearthed any of the many ingenious hiding places. A good thing, too—the discovery of just one false identity document would have been a dead giveaway to the planning for an escape.

As the tunnel approached its objective, a disturbing series of events took place involving visits by the Gestapo to Stalag Luft III. The Kommandant of the camp, von Lindeiner, had a sense that something was developing and asked for a visit from the special security department of the Gestapo that had been established to help prevent escapes by POWs. A representative visited the camp but made no inspection of the premises or the measures that were being taken by the guards to prevent such an eventuality. Even the seismographs, which had been removed for repair, were not reinstalled.

Around this time, an order had been issued by the German High Command that escaping officers were to be handed over to the Gestapo without reporting their recapture to other POWs, German military authorities, the Protecting Power or to the International Red Cross. A subsequent circular from the Gestapo specifically directed that all recaptured escapees, except British and Americans, were to be 'taken in chains to Mathausen Concentration Camp and there executed by any convenient means.'[86] Whether the prisoners were generally aware of the specifics of this sinister development is uncertain, but von Lindeiner no doubt knew; indeed, he had been told the Gestapo might shoot escaped prisoners in the camp compound. Von Lindeiner did his best to warn the senior representatives of the POWs of the potential dire consequences of any escape attempt, but to no avail.

By the third week of March, tunnel 'Harry' was finally ready, still undetected. Jimmy James later recalled, 'The real astonishment was not that it was done, but that it was possible to do it without the Germans discovering it.' But Skeets described how close they came:

> A short period after the work had been completed, our 'duty pilot' reported a large party of goons approaching the gate on the run. This could only mean one thing—a search. This was a routine occurrence and we were not unduly upset until the search party headed straight to the hut. Great was our despair; it seemed just too much to lose out at this stage. However, a few hours later the searchers withdrew with the usual collection of assorted nails and bits of string and it was all too good to be true—our secret was intact.

Unfortunately—or perhaps fortunately for them—several of the key members of the tunnel committee, including Wally Floody, were moved without warning to another camp. Secrecy notwithstanding, the Germans had a good idea who might be involved in an escape and were increasingly nervous that something was going to happen. In the event, nothing could be done but move the escape forward to the earliest possible date.

24

LAST MAN OUT OF THE TUNNEL

The ideal timing for an escape was, naturally, as dark a night as possible. 'Harry' was complete, tension in the camp was high and the risks of discovery were increasing greatly. It was decided that the moonless night of March 24–25 would be the best opportunity for opening the tunnel, despite the extremely cold weather. A list of 200 names was prepared. The first 100 were selected because of their greater chances of successful escape, for the length of time they had been in the camp or due to their contribution to the tunnel's construction. The second 100 were identified by drawing names from a hat. Some prisoners—those who were claustrophobic or others who wanted to complete their study activities—declined to be included, but they were in a minority.[87]

Men who could speak German or another European language or who otherwise had the greatest chance of getting away were given the first positions in line and received the most authentic clothing and escape materials. Some had elaborate instructions on how to make their way away from the camp, planned in detail based on collective intelligence gathered by other inmates, information gleaned from camp workers and guards on train schedules and the like. The first thirty were to travel by train from Zagan station early on the morning of the escape.

However, those following a defined plan were relatively few. Most escapees were simply being given the chance to get out from behind the wire and make their way, any way they could, toward neutral or friendly territory. Their uniforms were slightly modified to make them appear mainly as labourers, usually non-Germans, and they had related papers and extra food rations. Mostly travelling on foot, they won the nickname 'hardarsers'

187

for obvious reasons. While they were deadly serious about getting away, their function was mainly to create a smokescreen to enable those who were better equipped with civilian clothes and passes to get away on the trains.

Skeets was one of the 'hardarsers,' number seventy-six on the list, and happy to go: 'One of the boys from the committee came in and said, "Your name has been picked as one who has a chance to go out in the tunnel." I was of course pretty excited at the prospect of getting outside the camp. Getting out and walking around seemed like a pretty good idea at the time. I'd never won anything in the lottery before and this was as close as I was about to come.' His aspiration was to get into Yugoslavia and meet up with Tito's partisans in the mountains, hoping either to fight or return to England with their help. Like the other prospective escapees who hadn't done this sort of thing before, he had all kinds of questions but no one to ask—there could be absolutely no conversations about the escape because of the need for the strictest security. Nonetheless, whatever their position in the line-up and whatever their perceived chances, the chosen escapers were optimistic, excited by the prospect of an adventure to break the stifling boredom of their existence and utterly committed to making their best effort to get home by whatever means possible. It was still a bit unreal, almost a game—serious, but still a game. Not every escapee could hope to have complete disguises, but according to Skeets, all of the escapers, hardarsers or serious prospects for evasion, had maps, money, compasses and a good supply of 'iron ration' made of a sustaining mixture of cocoa, porridge, vitamins and other ingredients cooked into a block.

The night of the escape was a Friday. Arthur Crighton learned of the intended breakout that afternoon when 'the Wing Commander, he was in charge of Security, he said (in a low voice), "Art, we're going tonight." That's all he said to me, I remember it now. He said, "We're going tonight." That was the hottest news of course in the camp.'

At a final briefing for the escapers, those who had been involved in previous attempts passed on a number of pointers. Skeets remembered two in particular:

One of the boys remarked that the woods through which the 'hardarsers' hoped to make their way into Yugoslavia were fairly well populated with deer which barked at night, similar to dogs. I had never heard of this before, nor have I since, but, so help me, German deer sound more like a dog in the lonely woods at night than a dog does, this I know!

His second memory of the briefing was more serious:

'Big X,'[88] the brains behind our intelligence, assured us that when, as, and if we were caught, the Germans would make every effort to discover the organization behind our activities. They might go to any length to find out, even by standing us against a wall and threatening to shoot us . . . but they would not carry it out. In view of what happened this was a most unfortunate underestimation of the German mentality. 'Big X' was shot following his capture on the French border.

Ogilvie remembered, 'You could smell the suspense.' The tension was palpable throughout the day as hidden supplies were recovered and distributed, last-minute preparations were made and those who were among the 200 on the list made their way in the dark to Hut 104 where the tunnel entrance was located. They crowded in together, twice as many as the hut was designed to hold, dressed in their diverse escape clothing and clutching an assortment of maps, documents, food and whatever else they felt they could take with them—not much, given the tiny confines of the tunnel. The scene inside Hut 104 was surreal, with well-dressed civilians, some with suitcases, apparently mixing with workmen in the meanest clothing, and a large group of military personnel carrying knapsacks. At one point, into this tense atmosphere came Paul Tobolski, a Polish RAF officer who spoke perfect German, in the uniform of a German Luftwaffe corporal. After a deafening silence, there was incipient chaos until Tobolski was recognized, just in time to avoid any unpleasant consequences of his excellent disguise.

At ten o'clock, the guards closed the shutters and locked up the huts as they did every night. No one looked inside Hut 104. All was in readiness as the escapees sat impatiently waiting for the action to start.

Then, the diggers at the front of the tunnel reported disaster. After unexpected delays opening the last 2 feet of the tunnel through frozen ground, the first tunneller cautiously poked his head above ground and discovered a disastrous error. Despite the best efforts at estimating their position, the opening—intended to come up just inside the woods—was found to be several feet short of its objective, in the open and very near a watch tower. More discussion ensued. It was decided that delaying the escape and extending the tunnel would be impossible; the forged passes were good for that particular time, everything was in place, and the momentum was with the escapers. The night was dark and a cold wind pushed around the light snowfall, which would help disguise any unwanted noise. The escape would continue, with a modified system of exiting the tunnel. A rope would be strung between the tunnel and the edge of the woods, and as each escapee made his way to the woods, he would survey the scene, make certain there was no risk, and signal the next escaper to move up by tugging on the rope.

So the escape began—but more problems ensued. Some nights, the inmates could actually see fires and occasionally hear aircraft and feel the thump of explosions as the Allies bombed the area around Berlin, 100 miles away. On these occasions, the camp's electricity supply was shut off to avoid detection. The night of the escape, an air-raid siren sounded and the camp lights were turned out as a huge air assault on Berlin and environs unfolded. The tunnel was immediately plunged into darkness. Fat lamps had to be lit and passed down to illuminate it until the electricity returned, sometime after midnight. At several points, there were near-disasters. Ken Rees (number seventy-eight on the escape list) recalled, 'A lot of the chaps escaping hadn't been down the tunnel before, and some of them didn't like it very much. They tended to, you know, disturb the fittings, and caused small sand falls and all of those damages had to be repaired on the spot, and that took time as well.' Skeets remembered an army officer in the camp who was a cousin of Churchill's, a Major Dodge.[89] He, unfortunately, had a suitcase with him that caught one of the props and caused a cave-in. Movement stopped 'while they dug the old Major out, propped things up and started off again.'

The escape proceeded, more or less as planned. One by one, the escapees made their way to the entry to the tunnel, descended with their small parcels of gear and moved through the passage to await the all-clear signal and ease their way into the woods, where they would form their travelling groups. However, with all the hold-ups, it was slow going. Those overseeing the progress of the escape recognized that the delays were going to make it impossible for the original plan of freeing 200 prisoners to be completed before daylight. They decided that after eighty had gone, the tunnel would be closed, with the hope that nothing would be discovered before the prisoners were counted at morning appell. As number seventy-six on the list, Skeets would be part of that night's attempt, whatever happened.

So on this cold and miserable March night, laden with maps, papers and food, he made his way in his turn through the hatch and down the 30-foot ladder, climbed on to a cart and was pulled one-third of the way down the length of the tunnel. There, he changed to a second cart to be pulled to the next stop, while the first cart was returned to the starting point for the following escaper. The third stop in the underground journey was the bottom of the exit shaft. Just before 5:00 in the morning, Skeets looked up and saw the cloudy sky outside the fence for the first time in three years, and welcomed a breath of fresh, cold air after the fetid environment of the tunnel.

One of his planned partners on the run, Squadron Leader Laurence Revell-Carter, had preceded him in the tunnel and had already made his way into the woods. On receiving the 'go' signal, Skeets poked his head out and 'could see the wire not far off. It was starting to snow outside. I just pulled myself out and crawled over to the trees to wait for the next guy.' The 'next guy'[90] was Mick Shand, a New Zealander. At that point, fate stepped in the way.

Different accounts agree that a guard, moving away from his normal routine to 'spend a penny'—as one of the escapers later recalled—nearly trod on the open exit to the tunnel. Shand was halfway to the woods and Len Trent, who was following Shand, had just nudged his head out of the ground. Skeets was watching from the woods as the guard came closer and closer to the hole in the ground, and was praying quietly that he would turn around and go back again. His attention to his now completed ablutions turning elsewhere, the guard suddenly noticed steam rising from the ground and the slushy trail made by the escapers as they crawled to the trees. He looked down to see a figure emerging from a hole, nearly at his feet. 'The guy jumped up and the old Jerry nearly pooped himself,' said Skeets. 'He swung his rifle from his shoulder and I heard the bolt click.' Revell-Carter, now the 'controller' who had been signalling to each new escapee from the woods, could speak German. He heard the gun being cocked as well, stood up, and while Shand headed for cover, ran back with his hands in the air, shouting, 'Nicht schiessen! Nicht schiessen!—Don't shoot! Don't shoot!' The startled guard jerked his rifle up in the air and fired. And with that rifle shot, 'Harry' passed into an exalted position in the annals of escape history.

Meanwhile, Skeets was among the trees momentarily savouring his freedom and waiting for his group of POWs to form up. Escapees were to assemble in groups of ten. Each group had one man who was to act as a guide in taking a circuitous route around the camp and into the dense woods, where they would split up into pairs and take off for their predetermined destinations. 'That was the plan. Too bad it didn't work,' Skeets later said. Revell-Carter would have been his intended companion when his group split up. But when the guard fired his gun and the chaos started, it was clear to Skeets that he was on his own. 'I took off and was pretty well clear by the time the other guards got there.' Shand also bolted.

As they streaked away, Ogilvie was trying to do so with a minimum of noise, but remembered 'the Newzie barrelling along with the deftness of a runaway truck. The resulting commotion naturally attracted a few rifle shots in our direction. I thought I was moving at top speed but, with this added incentive, I practically doubled my velocity.' With his disappearance into the woods, tossing excess kit and papers he didn't want to be caught with as he ran, the last of the seventy-six men who had escaped from the supposedly escape-proof camp was gone . . . at least for the time being.

25

OUTSIDE THE WIRE

Every one of those who actually got through the tunnel had a tale to tell of their adventures outside the wire, but not all would have the opportunity to do so. Three men actually made it home: a Dutch officer who was helped by the underground to escape through France and Spain, and two Norwegians who were hidden by Swedish sailors on a ship sailing for neutral Sweden. The rest of the seventy-six were recaptured, some painfully close to achieving their freedom. Several were able to catch trains to various destinations from Sagan station, only to be captured in the intensive countrywide sweep by the German authorities that followed the 'Great Escape.' Minor discrepancies in their papers were the downfall of some. Others had trouble with the language; ironically, two who had been travelling as Yugoslavian workers were found out when a Yugoslav sympathetic to the Nazi regime tried to speak to them in Serbo-Croat and couldn't elicit a response.

Skeets had his own story about freedom, but it turned out to be a fairly short one. He quickly became separated from Mick Shand but kept going into the woods, skirting the POW camp as they had been briefed before going into the tunnel. He was on his own in a hostile country, wearing a slightly disguised enemy uniform, with limited supplies, no local knowledge and unable to speak the language. It was cold and snowy, much like it would have been in his home in Canada. Potential escape routes were quickly blocked as the news of the tunnel discovery got out, and thousands of armed Germans in search parties were working an expanding radius from the camp.

He 'ran for hours' to put as much distance between himself and Stalag Luft III as possible. Taking a chance in coming out of the woods, he followed a rough road through a small town until finally slowing to a walk, utterly out of breath. To add to the misery, it started to pour with cold rain. From that point, he gives the account in his own words, as the euphoria and excitement of escape began to be tempered by the reality of being on his own, in an enemy country, with neither supplies nor shelter:

My heart had just about returned to normal when a cyclist came riding up to me, chattering angrily away in German. He rode off as fast as he could in the direction of the town. It was obvious that he was going to call the police so I took off on the double. Back in the woods again I hid under heavy underbrush, but it was frustrating knowing that I was barely out of sight of the camp. I thought the woods would be teeming with soldiers, prison guards, police and dogs all looking for me but there was nothing but deathly silence.

At nightfall I started off, navigating with my escaper's compass. Conditions couldn't have been much worse for travelling through the woods. It was like Canada in March: cold, lots of snow and, in some places, slush. I walked all night, crashing into trees and stumbling into swamps. By dawn, I was cold, wet and miserable and found that I was in a farmyard. Dogs started barking as I faded into the trees at the far side of the clearing. Some time later I heard barking again. If I hadn't been briefed on this peculiar habit of local deer, I would have thought there were more dogs around. By midday I reached the autobahn, which the escape committee had told us we should have crossed the first night. The idea was to get across the autobahn before the Germans had time to get troops on the road. Even though I was hours late and it was broad daylight, there wasn't a person or vehicle in sight. I crossed the superhighway unmolested and slipped again into the woods.

It was a strange feeling to be absolutely alone after almost three years of crowded confinement in a POW camp. I spent all of my second day 'on the loose' hiding in underbrush waiting for nightfall. When darkness came I started off again, ricocheting into trees I couldn't see and splashing into swamps I couldn't anticipate. To add to the discomfort, snow began to fall. After some hours of this floundering around and getting practically nowhere I came to a road running in the direction I wanted to go. Taking that road in order to make better time was where I made my mistake. About one-half hour later I was crossing a small bridge when two members of the German home guard came along. There was nowhere to go—they had me. As it turned out, almost all of the escapees were recaptured the same way I was. No wonder it had been so quiet in the woods—the Germans hadn't even bothered to search the bush. They knew that, sooner or later, we would be forced out of the snow-choked forests onto the roads where they would be waiting for us.

Indeed, most of the other 'hardarsers' had similar experiences, being captured after suffering very badly from exposure through two or three nights in the open. Skeets continued:

The home guard personnel took me to the local police station,[91] placed me in a room, then ignored me for a full day. The following morning two civilian policemen took me to a jail in Sagan where I was reunited with 23 fellow escapees. We learned that a Panzer division, numerous civilian police, military provost and home guard had been diverted from all other activity and employed exclusively in the task of recapturing us. This fact gave us the satisfaction of knowing that we had done our bit to hamper the German war effort.[92]

In the middle of Monday night, three days after the escape, the cell door of the Sagan jail was roughly opened by a dangerous-looking group of men. Skeets recalled them as Sicherheitsdienst, the SS intelligence people, 'Hitler's black cross boys.' They gathered the prisoners together and pushed them outside and into the back of a covered truck. Several hours later, without a word of explanation from their captors as to where they were going and imagining the worst, the truck stopped and the group was discharged into a stone-walled courtyard. Skeets described their arrival: 'At dawn we pulled up in front of a forbidding-looking prison surrounded by high grey stone walls.' Their destination turned out to be the Gestapo prison at Görlitz, Czechoslovakia.

The prisoners were unceremoniously herded at gunpoint into the prison and deposited into tiny cells on the third floor, each holding a group of up to four prisoners. Skeets's initial companions were Pilot Officer Paul Royle and Flight Lieutenant Charles Hall, both of the RAF. They found the place thoroughly medieval, with narrow stone corridors and tiny cells, about 6 feet by 9 feet. Most of the space in the cell was occupied by boards that constituted a communal bed. Rations were limited to twice-daily issues of black bread and a thin, unidentifiable soup. It was a big change from the relative comforts and space of the 'Rackets Room' in Stalag Luft III.

26

AFTERMATH AND CONSEQUENCES

Back in the camp, all hell had broken loose. Arthur Crighton opted to stay out of the way: 'What was going through my mind that night? I better get into my bed and stay there, which I did.' But the wild gunshot from the guard was the signal that the escape had been discovered. Crighton said, 'I knew it was all up.'

Those in the tunnel began to reverse their course and tried to get out of the narrow passageway as quickly as they could. Ken Rees, number seventy-eight in line and waiting at the foot of the tunnel exit, was devastated when he heard the shot, knowing that given another ten minutes or so he and his fellow escapees would have disappeared into the woods and the tunnel could have been closed, with no one the wiser. He later admitted, 'I was really almost in tears. I don't think I've ever been so disappointed in my life.' When the chaotic clearance of the tunnel was finally complete, the trap door was closed and the stove over the entrance was replaced.

Those waiting their turns above ground started to eat their food supplies and get rid of all other potentially incriminating evidence. Some who held later numbers in the list had gone to sleep as they waited their turns while the escape progressed. John Colwell woke around 5:15 with two 'goons' in the hut with their dogs, and immediately burned his papers and threw his chocolate and food out the window. Other German guards were by now working their way back from the open end of the tunnel. About 6:00, some seventy regular German soldiers tramped their way into the compound in full combat gear, and in silence began setting up machine guns around Hut 104.

By 6:30 on Saturday morning everyone had been taken outside into the cold, driving snow, counted, stripped and individually searched, with anything that looked as if it could be used in the escape tossed on a pile to one side. All the 'ferrets' and guards surrounding the prisoners had drawn and cocked their weapons. Extra guards were brought in to man the machine guns in the towers. Finally, around 11:00 the Germans allowed the remaining prisoners, now half frozen, to return to their huts. The new, stricter lockdown rules included three regular and other additional random appells every day, together with curtailment of most recreational activities.

Most seriously for the remaining inmates, the Luftwaffe's administration and guards were replaced almost immediately by members of the SS, who were not nearly as compliant as their predecessors. Von Lindeiner, the camp Kommandant, was arrested and confined to his room on Göring's personal orders.[93] Before this happened, however, and in anticipation of what might follow, he tried to have the escapees who were being held in the Sagan civil jail (including Skeets) returned to Stalag Luft III. His efforts were summarily dismissed. The camp remained in a tense state as the POWs, with even less freedom than they had before, awaited word on the outcome and consequences of the breakout.

Meanwhile, news of the escape spread like wildfire through the German High Command. The Germans eventually mobilized nearly five million people over a period of three weeks[94] in response to it, at great cost to the German war effort. Gestapo, Polizei and border police were all put on high alert and those on leave recalled. The Landwehr and Landwacht—the Home Guard consisting of boys and men too young or old to be conscripted into the regular army—were called out to keep an eye on any potential escape routes in the countryside.

Wally Floody, in a 1980 interview with the Canadian Broadcasting Corporation,[95] remarked:

> The basic reason [for the escape attempt] wasn't because we needed to get those pilots . . . or observers back to England, it was to cause consternation among the enemy, and of course it did do that, because on the day of the escape when the Germans found out there were nearly a hundred people loose, Hitler himself panicked, every train was stopped in Germany and every 15 minutes on the air, Germans were warned that the 'Terrorfliegers,' as they called us, were loose, and all the German forces were called back from

leave. It was the first time this had happened. So we did a little bit to help the war.

Hitler was livid on receiving the news of the breakout at his mountain residence in Berchtesgaden, near the former border between Austria and Germany. Summoning his senior military staff on to the carpet, he immediately ordered that all recaptured escapees were to be shot. General Göring, the head of the Luftwaffe, protested as tactfully as he could, arguing that this would make it too obvious that the Germans were committing a crime against humanity. After long discussion, Hitler reluctantly agreed that 'more than half' should be shot. According to documents relating to the post-war interrogation by British intelligence of General Major Adolf Westhoff, Göring berated Field Marshal Wilhelm Keitel in front of SS head Heinrich Himmler. Keitel in turn warned Westhoff and other senior officers that they must 'set an example' to other prisoners. General von Graevenitz replied that it was out of the question to shoot prisoners and contrary to signed conventions, but the field marshal replied, 'I don't care a damn. We discussed it in the Führer's presence and it cannot be altered.'[96]

Himmler, head of the SS and architect of the Holocaust, later signed the 'Sagan Order' directing the police to hand over two-thirds of the escapees to the Gestapo for execution. According to Paul Brickhill, the choice of who was to live and who was to die was made by General Nebe, the Kriminalpolizei chief. Nebe reviewed the records of the escapees one by one and made his decision on each. A special execution squad formed by the Gestapo was to do the rest, and the whole operation was to be carried out in the greatest of secrecy.

A week after the escape, the Gestapo arrived to undertake their own search of the camp, including the other compounds, but found little of consequence. However, in searching for an explanation of how the tunnel had been lit electrically, they discovered the loss of the roll of electrical cable. The electricians from whom it had been stolen were identified as traitors and shot.

Shortly after, a new Kommandant arrived at the camp. Oberst Braune was expected to implement severe reprisals but in the end limited them to the closing of the camp theatre, increasing the number of appells and denying the inmates Red Cross boxes or food tins—each of these measures making the inmates' world that much smaller than it had been before.

27

INTERROGATION

I n their tiny cell, Ogilvie and the other foiled escapees at Görlitz were unaware of these machinations, or the more sinister and brutal consequences of their breakout.

For reasons best known to themselves, our hosts kept juggling the prisoners in the cells and with each new face, conversation and speculation began anew. I well remember one officer, an RAF Spitfire pilot, who passed through our cell on one of these exchange visits. The walls of the cells were covered with the writings of former inmates and this lad in a spirit of bravado wrote 'Morature Te Salute' (I salute death).[97] This sombre greeting was more prophetic than we realized, for he was one of those who did not return.

After several days of inactivity we were taken individually to the Gestapo headquarters for questioning. At least in my case, there was nothing too formidable about this interrogation. The questioning was mainly on the tunnel construction, our sources of information, etc. I stated that I was a career officer, it was my duty to escape if possible and that as a 'Kriegie' of some vintage I was happy to get out if only to see the wire from the other side. Of course, I maintained I knew nothing of the tunnel construction. The fact that I was still in uniform supported my story and after two or three sessions my questioners lost interest in me.[98]

Skeets's cross-examiners were never abusive in their interrogation. They wanted to know everything about the circumstances of the escape, but there was little Skeets could or would tell them, beyond that he had been offered a chance at freedom and had taken it, as any of them would have in the same circumstances. He recalled a female stenographer and 'this funny, wizened up fellow' who was his interrogator. At one point the girl sort of laughed and said something in a low voice to him. Skeets asked, 'What was that about?' His 'interviewer' replied simply, 'You're lucky.'

It seemed each time he was returned to his tiny cell, there had been some turnover in the inmates. Skeets saw leather-coated Gestapo men take other prisoners out, one at a time, presumably for questioning. As they came back from their final interrogation sessions, the prisoners were reassigned to different cells. Ogilvie's roommates in the new arrangement were Alistair McDonald, Paul Royle and H.C. 'Johnny' Marshall, all downed flyers who had been in the RAF.

On the morning of March 30, the day after the 'sorting out' had taken place, Ogilvie heard the shuffling sounds of some of the other prisoners who appeared to be leaving. According to Brickhill's account,[99] Skeets banged on the door until the warders came to take him to the latrine bucket. On the way he encountered a group of six prisoners being escorted out by heavily armed men and managed a brief whispered conversation with one of them, Al Hake, who thought they were being taken for interrogation. On his return to his own cell, Ogilvie said to the others, 'By God, they're plug-uglies. Looks like the same bunch that brought us from Sagan; same coats and black hats over their eyes. Must be Gestapo.'[100]

The next morning, ten more escapees were marched out of the prison in a similar fashion, piled into a covered truck by armed guards and driven away. Wondering whether they would be next, the four prisoners in Ogilvie's cell noticed when their evening meal of bread and weak cabbage soup was brought to them that a big 'S' was chalked on their door. Marshall opined that it meant they were to return to Sagan. One of the others suggested it might mean 'S for schiessen [shoot],' a morbid joke that brought little laughter.

That same day, Skeets had seen a group of Luftwaffe guards walking down the hall and recognized one of them as one of the guards who had been overseeing work in parcel storage. Skeets called out to him, 'Hey, Hans, when are you going to get me out of this rat trap?'

'Ah, Mr Ogilvie,' the answer came back. 'Tomorrow, tomorrow we'll take you out.'

To the delight and relief of the group of four, three Luftwaffe guards from the camp escorted them out of the prison at 9:00 the next morning, to the train station and back to Sagan.

It was a welcome change to be back in the custody of the Luftwaffe. The railway station was crowded with people waiting for trains but they showed no hostility, only curiosity, when our armed guards brought us into the waiting room. An ominous hush fell over the crowd, however, with the appearance of the Gestapo. Even though the Luftwaffe personnel were obviously employed in the task of escorting prisoners, the Gestapo men demanded to see their papers.

After a train ride of several hours duration we were back at Stalag Luft III from where we had departed, somewhat hurriedly, some weeks previously. I was immediately put into solitary confinement for two weeks, and, while there, I heard the shattering news that 50 of my fellow escapees had been shot in cold blood. I found it hard to believe that such a thing could happen. Only two days before I had shared the same cell with some of those men.[101]

At first, Skeets and the other escapee survivors had had no inkling of the fate of the other men they had been with, but who had not returned with them from Görlitz, and wondered what had become of them. It was 'Red' Noble, one of the men who had been waiting just below the tunnel exit for his turn to get out when the tunnel was discovered, who broke the news to him in the cooler. Noble told him of the rumour that fifty men had been shot. 'Where'd you get that gory story?' Skeets asked, in disbelief. Later, he said: 'If I'd known what was going on in that Gestapo jail, I'd have died of fright.'

The sixteen prisoners who had been marched out of the prison at Görlitz following questioning by the Gestapo were actually being taken into the nearby woods to be summarily executed. They represented two-thirds of the twenty-four prisoners who had been brought to Görlitz; in all, fifty of the seventy-three recaptured escapees were to meet the same fate. Ten Canadians had been among the escapees. Ogilvie was one of only two who weren't executed.

But Skeets's luck had continued to hold. Only fifteen of the escaped POWs who survived were sent back to Stalag Luft III. The other recaptured survivors were dispersed, without notification to the Red Cross or other authorities, to less auspicious locations—four to Sachsenhausen concentration camp, others elsewhere. Like the others who returned, Skeets was never able to determine why he had been spared and his companions had not. In 1945, he said: 'The men who were shot were picked at random. I don't know why I wasn't chosen. Guess I'm just plain lucky.'

Two weeks after Ogilvie had vacated the tunnel, the new Kommandant, Oberst Braune, had asked for a meeting with Group Captain Herbert Massey, the senior British officer at the camp. In a tense and unhappy discussion, Massey was euphemistically informed that some officers who had tried to escape while being recaptured had been shot in the process. The news that none had been wounded was the giveaway of the real situation. The inmates in the camp were horrified, disbelieving. They too had wondered what had become of the other escapees who had not been returned to the camp.

In a later interview, Skeets acknowledged the suddenly deadly serious consequences of what had been 'the only occupation [a POW] had. The Germans' occupation was to try to keep us in there and ours was trying to get out.' But the deaths affected him deeply. 'They were all buddies. Some of those killed, in particular a couple of the Canadian boys killed, were good friends of mine, and it shook me . . . you can see their faces, and hear their voices, you know?'

In Ogilvie's collection of clippings and documents is a certified true copy of a translated German document, dated May 8, 1944. It states:

> The prisoners of War are to be informed of the following Statement orally and on the notice-board as well: 'In the course of an enterprise to recapture British Air Force Officers, who had escaped in a large number, some of them offered resistance on being arrested. After recapture others tried again to escape on the transport back to their camp. In these cases the fire-arms had to be made use of. 50 Prisoners of War were hereby shot.'

As is often the case in war, the German people were given a sanitized version of events. John Colwell's diary contains a translation of an article dated July 24, 1944, in *Deutsche Allgemeine Zeitung*:

In March of this year English Prisoners of War broke out of various camps in Germany in large numbers. The measures taken to capture the fugitives were completely successful. From the evidence it was apparent that a well planned action which had in part been prepared in conjunction with a foreign land, had been foiled. In the bringing back of the prisoners which fled from one camp the German security forces repeatedly had to make use of their arms because of the opposition or attempts to re-escape, as a result a number of POWs were killed.

Some weeks after the return of the fifteen escapees to the camp, the ashes of the victims of the mass murder were returned to the camp. The new Kommandant, who was also evidently concerned by the circumstances, allowed the prisoners to build a stone cairn under the direction of John Hartnell-Beavis in which the ashes of the fifty were interred.[102]

A short dedication ceremony took place on December 1, 1944, under the direction of a Catholic priest and a Protestant padre, with the German camp adjutant participating. On the day of the service, Arthur Crighton, who had remained in the camp at the time of the escape to continue his oversight of the camp orchestra's activities, was called on to participate in the ceremony at the memorial cairn. It was his first time out of the camp since his own capture. 'I can still remember my first walk out in the woods,' he recalled.

> I was excited as hell, real trees, I could touch it. I still remember those events. I went out on a funeral march. Well, I had to play Last Post out at that monument we built. We had a dedication ceremony for the fifty shot, quite an experience for me. It was a reasonably warm day, not a cold day. There were not many, 20 or 30 or 40 'invited guests' we called them, involved in the escape activity. I remember going back through the gate.

Skeets must have been one of the 'invited guests.' In an interview on the occasion of Remembrance Day, November 11, fifty years later, Skeets acknowledged the great cost of the escape was still with him. 'I'll be thinking about the chaps who didn't come back,' he said. 'I'll be thinking about the luck I had and the fact that their luck ran out.'

There were many escapes from prisoner of war camps over the course of the Second World War. Just what was it that made this one deserving of the indelible 'Great Escape' label? In part, it was the sheer audacity of the endeavour, its size and complexity. Imagining, then planning the collection of materials and carrying out the physical work of constructing three tunnels without detection, along with making the necessary preparations for up to 500 potential escapees—all in secret—bordered on the unthinkable, the outrageous. Even in its reduced form, with only one tunnel completed, it was almost unbelievable. In part, it was the context—the supposedly 'escape proof' camp, built on sand so loose and treacherous that it has foiled all subsequent attempts to unearth the tunnel 'Harry.' It was also the brutal and ugly consequences of the escape itself that made it notorious, and that keep it high in the annals of heroic undertakings during the conflict.

Fifty years after the Great Escape, after a commemorative ceremony at the National War Memorial in Ottawa, Skeets was asked by an interviewer whether it was all worth it. He paused, and replied, 'As a project, it was great. But not in what it cost.' That view was shared by his fellow escaper, Bob Nelson, who said, 'With that casualty rate, 50 people dead, I don't really think it was a great escape. It would have been a great escape if we'd got 50 back to England with only 3 killed.' From the distance of decades, for those close to the event, the horror could finally take its place in the broad and ugly landscape of the Second World War. Ken Rees, who had almost made it out of the tunnel to an unknown fate, later said, 'I think the world at large should remember Belsen and Auschwitz much more than the fifty; those of us who were in the escape should remember the fifty.'

28

RETURN TO CUSTODY

In the camp, Skeets and his colleagues settled in for the balance of the war. His personal account gives a solid reason for doing so: 'From the hidden radios in camp we received word from the BBC that there were to be no more escape attempts. We were to stay in our camps until liberated. The Germans apparently felt the same way for they put up posters throughout the camp stating that, in future, they would shoot all escaping POWs.' After the experience and tragic consequences of the Great Escape, Ogilvie and his fellow returnees were willing, if not happy, to comply with the order to stay put.

Those same radios continued to give the Kriegies heartening news of the progress of the war, and allowed them to discount the German claims of victories and strategic withdrawals. Life gradually returned to a semblance of what it had been before the breakout, waiting and watching, but it was clear that things were beginning to move in a new direction.

Skeets renewed his correspondence with family and friends. He must have written home wondering about whether he might receive a 'Caterpillar' pin, the item awarded to aircrew who had survived bailing out of their aircraft thanks to their silk parachutes. On August 6, 1944, his stepmother Margaret wrote to the Irving Air Chute Co. Inc. in Buffalo, New York, enquiring as follows: 'On the 4th July, 1941, our son, Flight Lieutenant A. Keith Ogilvie, DFC (RAF) went down over northern France. So far we have not received his Caterpillar pin. He has enquired about it and we shall be very much obliged if you will have it forwarded to us. He was a member of the 609 Squadron.' The company quickly replied that up to the present time, the lists received from England have not included the name of your son. However, we feel that your letter justifies the enrolment of his name on the roster of the Club, which will be accomplished. Re the date, if this is correct—July 4th, 1941? As soon as you advise relative date, we shall also be pleased to have the insignia made and engraved, and forward it to you to be held until his return.

Margaret confirmed the date and the pin was duly sent to Skeets's family home. It was always one of his most prized possessions, along with the precious Caterpillar Club membership card that was taped into his flying log following the final wartime entry of July 4, 1941.

Back in England, Irene continued to live a busy life as the war wore on, both socially and in her photographic service with the RCAF. On leave in the Torquay area of England in October/November 1944, she went to visit 'Madame Valerie, Clairvoyant,' an experience she thought was 'remarkable.' Among other things, the seer predicted that she would be 'crossing the ocean in three months.' The timing was about a year off, but that voyage was definitely in her future. In a postcard to her mother from the Queen's Hotel in Paignton she commented on another vision of the future, this time her own premonition: 'Dreamt about the old man [her father] last nite [*sic*],' she wrote. 'Had my palm read (big laugh) and he was going to kick the proverbial bucket. Any news?!!' The timing of that prediction was off, as well, by quite a bit more than the one-year error of Madame Valerie.

29

THE LONG MARCH

Skeets didn't have long to wait after his return to the camp before he would face more challenges. As the war drew to its increasingly obvious conclusion, the Russian army and the Allies were racing each other to reach the ultimate objective—Berlin. The Russians had a reputation for fighting an ugly, 'take no prisoners' war. The Germans were terrified of being overrun by Russian troops, and many of the Allied POWs shared this fear.

The prisoners in Stalag Luft III devoted a great deal of time to preparing for the unknown. Whatever was going to happen when the Germans finally capitulated, they decided that they would be prepared. After the dust had settled from the escape, the POWs began to store food, clothing and other supplies that had been husbanded and set aside in the tunnel built under the camp theatre.

Arthur Crighton, still committed to the camp's theatrical and orchestral events, was worried about the implications of using the theatre for future escape attempts even though the prisoners had given their undertaking that this would not be the case.

> I was aware of course that they were using the theatre when they shouldn't have been using it. We had 'given our parole [word of honour]' that we would not use the theatre for escape purposes. They were digging a tunnel there. I didn't know that, I suspected it, but I simply ignored it. They were using seat number thirteen to go down in the tunnel, and I knew that was happening, but I didn't look at it, I didn't talk about it, I simply ignored it. Because

I believe that parole was parole. Your giving parole to an enemy . . . you still behave, you do as you say. And I think although they broke their parole by going ahead and digging that tunnel, they knew and we knew, we all knew, they were not digging it for the purpose of escape. It was purely a tunnel for . . . We were afraid of the Russians coming in there and just slaughtering us; that could have happened, Germans and Prisoners. And, I didn't ask about the tunnel, I didn't tell anybody. I didn't know anything, because parole is parole, you don't talk about these things.

But the actual intent of the digging beneath the theatre was unrelated to a specific escape plan. It was rather a simple matter of prudence—being prepared for whatever might befall those who had managed to survive so far. There were rumours that when Germany fell, the camp might be wiped out, so intense effort went into planning for a camp self-defence unit, innocuously dubbed the 'Klim Klub,' which would at least provide some organized opportunity for resistance. Plans were even made to storm the guards' barracks to secure arms, if need be.

The Russian offensive into Germany started in the middle of January 1945. As they advanced rapidly south along the Oder River, the Germans became increasingly nervous. Camp inmates began to hear the Russian artillery and could occasionally catch glimpses of their spotter planes.

It was not clear exactly how the German High Command viewed their prisoners of war at this point—whether the inmates of Stalag Luft III and the other camps were simply to be kept from reuniting with the Allied forces, or, more likely, were seen as potential hostages or bargaining chips. Whatever the rationale, the German High Command ordered a mass transfer of prisoners to locations less at risk of being overrun. More than 100,000 prisoners from many different camps ultimately were put on the move into the heart of Germany as the advancing Red Army began to progress into German territory. This shift took place over objections from the Swiss, who were acting as the Protecting Power for Allied POWs, and who felt that it was too late in the war and that conditions were too changeable to permit the relocation to take place safely.

For Skeets and the others in the North Compound, unaware of the high-level machinations, it was the beginning of their last, dangerous adventure of the war. Their German guards gave the inmates only a short warning that they should prepare to be moved at any minute. Then, around 9:15 p.m. on the night of January 27, 1945, the order was given for POWs to be ready to march out of the camp within an hour. There was much feverish last-minute activity as everyone tried to pull together the clothing and hoarded food they might need and organize it into a bundle that could be carried. Some constructed rough sleds on which they hoped to tow their loads. One of Skeets's fellow camp-mates was an ex-Mountie (member of the Royal Canadian Mounted Police) who showed them how to make backpacks so they could carry twice as much as they would have been able to in their arms. Those who were too sick to walk remained in the camp hospital. In the last minutes, the rest of the men worked to get their boots into the best condition possible and treated themselves to a last, opulent meal of whatever they wouldn't be able to carry. The remaining supplies were simply abandoned, along with precious personal effects, books and, by one account, at least two million cigarettes. Determined that the Germans wouldn't get this last bounty, some of the prisoners threw most of them into the fire pond.

After a number of false starts, the Kriegies of the North Compound were lined up in the first hour of January 28, in a heavy snowfall. The temperature was later estimated to be minus 17 degrees Fahrenheit. The gates were opened and the march began at 1:00 a.m. with the last man having cleared the North Compound by 3:15, according to the senior British officer. For almost all the prisoners, it was the first time they had been outside the wire since being taken into captivity and their initial mood was high. But this was to be only temporary. Those who had managed to construct makeshift sledges had piled on their blankets, cooking pots and whatever food they could put together. Each man was given a Red Cross parcel, yet many could not carry all the contents; John Colwell recorded in his diary that it was only a short way before the marchers came upon the first broken-down sleigh, followed by articles of clothing and food discarded by those who were finding their packs too heavy to carry. Both German guards and civilians were foraging along the sides of the road among the items tossed aside. According to Colwell, the temperature continued to drop. It was simply too cold to stop so the column slowly moved ahead, passing through small towns and villages that made a welcome, if strange, change of scenery from the camp, despite the gruelling conditions of the march.

Some 1,920 POWs from the North Camp were in Skeets's group, making a straggling column that sometimes stretched out 3 miles. Many of the guards were in as bad shape as the POWs, and in the cold and blowing snow, Colwell recorded that 'except for their uniforms and rifles, you couldn't distinguish them from the prisoners.' One survivor recalled,

> You just followed in the footsteps of the guy in front of you. You bowed your head because snow was falling and somebody said if you bowed your head as you walked or shuffled you'd be less affected by the wind coming at you. You didn't talk because that was an effort. You concentrated on walking. You concentrated on putting your foot into the footmark in the snow of the person in front of you. You didn't think.[103]

One of the guards, an older man who was popular with the inmates and whom they had nicknamed Shorty, suffered from an injured leg and eventually collapsed. He ended up being carried by prisoners until a German staff car came along and took him away.

To Skeets, the further they marched, the more it 'looked like the retreat from Moscow. There were parcels, clothes, band instruments, everything the chaps had tried to save, in the ditches. Everyone was simply jettisoning everything they simply didn't need.'

Around noon the column—which had marched in grim conditions for some 28 kilometres without rest or eating—stopped in the town of Freiwalden. There was inadequate accommodation for the POWs so the German officer commanding the march, (Luftwaffe) Major Rostek, ordered the trek to continue another 6 kilometres to the Polish village of Leippa. After thirty-six hours of almost continuously trudging through the snow, 700 of the prisoners were herded into a large stone barn for the night.[104] The rest, including Skeets, were left in a field, huddled together against the cold in the foot-deep snow. He later recalled the experience:

> I will never forget the first night. It was below zero and we came to a farmer's field, and the Germans said, 'That's where you're staying

tonight.' We went into the field, and fortunately one of the boys from my room, Sam Pepys, a direct descendant of the original, had a sleeping bag. I had absolutely had it. This was my lowest point on this whole affair, this night in the field. Sam got me into his sleeping bag and the two of us huddled in that thing and we made it through the night.

Even for those under shelter, the conditions were frightful. They had had nothing to eat for the first two days, other than what was in their packs, and what little they were carrying was frozen solid—it was the coldest night of the year, with a strong wind blowing. Many of the marchers suffered from dysentery, frostbite or diphtheria, with no hope of medical treatment. They were overcrowded and had almost no access to water.

Arthur Crighton later recalled his own ordeal, which was remarkably similar to that of Skeets: 'Etched in my memory is that second dreadful night, which was the coldest night of my life. I'm sure I would have died had it not been for a compassionate friend, who shared with me his roughly sewn sleeping bag.'

Early on the morning of January 29, at 8:00 a.m., they were called out and put on the road again, after a failed attempt by the Germans to count the prisoners. Whatever organisation of the marchers existed was thanks to the prisoners themselves, who tried to keep their group as orderly as they could as they marched at their own pace. A halt was made at Priebus in the late morning, and John Colwell was surprised to find the civilians very friendly towards them, offering them hot water or sometimes ersatz coffee to drink. One woman told him she had a son who was a POW in Canada.

For many of the POWs, any thought of escape was tempered by the fear of being 'liberated' by the Russians and the sheer impracticality of escape—most of the POWs, suffering as they were, realized they would have no chance of survival on their own in those conditions. Skeets admitted: 'We had no idea where we were going, just away from the Russians. Across the river we could hear the rumble of guns in the distance. We just kept walking.' He and Pepys kept browbeating each other into continuing whenever one of them felt he could no longer go on.

The column finally reached Bad Muskau, 40 kilometres west of Sagan, around 6:00 p.m. and for the first time on the march, decent billets had been arranged by the German military. For Skeets and a large number of others, it was finally a chance for at least a little recuperation: 'They got us all into this brick factory, nice and warm, where we were finally able to make some cups of tea and this sort of thing.' Still, there were no sanitary arrangements and by now most of the marchers were suffering from at least a mild form of dysentery. The civilians in charge were credited with making conditions at least as tolerable as circumstances allowed, some even expressing the hope that the prisoners might be going home soon. During this stopover, there was what H.P. Clark called a 'frenzy of sledge building' as the marching prisoners tried to make their burdens easier to manage.

A day later, on the evening of January 31 at 6:15 in the evening, the German English radio service announced that Allied prisoners from Stalag Luft III were marching westward after demanding to be withdrawn from the danger zone where they risked being overrun by the invading Russian troops. The propaganda was clearly a unique interpretation of the situation, meant as insurance in the event of the march turning into a significant disaster—a real risk, given the conditions.

At 10:45 p.m. that same day, two days after the arrival at Muskau, the march resumed in total darkness. A number of prisoners who were no longer capable of going on were left behind. There was a perfunctory issue of food before the column departed, but not all of the prisoners received their rations. Complicating matters was an unexpected thaw the night before, which made it impossible to continue to use the makeshift sleds. Most were abandoned, along with much of their load, shortly after the slow trek once again got under way.

The column finally reached its immediate objective of Spremberg, a rail hub, around 3:00 the following afternoon. After a brief stop the men were allotted to rail cars designed to carry six horses or cattle, or 40 to 45 prisoners. Accounts vary on how many were crammed into each rail car, but they agree that there was room only to sit or stand and not to lie down. Most of the cars were not clean, and the men had to clear out animal manure by hand to achieve even a minimum standard of cleanliness. The marginally improved conditions quickly degenerated into an unspeakable state as the men, many suffering from dysentery, were forced to relieve themselves in a filthy bucket or hole in the floor of the rail car.

Rolling out of the Spremberg station, the groups from the various Stalag Luft III compounds were directed to different destinations. The North Compound company was sent north-east on a journey of two days and two nights, including one night while the train sat in Hanover station during an air raid. They were without sustenance or relief. Paul Brickhill recalled, 'After thirty-six hours they did give us each a cup of water drained off the engine.'[105] All in all, he noted with succinct understatement, 'It was a fairly grim trip' from the start of the march to their ultimate arrival and unloading at the town of Tarmstedt, a town about 30 kilometres from Bremen, in the late afternoon. The men, cramped, exhausted and filthy after their ordeal in the cattle cars, faced a further march of 4 kilometers to an abandoned prison camp.

Marlag und Milag Nord had been formerly occupied by navy and merchant marine prisoners, but had been emptied when it was condemned some time previously. To add insult to the suffering the men had so far endured during their ordeal since leaving Stalag Luft III, the German guards were under orders to search each man before allowing him entry to the camp. The column stood in the rain for nearly six hours while individual searches were carried out and the last man could finally stumble into his assigned hut. It was early morning on February 5, 1945.

Group Captain D.E.L. Wilson, camp senior British officer, reported that 'more than seventy percent of the inmates ended up suffering gastritis, dysentery, colds, influenza and other illnesses during the first week'[106] as a result of the hardships they had endured. Paul Brickhill noted that 'everyone had lost . . . weight, up to thirty pounds. We really hadn't had that much to spare and most of us were looking a little bony.'[107] To make matters worse, the camp was polluted with bed bugs and many prisoners preferred to sleep outdoors rather than struggle with these pests.

However, the POWs gradually settled back into camp life and tried to make themselves more comfortable in their new surroundings. John Colwell, needing to keep himself occupied, almost immediately began producing more tin ware, starting with pots and a makeshift stove to allow the inmates to do some basic cooking and keep warm. On March 25, the prisoners organized what must have been a poignant ceremony—a memorial service for the fifty escapees who had been murdered a year before. The usual tussles with the guards went on. Colwell reported to his diary on March 19 that he was on a 'parcel war with the goons. They want to open and dump all the cans—we refuse to accept.'[108]

As quickly as the Kriegies developed their routines in the new camp, though, it would be only temporary. With the Allies once again closing in, the camp was called to early appell at 3:30 on the afternoon of April 9 and told to be ready to leave by 6:30. They started out around 8:00 into thickening fog, but returned when conditions deteriorated to near zero-visibility conditions. The next morning a second departure was made in better weather conditions, the column heading north-east toward an unknown destination. The hazards of being in the open quickly became apparent to the fleeing prisoners. Skeets described the circumstances:

> That first day we were out, we were attacked by our own airplanes [sic]. They shot up the supply wagon that had our rations and everything on it and killed several chaps who had been in the camp then for four or five years and had the bad luck . . . These were Navy guys, I forget how they got into the camp. But as soon as the Air Force boys saw these planes coming, we got out of the road, into the ditches or fields while our planes strafed the road. They thought we were German troops or something. After that, I think we got word back to the Red Cross and they put red crosses on the wagons that were being pulled. They were told not to attack anything with red crosses. Apparently this was going on all over Germany, they had prisoners marching all over the place.

But it took time for information to get to the right quarters, and it turned out to be a terrible mistake that would be repeated several times in the next few days. As Skeets's account makes clear, part of the reason for this tragedy was the great confusion and concern among the Allies regarding the whereabouts and well-being of their POWs. No precise intelligence on their positions was provided by the Germans, resulting in repeated occurrences of Skeets's experience. The Allies also feared the possible mass executions of prisoners of war, particularly after the mid-February bombing raids on Dresden that claimed tens of thousands of victims, many of them civilian refugees from other parts of Germany. The Allies actually made preparations for air drops of weapons and possibly troops to help liberate the prisoners who were still in identified locations, but there was little that could be planned for those on the move, like the POWs from Stalag Luft III.

The column trudged north-east from Marlag und Milag Nord day after day, through the countryside and small towns. It must have been an extraordinary sight, this motley, straggling line of men and their paraphernalia. As they tramped their way along, the prisoners traded cigarettes for food and wheeled vehicles to help them carry their loads—carts, baby carriages and wheelbarrows. Sometimes it worked the other way. Passing through the town of Lüneburg, where the young Johann Sebastian Bach had been a choirboy, Arthur Crighton wondered what Bach would have thought of the woman and small child who approached him, begging for bread.

The guards found it impossible to keep an eye on everyone, and some prisoners slipped away from the main group. For the most part, however, they recognized they were still at considerable risk on their own. Either way, there were hazards, some unknown at the time. In addition to trigger-happy guards and the risk of being killed by Allied strafing, it was later learned that the guards had been ordered to execute all of the escapees if they failed to reach the Elbe River by a certain day. Brickhill says, 'We didn't reach the Elbe by that day, but at this late stage the guards were getting rather prudent about mass murders, so they decided to overlook the order.' It was a good thing the guards weren't members of the Gestapo.

Occasionally, the prisoners would witness Mosquitoes, twin-engined fighter-bombers, shooting up the nearby towns as they rested overnight in fields or on farms. The weather turned filthy, with rain and sometimes hail, making progress difficult and uncomfortable.

Finally, by April 23 the column reached Hamberge, six kilometres short of Lübeck, not far from the Baltic Sea. The senior British officer inspected the proposed quarters in Lübeck with the German Kommandant and a Red Cross medical officer, and found them to be uninhabitable. An epidemic of typhus had broken out among the thousands of prisoners already there and it was unthinkable to move into such appalling conditions. The decision was made to billet most of the POWs on a large tobacco plantation at Trenthorst, near Westerau, for the rest of the war. Some were taken to

Oflag X-C, an officers' prison camp north-east of Lübeck. Skeets was one of those housed in the 'lovely clean barns' on the property, in a beautiful pastoral setting.

After two or three days the German Kommandant came in and declared, 'We're on our way again.'

At that time, the prisoners' senior officer was Group Captain Larry Wray, a Canadian from Ottawa. He stated emphatically, 'We are not moving from here. If you move us out . . . You know the war is over, I know the war is over, and if you move us I guarantee we will have you shot.'

The Kommandant simply shrugged his shoulders and replied, 'Well, it doesn't matter to me. If I take you out there your people will shoot me; if I leave you here my people will shoot me.' So he just took off on his own.

30

FREEDOM AND REPATRIATION

According to Skeets, by that time most of the German guards had departed, often leaving their rifles behind. Then, after another week of mostly rain and watching many German troops trail by without guns, ammunition or food, Skeets saw a jeep come careering down the road.

Some of our chaps were out and stopped it, and asked them who they were and what they were doing there. It was the advance party for the British 8th Army, just barrelling through there. They said, 'You fellows stay where you are, things are still not finished, the Hitler Youth are around and have been armed and it is just too dangerous to try to get out of here. Our chaps will be through here soon anyway.'

The next day or two, there was an awful racket outside and British tanks started going through, just as fast as they could go, barrelling up this road. A little pothole here or there, and in two minutes the pothole was big enough to lose a car in. They'd just swing around and go across the front lawn of anyone's home. They'd come to a village and tell the mayor, 'Phone the next village ahead and tell them we're coming through, and if there's a rifle shot or any sign of resistance, you're done.' If there was a sniper, the tanks would just turn around and blow the house right off the map and go on their way. So we stayed there another two or three days, I guess, and then they sent some army vehicles in to pick us up.

Brickhill described the scene where he was camped.

On May 2nd, we heard firing down the road and two tanks rumbled through the trees from the south. We didn't know whether they were Germans or British and you could practically see the nerves sticking out of everyone's skin and vibrating like piano wire. The hatch of the front tank opened and two Tommies stuck their heads out. We ran up to them screaming at the top of our voices.

Another former inmate of Stalag Luft III carried the story on:

The lead tank stopped opposite the camp. The turret opened, and a khaki-clad figure popped out and waved in our direction. The tension broke. A roar of cheers; crudely made flags waving; laughter and tears mingling; the guards running off, weaponless; men climbing the wire to run to the tanks; men embracing each other, shouting incoherently; men kneeling to pray; men staring vacantly, bewildered; thousands of men in a state of hysterical, blessed release.

Colwell simply recorded at the end of his extraordinary diary: 'Goons deserting. Tanks arrived at noon—FREE!'

They were almost certainly two Comet tanks, from 'A' Squadron of the 2nd Fife and Forfar Yeomanry, 11th Armoured Division of the British Army. Lieutenant Tom Heald, the commander of the tank squadron, provided a wonderful account from his perspective of the liberation of the temporary camp:

It was May 2nd 1945 and the 2 F&F Yeo. had crossed the Elbe the day before and advanced about 20 miles. For once the petrol lorries had failed to get through the night before and 2 of my 3 tanks were the only ones in the Squadron who would admit to having sufficient fuel for an operation.

It was reported that there was a POW Camp at Winsen about 6 miles away and I was ordered to free it. We got to the village, which was very small, where there was no sign of a camp or of life. However, by dint of getting out of the tanks and knocking on a door (very gentlemanly), I found the camp was down a narrow country lane. As the lane had high hedges we proceeded rather gingerly until we came to a large sign: 'Good Pull-In For Tanks 200 Yards Ahead.' Thus we came to the camp.

That was only the start of our problems. The Comets had been so quiet that no one had heard our approach. The guards must have opened the gates very quickly as we did not have to knock them down. Within a matter of seconds there were about 400 POWs on the two tanks. It was literally impossible to move for 5 minutes. Needless to say although we had been ordered to return immediately to the Squadron to advance on Lübeck, that was quite impossible.

My Army training had not taught me how to take over a POW camp. First I had to arrange for the handover of the Camp by the German Commander to the senior British Officer. They appeared to be on the best of terms but etiquette forbade the German Officer surrendering to his British counterpart, who was his prisoner. I accepted the German Officer's surrender and handed his pistol to the British Officer and told him he was in charge. By the time I got back to my tank I found my crew was being feasted on the contents of Red Cross parcels and the other tank had disappeared. I was told it had some trouble with its tracks, which the crew were dealing with. After about a quarter of an hour it turned up.

Only about 5 years ago I learnt from Gordon Fidler its story. Gordon, the driver, had been beguiled by some POWs to sample their fare. While he was away the very inexperienced tank commander (he had been made up to Corporal that week) and equally inexperienced co-driver were persuaded to drive down the Camp perimeter fencing. Instead of driving across the wire they had drove along the wire, which became inextricably entwined with the track and sprockets so that they had to take the track off to free the vehicle.

In fact they did very well to finish the job in about 20 minutes and keep me quite ignorant of what had happened for 45 years. We were in time to rejoin the Squadron, refuel and move off to capture Lübeck that afternoon.[109]

The same source goes on to note that years later Lieutenant Heald received a letter from one of the former POWs in the camp he had liberated:

Your letter in *The Times* about the Comet tanks struck a chord. Could it have been you, or your Troop, who liberated some POWs near Lübeck on 2nd May 1945? I was one of those fortunate ones and the events of that day remain very clear.

Obviously we knew freedom was near but the sight of tanks near the farm yard where we had found shelter was absolute proof that we were free. There had been little gunfire or noise of warfare for the few days prior to our release and the tanks arrived relatively silently except for their engine noise. I was one of many who clambered all over them and asked what they were called; Comets they said and were obviously proud of them. They certainly looked like what a tank should look like. The crews were obviously delighted to free us and stayed far too long because I remember instructions had been repeated a few times on the tank radio ordering them to press on to Lübeck.

The bulk of us had set out from Stalag Luft 3 near Breslau in January 1945, just keeping ahead of the Russian advance, and had arrived near Lübeck via Berlin, Bremen and Hamburg—most of the time walking. By the Spring of 1945 the Germans were only too anxious to keep away from the Russians and, in many ways, the prisoners controlled their captors. We had no intention of walking any further towards the East and had been 'resting' at the farm for about a week. We had established an early warning organisation to scout for signs of rescue but your tanks arrived almost without warning and I bless you for that.

For the rest of that day, the newly liberated prisoners relaxed and savoured the end of their three-month odyssey, and all that had gone before that. They were, once again, the lucky ones who had survived. A couple of days later, the prisoners climbed into trucks and sat down on the packs they had carried from Sagan and contemplated the first step of their journey home.

After the end of the war, it was revealed that the British and US governments had negotiated a policy of 'staying put' with the German command, whereby prisoners would simply remain in their camps when German troops withdrew, to be liberated by whichever Allied army was first to arrive.

Unfortunately, this agreement came too late for the inmates of Stalag Luft III and the other camps in Silesia. The policy did not take effect until late April, or early May, 1945, by which time an unknown number of prisoners—estimated to be in the thousands—had perished because they were unprepared for the challenges of weather, food shortages, lack of shelter and, most sadly, the strafing attacks from their own aircraft. Some 10,000 of the many POWs who had been removed from their original locations were from Stalag Luft III, and more than 300 of these men died in temperatures that had reached minus 25 degrees centigrade during the marches to Spremberg and Lübeck. Most of those who survived the long trek suffered terribly from the conditions they had endured.

That included Skeets. Unhappily, by the time the 8th Army arrived, he had developed a bad infection in his foot and was in some distress, unable to walk. So while the rest of his group was en route to England, Skeets's flying log book, on the page after the entry describing his last flight in 1941, records a flight as passenger on May 6, 1945, in an RAF C47 Dakota from Lübeck to Brussels, where he could receive the necessary medical attention that had been lacking for so long. Ironically, he was destined for treatment in the very same hospital in which he had convalesced at the beginning of his prisoner of war experience, four years before. He stayed in hospital long enough to see VE Day come and go, and finally left the continent to return in an RAF ambulance aircraft to the POW repatriation centre at Cosford in England on May 16. He wryly noted that he had started the war in his uniform, but left it in his pyjamas, without any of the souvenirs most of his colleagues had managed to find.

The former prisoners repatriated to Cosford arrived to a wonderful welcome from the RAF, with bunting, a brass band and tables laid with cakes and sandwiches. They were given clean sheets and a radio in each room, a new uniform and an advance on their pay, and were driven wherever they wanted to go. Not Skeets, though—he was taken straight to hospital for continued treatment for blood poisoning in his leg.

But the doctors weren't his only visitors. As one of the few survivors of the Great Escape, his account of the circumstances and results was critical to fulfilment of the British promise to bring to justice those responsible for the murder of the fifty. While he was still in hospital, Skeets was interrogated —his word—by British intelligence. He claimed they gave him a 'worse going over than the Gestapo, by far, inasmuch as they wanted to know everything, every little thing. They said that as they had promised, they were going to get these fellows, one way or another.'

With the help of his questioners, Skeets set out to document that part of his experience in Stalag Luft III as best he could, as accurately as memory permitted and in the most objective of terms. While he loathed the Gestapo and all they stood for, for the rest of his life, he never felt personally aggrieved by the treatment he had received from the Luftwaffe in the course of his daily life in the prison camp. To him, as to all the others, at least up to the time of the Great Escape, it was all a deadly serious game, to be played out according to the prescribed rules. It was the same for the Luftwaffe, who expected their charges to be constantly plotting for freedom as much as the prisoners themselves expected to try to escape. But the dreadful events that followed the Great Escape changed these rules, and the RAF was determined to have every detail that might help them bring the perpetrators of that war crime to justice. It was a quest that was ultimately successful in large part.

The commitment to pursue the matter was made almost as soon as the gruesome circumstances became known. Group Captain Massey had been repatriated to England not long after the escape took place, for reasons of ill health. After learning of the escape details from Massey, Foreign Secretary Anthony Eden had reported on the event and its sad aftermath to the British Parliament. In concluding his statement, Eden said: 'His Majesty's Government must . . . record their solemn protest against these cold-blooded acts of butchery. They will never cease in their efforts to collect the evidence to identify all those responsible. They are firmly resolved that these foul criminals shall be tracked down to the last man wherever they may take refuge. When the war is over they will be brought to exemplary justice.'[110]

The British government was as good as its word. The job of following through on this commitment was given to Wing Commander Wilfred Bowes of the RAF's Special Investigation Branch. His fifteen-man team, activated almost immediately on declaration of the armistice in Europe, spent two years doggedly searching for the truth about those responsible. More than 250,000 interviews were carried out and despite the chaotic post-war state Germany found itself in, the team unearthed and examined thousands upon thousands of obscure documents from across the country relating to the events of March 1944.

One of the team was Andrew Wiseman, a former Stalag Luft III inmate who was born in Berlin in 1923 of a Polish father and an American mother, and who spoke fluent German, Polish and probably several other languages as well as English. He would have been an incredibly valuable member of the investigating team given his language skills, and he undertook several of the primary interviews with perpetrators and various witnesses. Participating at the events in 2014 commemorating the seventieth anniversary of the Great Escape, Andy had described his experience of being on the trail of 'one of the worst,' who had somehow managed to disappear. Andy had tried to interview the man's wife, but she refused to speak to him. About a month later, Andy was suddenly summoned by her, calling him back for what was this time a fruitful conversation during which she told Andy exactly where her husband was hiding. He was arrested and later hanged for his crimes. When Andy asked the woman why she had changed her mind, she answered, 'When you came before, I didn't know he was shacked up with his 17-year-old girlfriend.'

In the end, through their unstinting efforts, the team identified and rounded up most of the Gestapo agents responsible for the murders of the fifty escapees who didn't return. Those who weren't arrested were already dead. Several of the perpetrators were jailed; thirteen were hanged for their parts in the war crime. Exemplary justice could indeed claim to have been done.

When asked to recall his four years as a POW, Skeets was generally sanguine. He observed in an interview for an November 11, 1983, newspaper article, 'It certainly taught you there are very few things in life that matter much. Just a few good friends, food and shelter.' In more private moments, he admitted that his time in the camp 'did nothing for me but waste my time.' But he consistently acknowledged his good fortune in having survived these extraordinary circumstances, saying, 'It was four years in prison I could have done without, but at least I was lucky and came home.'

In another, undocumented interview a somewhat broader question was posed: 'How did the war affect you?' His answer was similar. 'It made me realise what life meant. I saw some buddies of mine that I grew up with and went to war with get killed, and it made me very appreciative that I am still around and I've been able to enjoy all the things which were taken away from them. That is the most important thing, I think.'

But he held no romantic illusions about the victory achieved. When the same questioner went on to ask what he felt the war had accomplished, Skeets paused.

I guess, theoretically, we stopped Hitler from invading England, but it really didn't accomplish anything. Millions of people were killed, and nobody really won. Everyone lost on the war. So I would say that it didn't accomplish anything, because both sides lost almost everything that they had, and we were right back to where we were before the war, only we were worse off.

PART FIVE

AFTER THE WAR

31

A NEW LIFE

After medical treatment and a period of rest and recuperation had allowed his leg to mend, Skeets was given some clothes and money and put on indefinite leave. As soon as he could, after going through the formalities of repatriation, Skeets went to Irene's place of work, there discovering to his chagrin that she had gone on holiday to the Lake District. His disappointment was so obvious that Irene's boss took pity on him: 'I'm not supposed to do this,' he said, conspiratorially, 'but . . .' and passed him the name of the hotel that Irene had left as a contact point. Skeets immediately grabbed his bags and headed there himself, as fast as he could figure out the connections.

Irene was caught completely unawares by his arrival and broke down in tears. After getting over the initial shock of seeing him again so unexpectedly, she was delighted that he was all right after his POW experience, and amazed that he had sought her out. Remembering the meeting many years after, she recalled: 'He had so many girlfriends. . . .' There must have been some tentative moments for each of them, but in the end it turned out to be a memorable holiday for both, idyllic in the pastoral Lake District countryside and without worries of any kind to distract them.

But it didn't last long. When Irene returned to work, Skeets went to London as well and met up with some other Canadians who had been in the RAF and had been prisoners of war like himself. It was a celebration of sorts. 'We bummed around London for a while and spent all the money we had saved up during our years in the jug,' said Skeets. Then came an opportunity. 'One chap came back one day and said he had been to the RCAF headquarters and they were prepared to transfer any Canadians in the RAF into the RCAF and backdate their pay for a certain length of time. This was highly popular so a lot of us signed over at this time. About a week later, I was on a boat back to Canada.' He was no doubt anxious to get home, as it had been over six years since he had seen his family and friends.

Before he left England, he settled up with the RAF, an experience that rankled with him for a long time. In his latter years he talked about why.

> I got paid by the RAF . . . after they had deducted income tax, after they deducted prisoner of war pay, like the Germans were getting in Canada to use in the canteen. We never had anything like a canteen, they had nothing for us. Round figures, I probably came out of there with something like five thousand dollars. A Canadian, Harry something . . . a F/L, had something like $25,000 in his bank account when he came back.
>
> However . . . [some of the ex-POWs] tried to get some of this money [that had been deducted] back from the Brits, but I never got too excited about it. They won the war, but lost the peace, I think. Some of the prisoners actually wrote to the Queen to . . . get them to cancel at least the prisoner of war pay. That really hurt. What it was—the Germans gave us some funny looking money to spend in the canteen, and deducted this from the officers' pay, same as the German prisoners in Canada were given so much money to spend in the canteen. The first little while [while we were prisoners], we just threw it away. There was no canteen, there was nothing to spend it on. I didn't even keep it for a souvenir. They just deducted it from your pay, every month. So that's it, the war is over. They turned me loose on an unsuspecting population. But I'm getting even with them now, I'll draw my pension for a long time yet!

Andy Wiseman, in his reminiscences at the seventieth anniversary commemorations of the Great Escape, told a similar story, with something of a twist. He said that at the end of the war he and his fellow prisoners received 'a pile of back pay' that they never checked. However, someone in their number did the maths and discovered a significant shortfall. When he pursued the matter, he was told that their pay had been reduced because the Germans told the British the officers in this camp were getting extra rations—fruit, fresh vegetables and the like—and the British actually agreed to pay for this. When it was made clear this was not the case and that no special food privileges had been given to the Kriegies, the Air Ministry claimed to have 'lost the nominal roll of Stalag Luft III' and that they couldn't therefore be sure about who to pay what amount back to. Years later, at the Bomber Command memorial ceremony, Andy was one of the guests of honour and afterwards met the Chancellor of the Exchequer. Andy didn't waste any time, opening the conversation with, 'You owe me money!' After receiving a more detailed explanation, the Chancellor consulted his aide and, returning to Andy, said 'I'm being briefed.' Andy never heard anything more. 'Typical politician,' he concluded.

When Skeets set sail for home, Canada, it was the end of July. It was in the quiet days while he was on board SS *Stratheden*, a P&O liner, that he was finally able to catch up on his flying log book and diary, before facing a tumultuous homecoming. An article in the Ottawa Journal of Thursday, August 2, 1945, described the scene on his arrival:

Ottawa Flyers Home from War
Home after four years in Nazi prison camps, Flt. Lt. Keith 'Skeets' Ogilvie . . . reached Union Station with a draft of 13 RCAF 'repats' last night . . . Flt. Lt. Ogilvie, met by his parents at the train, was whisked to a side gate where the rest of his family and a large group of friends were waiting to shower their greetings on him. 'Wow!' exclaimed the flyer, as he planted a big kiss on the last girl of an admiring female circle of which he had made the rounds.

The accompanying picture shows no fewer than six young ladies surrounding the returning aviator. It's a good thing Irene wasn't there at the time, or her fond memories of that Lake District vacation might have faded more quickly. Skeets enjoyed the attention of his family and friends for a brief time until his RCAF duties called him to a base south of Montreal, RCAF Station Lachine, where he settled in to his new responsibility of looking after the repatriation of other Canadian airmen arriving back.

32

POST-WAR EUROPE: RCAF 'CARNIVAL'

Back in England in the immediate post-war period, Irene continued her photographic activities and the active social life that went with it. Although she didn't make much money, and was living on her own, she continued to support her mother as best she could.

The period of unfamiliar post-war quiet dragged on into the cold of the British winter as Canadian troops remained in outposts all over Europe. The RCAF was looking for ways of boosting the sagging morale of their troops still located on the continent and hit upon the idea of a travelling roadshow called 'Carnival,' basically a roving party and games room that would go from base to base and allow servicemen to gamble at blackjack, roulette and a myriad other normally frowned on activities—all without real betting, of course. This naïve notion aside, the masterminds behind the idea were probably closer to the mark when they decided to have the whole thing presented by a number of young women, in the end a more likely morale booster than the games themselves. When Irene was approached to join the troupe for a few months before she was mustered out of the RCAF, she saw her chance to see the European continent, even in its semi-apocalyptic post-war state, and agreed to participate.

In some ways she would find it the education of a lifetime, witnessing at first hand everything from the sometimes dubious pleasures of Paris to the horrors of Bergen-Belsen concentration camp. Irene kept a rather spare diary of that time, but regularly wrote to her mother—now living on St. John's Road in London—to tell her, briefly, about the things she was seeing, starting with a detailed account of her first-ever experience of flying as they prepared to load into a C47 in the early morning of December 8,

1945, for the hop across the English Channel. But first, there was a poignant reminder of friends past. Arriving at Biggin Hill for the flight, 'we found no one around—no fires in the hut where we were taken. Then while exploring, I heard a muffled "What the hell!" and found I had entered the duty N.C.O.'s sleeping quarters. He was very kind and got up immediately and began building a fire. While he was doing this I was wandering around and came upon a locker with Keith's name on it—and the boys told us how the Battle of Britain types had that hut as their Dispersal Hut.' The locker had remained unaltered for four years. It must have brought back memories of the last time she had seen him—and was supposed to have seen him, at the Eagle Club opening—but there was little time for reflection. She wrote in the letter to her mother,

A kite taxied to within a hundred feet of the hut and we were told to 'get goin.' The excitement was terrific. It was a Dakota, seated twenty-four of us and was certainly not built for comfort. We were all strapped in with our safety belts, farewell to the kids we knew and also to those whom we didn't know. Thought of you worrying your funny old head about our trip and only hoped you'd know, somehow, that all was going to be well.

Away we went along the perimeter, excitement shaking me from top to toe. Then we stopped again and I stopped feeling excited and just waited. When we finally did get going I had calmed down to just a speedy heart beat. Taking off was an odd sensation and not a happy one for me. When completely airborne we loosened our belts and had a good look around. Everything took on a toy-like appearance and England looked just as one imagines it, all patch-work with farms dotted here and there, winding roads and everything so very green.

Then came the dawn!!!! A quick dash to the end of the plane and—yes, I was sick!!!

Recovered and tried to sleep a while tho' the cold was intense. The windows became frosted and the plane became a weaving toy in the midst of a gale. Could not even bring myself to go into the co-pilot's seat where we were to take turns in getting warm. I knew if I moved I would 'give out.'

Then came time to land—we were to fasten our safety belts again. Mine got mixed so the Navigator said, 'C'mon down here, this one's okay.' You can guess what happened! As soon as the wheels landed on terra firma one of the lads yelled for the pail and away he went! The landing was perfect.

It was certainly not an auspicious first flight for someone in the air force. However, Irene was quickly revived by a cup of tea, a ginger biscuit and the cold air. The troupe was taken to their accommodation, starting at a club called 'The Malcolm.' Irene explained to her mother: 'There are a series of these everywhere, dedicated to a guy who won the VC in the earlier part of the war.[111] It is for Air Force personnel only—any nationality.' This one offered extra benefits to the new arrivals that still seemed very special after the privations of wartime rationing in London. 'Had cream cakes such as I have never tasted before and coffee. Then to our billets—and here comes a laugh! They are centrally heated, as much food as you wish and hot water, tho' not very much of it.'

They had landed in, and would start their touring from, Schleswig, in north-west Germany, near the Danish border. It was Irene's first sad glimpse of the people who had such a short time before been the enemy:

The population is composed of elderly types and legless and armless youths—and, of course, children. The young gals we see are mostly displaced persons, most of whom are working here or at the club. There is one fräulein here who belonged to the Hitler Youth—seems a harmless sort of gal tho' you can never tell! They each have their little RAF boyfriend and fratting is rife. Thinking of the many friends we have lost, I cannot agree with the lads tho' I suppose it is understandable. There are dances held here for civilians and anyone may attend.

The policemen are a scream. In light green outfits with matching helmets and covered in braid (silver) they look like some impressive figure out of a musical comedy!

It is pathetic to wander around the streets window shopping. There is nothing around at all. The black market is rife in the village square though I have not indulged as yet. Some of the kids are doing okay tho' I hope for big things in Hamburg around

Christmas time. Next week we are heading for the Isle of Sylt . . . just west of the mainland on the German/Danish border. It is not far from here so we are motoring. There is a terrific bridge connecting the Isle to the mainland.

And finally, she offered a glance at some of the less savoury aspects of the town:

The bread in the shops is a horrid brown colour . . .

We visited a biergarten which was a foul smelling, evil tenanted dive. Women—dirty and brazen—our lads fratting and laughing for all they were worth. Business deals in progress everywhere. An hour of that was enough for this chick so away we went. It was nauseating!

After this less than satisfactory introduction to the local night life, the troupe returned to their billets. Irene and her 'terrific' roommate for the whole Carnival experience, Audrey Locksley, retired for the night.[112]

A couple of weeks later, Irene sent a postcard to her mother from the island of Sylt, to which the troupe had moved on December 16, travelling in open trucks—no doubt a cold trip at that time of year! The picture, probably from Westerland, shows a sandy beach, a promenade and crowds of happy holidaymakers—obviously a picture taken before the advent of the destructive aggression that would grip Europe for six years. In her brief note to her mother, Irene opines that it 'looks a lot like Bournemouth, huh? The sands and sea are still lovely—everything else just dead.' Since then, Westerland has reclaimed its luxury holiday reputation and is now known as the 'Beverley Hills of Germany.'

The next day her diary briefly notes a trip to Westerland and then around the island where they saw U-boat bases and underground factories, now abandoned to the blowing sands. It was a powerful reminder of the scale of the effort and expense of the hostilities. The deathly quiet of these empty spaces so soon after the end of the frantic wartime activity they hosted, must have inspired a mix of awe and disquiet for someone who had so recently been in the heart of the conflict.

Back in Schleswig on December 20, Irene communicated again with her mother, who was planning to return to Canada in the near future. Jean apparently had determined to settle permanently in Victoria, where there were good family memories. Irene wrote:

> Am wondering if you have had any news re: your return. Hope you do very soon though I guess you won't make it for Christmas. Wish we could make a quick trip to the U.K. just for a day or so around Christmas.
>
> We shall be at 126 Airfield near Hamburg and the cook is the one that was on Eddie Geddes' station. He was the guy that cooked for the King and Queen on their tour of Canada—remember? So I guess we shall be spoiled as far as food is concerned—again. We are eating wonderfully—steaks, roast beef and all that goes with them. The veg[gie]s are the problem—beans and cabbage, mostly. Just wish I could pack up some of these luscious cream cakes and send them to you.

She goes on to describe her experience with the collapsed post-war currency markets and how people compensated—much as they did in Skeets's prison camp—with cigarettes. She admitted she was 'most anxious to get a good camera so refuse to spend my cigs until I do. We are not drawing our pay while here. When we run out of dough we sell a package of cigarettes for 2½ marks a cigarette—40 marks to the pound—so this keeps us going for some time.'

Before moving to Hamburg, the troupe spent four days in Lübeck. It was a little more than seven months earlier that Skeets had boarded his own flight here, for that ride to Brussels and eventually back to England. Here, Irene met RAF pilot Johnny Johnson. Johnson was obviously taken with the young woman, and she must have been impressed with his record as the highest-scoring Western ace against the Luftwaffe. Her diary is noncommittal, though; she simply writes, 'Met Johnny Johnson—hmmmm. Dated me but I was sceptical.' With good reason; she may not have known that he was already married.

Irene sent another postcard from Hamburg, as the troupe settled in for Christmas. This card shows a night view across the river of the city, lights from the buildings and several tall church spires beautifully reflected in the waters of the lake in the centre of that city. The message is short: 'Dearest moms: It certainly is not like this now!! What a mess!! Hope you are well.'

She kept a copy of the menu for Christmas dinner at the officers' mess, 124 Wing, RAF Station, Lübeck, complete with several signatures and including a rather formal one by J.E. Johnson, with a parenthetical note below it: '("Jackson" to you, dear).'

New Year's Eve found them back in Lübeck. Irene's adventures this time went unreported to her mother, but she confided in her diary that she greeted in the New Year with Audrey and Dave from their troupe, along with Johnny Johnson. The next day the pilot invited her to go for a flight with him in a captured Fieseler Storch, the remarkable and versatile two-seater aircraft used by the Luftwaffe for forward air support and other duties during the war. Irene doesn't record her impressions of the flight . . . or the rest of her time with Johnson.

As they moved south, Irene sent her mother another card from Celle, a 'lovely old town—fifteen miles from Belsen!! Wish I could speak German and find out what these characters think of it all.' Even months after the end of the war, the place held a special horror that affected Irene and her colleagues. They took the time to visit Belsen concentration camp, empty of humanity but with the infrastructure still standing. It was an experience Irene found profoundly emotional and sobering and that she remembered in later years with mixed feelings.

The next stop was Bückeburg, a historic town where the troupe was put up in the palace, Schloss Bückeburg, the traditional residence of the princes of the region. Irene and Audrey were given a room in the 700-year-old building to themselves, but found the historic surroundings to be . . . interesting. Their enormous room turned out to be empty, save for two beds and a tin wardrobe, with enormous draughty windows.

> Audrey and I have a huge room (approximately six times the size of your living room), no heating except a paraffin stove which we pinched and which refuses to operate more than ten minutes at a time . . . We thought we would throw a party and have a band, bar and floor show. The space is adequate and it would warm up with a few hundred people in it!
>
> We are about half an hour's drive from Hamelin [sic] of Pied Piper fame—also that is where Irma Grese and Kramer[113] were imprisoned during the War Trials. Shall endeavour to cadge a ride today, I think.

Despite their frigid accommodation, Irene and Audrey made the best of the place. 'It is as cold as heck here but the sun is glorious and the clubs are centrally heated and it is easy enough to warm your tum with a coffee prettied up with rum!'

The next stage in their journey offered the troupe the promise of spending a bit of time in the Harz mountains for a long-anticipated chance at some skating and skiing. Irene describes the journey in another letter to her mother, sent in mid-January 1946. She leaves out the note from her diary in which she records tersely, 'Pass many Jerry graves on the way. Small drawing of cross with helmet on top.' Once again, her mother got the censored version of the trip:

> We left Bückeburg on Wednesday morning and started on a four hour journey. Climbing all the time—it got colder and colder—more and more snow—fir trees in abundance. Finally, after a very precarious ride up a slippery mountain road we landed at Braunlage . . . We were all so excited at the thought of skiing, skating and general icecapades. There was a lovely rink just outside the chalet where we were staying—skates and/or skis were to be had from Canada House, which was about two miles away.
>
> The chalet was built on the side of a mountain in front of a small forest. Skiing hills and tracks everywhere—skating just in front of the chalet. All in all we were looking forward to a strenuous two days with loads of sleep!

As chance would have it, their plans were foiled when they woke the next morning to two days of rain that turned the village, and all their intentions for enjoying the winter sports scene, to slush. However, they made the best of it, eating well, relaxing in their comfortable accommodation and enjoying the warmth until it was time to head back to catch their transport to Aurich, near the Dutch border. Their route took them through areas that would have been travelled by Skeets, by foot and cattle car, just over a year previously, following his evacuation from the prison camp. But Irene had more opportunity than Skeets would have had to observe and absorb the ravages of the war and describe them to her mother: 'Our journey was through Hildesheim, which is no more, Hannover, which is a wreck, Bremen, which is also horrible except the IKE Stadium which is a super job!'

From Aurich the troupe went to Brussels for two days of shopping, and then to Paris. Between their shows the group made side trips to Fontainbleau for a visit to the palace retreat of the French kings, and experienced more racy adventures in the famous Parisian nightlife. A couple of the 'boys' in the troupe somehow convinced Irene and Audrey, both fairly prim in their attitudes, to accompany them to the Folies-Bergère and subsequently to some of the seedier parts of the city. How this was accomplished was never clear—champagne and the excitement of Paris at night may have had something to do with it—but the evening was a memorable one for the two women, who found it to be . . . well, not to their taste.

Then on Tuesday, January 29, it was back to Brussels, a place that the young woman found 'lively and interesting,' and that she expressed a desire to revisit later, with her mother. In her last postcard to her mother from Paris, Irene informs her: 'Flying home Thursday, I think—ship sails for Canada two or three days later!!!' It was actually more like a week. The final brief note in her little diary is dated February 5 and describes having dinner with her mother at Challinor Mansions: 'Chatter and plan our life in Canada. Surely hope she follows soon!'

Before she set off for Canada, Irene had one more errand to run, pursuing her own dreams and demons. By now the young woman was more worldly, very much more self-possessed and thinking about her own imminent return to her homeland. She was concerned over her mother's future and decided to take the time to visit her father in Leeds. Her intention was to tell him that she was perfectly able to look after herself but that his wife's prospects remained uncertain, and that he should honour the obligations the court had set upon him. He still owed Jean court-awarded financial support that he had never paid and which, even if small, might help her to re-establish herself in Canada. Taking a deep breath and knocking on the door of the family house in Leeds, she was met by Arthur's sister, a short, ardently religious woman with a filthy kitchen and a nasty manner, and the ironic name of Grace.

The visit was unproductive. Irene asked her father whether he could see his way to paying her mother at least a little of the money he owed her, so that she could return to Canada and not have to find a job immediately, perhaps be able to relax a bit. Her father's answer, predictably, was, 'absolutely not.' In spite of the clarity of the court records, Arthur adamantly claimed he didn't owe Irene's mother a penny. Irene was angry as she knew he had money and still owned properties in Regina, but she was unable to change his mind—there was just too much bad blood between her parents. The young woman returned to London empty handed, but at least assured in herself that she had done what she could on behalf of her mother. It was very much the end of a chapter with regard to her family, as well as her life in England.

33

HOMEWARD BOUND

Skeets wrote to Irene care of 'Carnival' from Lachine, Quebec, on February 8, 1946, replying to her January letter telling him about the good time she had had over Christmas in Lübeck. His Christmas hadn't been nearly as much fun. He responded: 'To make a long story short I have been put in charge of Reception here, over the heads of some other boys, so when it came to a question of sticking someone for a job over Xmas I was on the spot. So I spent nine days in New York waiting for the *Lizzie* [the Cunard liner *Queen Elizabeth*] and came home with the near DTs.'[114] He goes on to say how busy his work is 'as they rush the boys home,' and wonders when she is going to return.

When and how Irene got this letter isn't clear, however, as she was likely on the boat on her way home by the time he posted it. Although Irene had opted to return to Canada after her discharge from the RCAF, she had not yet told Skeets when she would be doing so. The rough endearments in his letter reflected his strong affection for her and his fear that she may have found someone else. He warned her that she would certainly not be able to sneak back into Canada without him knowing of her arrival!

Ogilvie was making fairly regular trips to New York to meet, and arrange the transfer back to Canada of, returning RCAF personnel. While he was stuck with what must quickly have become a repetitive and tedious desk job, he valued every opportunity he had to fly, whether on commercial flights or especially on trips on military aircraft. Every flight he managed to get on, even as a passenger, was carefully entered in his log book.

Along with so many other repatriated servicemen and women, Irene's journey back to Canada took her first from London to New York on the

Queen Elizabeth. As the ship came into the American harbour, Irene, excited to be returning to her home country, was disappointed to hear that it would be several hours before the arriving passengers could be disembarked. Everyone was ordered to stay aboard until they could be taken off in an orderly manner, sorted into their various channels and directed on to transportation to take them home. Then came a surprise announcement over the tannoy loudspeaker system: 'Would Irene Lockwood please gather her kit and come immediately to the purser's office.' Arriving as requested, to her utter astonishment she was told she should get ready to leave the boat straightaway. No one else could understand why she was to get off when they couldn't, and it caused some grumbling.

Even Irene was in the dark. But after disembarking, she immediately found Skeets—who had come by train from Montreal to meet her, clearly with serious intent! They went together into New York to explore the city. That evening they saw the Rockettes at Radio City Music Hall in Manhattan, then caught a very late train for Montreal.

As far as Irene was concerned, they weren't in a serious relationship. She was adamant that she was never going to be married; her parents' experience had put her permanently off the idea. In any case, she agreed to accompany Skeets to meet his family in Ottawa, with whom she had had occasional correspondence over the course of the war, and who had sent her much appreciated parcels of small things that were unavailable in England. The initial meeting passed into family legend. Skeets's father, Charlie, had had a heart attack not too long before and was relegated to staying in bed, recuperating. Irene recalled going upstairs in the family home to meet him:

> I had another hat on with a veil, and was going to be introduced to my friend's father. I put it on top of the dresser, said how do you do, and we talked about Keith. I was shown my room—I was going to stay there—then came back and chatted some more. I picked up my hat and with it came my future father-in-law's teeth!

Somehow Charlie's dentures had become entangled with the net on her prized hat, fell on the floor and broke. Irene was mortified. When she was later asked whether Charlie had ever spoken to her again, Skeets, with characteristic wit, said, 'Not with the same teeth!' But Charlie and Irene got along famously. She found him to be a gentle and engaging man, to whom she could talk about anything. After his retirement from the railroad for medical reasons, he claimed to have had the most marvellous life, reading all the books he had always wanted to, and never had time for. It must have been an eye opener for the young woman whose own family history had been so difficult in comparison, to be exposed to such a loving family.

After a brief stay in Ottawa, they parted again. While Skeets continued his work in Lachine, Irene pressed on for Niagara Falls and the home of her aunt and uncle and two younger cousins. They had always got along well together and at this point were the only real relatives Irene had in Canada. It was a quiet and relaxing stay for her, despite being without work, and gave her a chance to catch up on family events during her absence in England. They were all wonderful to her, treating her like another daughter, and she had the fondest of memories of that interlude.

Then, on June 24, 1946, Skeets posted a letter to Irene in Niagara Falls from Ottawa, where he was waiting for more troops flying in from the UK. His letter is a bit confused and reflects what, for Skeets, was an unusual degree of introspection—at least, the kinds of thoughts he was usually reluctant to share. The letter read: 'This morning I got to looking through some old scrapbooks and pictures and stuff. Gee, it all seems so far away. Wonder if I should have stayed there? And so much time has been wasted. Why don't I smarten up?' The missive goes on to say that he has some time off and would like to come to Niagara Falls to see Irene on the weekend, apologizing for the short notice. He tells her of his plans to take a couple of weeks' holiday at the end of July and remarks, 'I'd like to just go somewhere and lie around and laze, much like we did up at the Lakes. No kidding. I think that is the only time I have really relaxed since I got out of the jug.'

Irene obviously agreed to the visit—an auspicious decision. They went for a walk and were sitting on the grass on the levee over the canal when Skeets finally mustered the courage to say, 'Would you mind if we eloped?' Without a second thought, and forgetting her determination to remain single, she replied, 'I'd love to,' and that was that.

Skeets's timing turned out to be all-important. They returned to her aunt's and uncle's house and announced their engagement. In the middle of the family's toast to the young couple, the telephone rang. It was another RCAF photographer friend from London who had come to Niagara Falls unannounced and wanted to come over because, Irene said, he 'had a special question to ask me.' When Irene told him they were having dinner and celebrating their engagement, there was dead silence on the line. He had come to pop the question as well and had to leave, disappointed, with a ring still in his pocket.

Irene and Skeets didn't exactly elope, but married quickly a month later, on July 31, 1946, in a ceremony at the chapel of St Matthew's Anglican church in the Glebe. It was a small ceremony, witnessed by Skeets's old friend, Norm Hurd and his wife Emily, and was followed by a memorable lunch at what then was known as the Ottawa area's best restaurant, Mme Burgher's, in Hull. Irene remembers the people from her new father-in-law's work making a row at the wedding party, and the newly married couple were happy to make an exit from the festivities.

They had planned a honeymoon in Sainte-Agathe, a quiet town north of Montreal. The first step was a train ride to Montreal and overnight at the Windsor Hotel. It wasn't the best accommodation, but there was a convention of some kind happening in the city and all the top-flight hotels were already booked—in fact, they were lucky to find anything at all.

The next morning they were back at the train station, waiting for the local train that would take them north to Sainte-Agathe in the Laurentians when, to the new bride's chagrin, a beautiful blonde woman came up to Skeets and embraced him. 'She was all over him . . . and he was all over her,' Irene recalled, and was only partly mollified when she was introduced as another cousin from Ottawa, working as a model in Montreal. However, Irene had cooled down (or perhaps, warmed up) by the time they arrived at Sainte-Agathe and the small inn, a converted house, where they were staying. There were no more family encounters . . . and no more complaints.

34

BACK IN THE AIR

They didn't have time to settle in Montreal, as Skeets was posted almost immediately on return from his honeymoon to the RCAF station at Trenton, to take on new flying-related responsibilities in the control tower. The following year, on June 4, 1947, nearly six years after being shot down over occupied France, he was back in the cockpit of a Harvard for a series of check-out flights. It was the start of a new phase in his aviation career that would take him through another fifteen years of flying in twenty-five different aircraft makes, single- and multi-engined, piston and jet.

It was to be a predictably peripatetic life and it didn't take long for his flying obligations to take him away from his new spouse. For most of July, after getting checked out again on the Harvard, he was co-piloting a C47 Dakota, the transport workhorse of the RCAF, in support of navy activity on the east coast. Two consecutive entries in his flying log during this trip make note of 'Glider towing experiments,' with the comment after the first one that 'glider broke away—rammed barn.' The second trial turned out better—'glider landed successfully.' Then it was almost immediately out to the west coast, still in the C47, towing drogues for gunnery practice from Sea Island, now the home of Vancouver International Airport.

About the middle of July, Irene mailed a letter to Jean informing her that she would be a grandmother in January. 'The idea of waiting until we were settled was no use as in this job we'd never be settled,' she says, a pretty realistic assessment of the kind of life they would lead over the course of Skeets's RCAF flying career.

At the end of that month away from his new bride, Skeets took the opportunity of some time off from his Vancouver duties to visit his mother-in-law, who was by now back in Canada and re-settled in Victoria. Perhaps in light of the recent news he felt he had best make an appearance! Returning to his temporary room at the officers' mess on the evening of the day of their first anniversary, he picked up his pen and sat down at the desk in his room to write Irene a letter. He poured out his feelings for her and expressed no little wonder that they were able to be together. It was an uncharacteristically sober letter, heartfelt and reflective, and is a lasting testament to his love and commitment to her.

More or less as predicted, son Keith junior arrived in January, on one of the coldest and snowiest nights of the winter. They had little time to adjust to their new family dynamic, however; in March 1948 they moved up to Ontario's cottage country. Skeets was attached to the School of Flying Control (SFCO) at Centralia, Ontario, logging hours on Harvards, C45 Beechcraft Expeditors and C47 Dakotas, then finishing his tour there on a two-month course at the No. 1 Instrument Flying School (IFS). Centralia was a great place in the summer; he and his new family of three lived in what amounted to an add-on to a cottage at Grand Bend, home of beautiful sandy beaches, plenty of poison ivy and an active social life.

At the end of his IFS training, Skeets packed up the family for a move to Ottawa's Rockcliffe Air Base, beautifully situated by the Ottawa River, where he joined 412 Transport Squadron. Ironically, 412 had been a Canadian fighter squadron during the war, but had since been re-equipped to carry out VIP transportation as well as more routine duties of flying cadets, paratroopers, pipe bands and boxes with unknown but urgently needed contents about the country. Skeets got his share of both types of duty. His aircraft was occasionally host to some of the key figures in the Canadian government of the day—cabinet ministers, invited peers of the realm, RCAF brass and, on one occasion, royal guests during the 1951 royal visit to Canada by (the then) Princess Elizabeth. In addition to this exalted passenger list, his growing number of flying hours also included an assortment of urgent medical evacuations, compassionate flights for servicemen with family difficulties and travels in the north with Canadian celebrities who were entertaining troops. Skeets recalled several flights to the Canadian north carrying Tommy Hunter, the tall and talented country singer and television personality, who hated and feared flying. Hunter was invariably sick on these flights, always disembarking white as a ghost. Skeets always felt great admiration for the fact that he still got on the plane every time, probably out of a strong sense of duty and the desire to contribute to the well-being of the men and women who served in the armed forces.

As well, there were the usual adventures served up by the fates. A loose gas cap, lost on take-off, resulted in a brief twenty-minute entry in his log as the pilots returned to base to rectify the problem, fuel streaming over the wing. But, by and large, this kind of incident was as serious as it got—the two years with 412 were relatively uneventful even while they filled his flying log with the names of distinguished visitors and airport destinations across the continent.

More memorable was the birth in March 1952 of a daughter, Linda Jean. Through it all and in addition to keeping her kids healthy and busy, Irene took on what was then the traditional role of wife and mother, keeping herself busy with an active social life and volunteer work.

In December 1952, Skeets got the posting of his dreams, as the first officer commanding 129 Acceptance and Ferry Flight (A&FF) at No. 6 Repair Depot (6RD), back in Trenton. It would be as close to heaven as a pilot could want—a variety of aircraft limited only by what the air force was still flying, and assignments that would take him all over Canada and the US, delivering and picking up aircraft from overhaul, repair and servicing locations. A couple of days after settling into the Trenton permanent married quarters (PMQs) and getting a quick local check flight in a Harvard, Skeets climbed into the cockpit of an ungainly C119 Flying Boxcar for the long flight to Edmonton. It was to be the predominant pattern for the next couple of years, again punctuated by the odd memorable incident. He admitted that he kept his flying and desk duties just about even. On those days he wanted to fly, he delegated the desk duties to others. When he didn't want to fly, he claimed exemption because of the same work.

In February 1953, Skeets was one of the first Canadians to sit at the controls of a jet, a Canadian-built T-33, nicknamed the 'T-Bird.' His description was slightly disparaging. 'It hums like a vacuum cleaner,' he said, 'and there is no sensation of speed whatsoever.' Not quite the same as the vaunted Spitfire. It was the first of his rides in several different types of jets, including the low-slung Vampire, the RCAF's first jet fighter, and its successor, the F-86 Sabre. These latter types were not easy aircraft to learn to fly, but as single-seaters, there was only one way to learn: that was to read and try to remember as much as possible about the aircraft systems and how to handle emergencies, then head out to the flight line and climb in.

But the books never gave the pilot the 'feel' of the aircraft. Some of these aircraft were brand new and had peculiarities yet to be explored. Skeets described flying the Vampire as an ungainly, tiny aircraft with short landing gear in which the pilot sat in front of the twin boom tail section in a seat very close to the ground. His conversion training took place at Trenton and consisted of a few high-speed landings in a Harvard followed by a solo in the Vampire. He said it was great fun until you came to land. It was a fast aircraft, and the proximity of the pilot to the ground greatly amplified the feeling of speed. Skeets admitted he was never able to overcome the impulse to raise his backside out of the bucket seat as he came in to land. It was what he called a 'high pucker' aircraft.

He was also one of the first to experience the vagaries of the F-86 Sabre's hydraulic controls. It was one of the first planes to use these controls, and the lack of direct feedback made them highly susceptible and sensitive to overcorrection. Going through some bumps in the summer air on a trip in one of the early models, Skeets got into a 'porpoising' pattern while trying to maintain level flight. The aircraft bounced up, and he pushed the stick forward; the nose went down and he pulled the stick back; up went the nose—and so on. It got worse and worse until his helmet cracked hard enough on the canopy of the aircraft that it cut his nose and knocked him out for a few seconds. He let go of the stick and the aircraft settled itself down, leaving him with a bloody face and a hard-earned lesson on how to avoid repeating the error.

Although he made his first jet solo in the 'T-Bird' in June 1953, Skeets always preferred the comforting noise and bustle of a piston engine. During a later posting at Rockcliffe, he was known to take younger pilots under his wing, often deferring to their abilities in a way that acknowledged the way things had changed over the course of his career. One of these young pilots, Warren Maybee, was happy to work out an arrangement with his senior officer early in their flying relationship to build up his jet time. The rule Skeets set out from the start was, 'If it's got a propeller, I'll fly it. If it doesn't, you fly it.'

He got plenty of propeller time at Trenton, including getting airborne in Mustangs and B-25 Mitchell bombers before they left the RCAF's postwar inventory, as well as the ubiquitous C-119s and Dakotas. The Mustang flights must have been a bit of nostalgic magic for him, offering an experience akin to flying the Spitfire a dozen years before, in a high-powered piston-engined fighter with similar manoeuvrability—simply a joy to fly. Along with the routine trips, his flying log reports incidents of blown tyres, single-engined landings in B-25s and electrical failure in a T-33, all recorded in the same professional, anodyne way with a minimum of descriptive remarks. Asked to comment on this much later, Skeets hesitated, then opined dryly that 'some flights were more significant than others.'

One of the more weighty and saddest incidents in his memory centred on the crash of a B-25 and the loss of one of his colleagues with whom he had flown many times. He recorded a fifteen-minute local flight in a C-45 Beechcraft to 'Check Crash.' In a simple annotation on the same line, he noted 'Terry O'Byrne/Cpl. Aubry killed.' It was a stark reminder of the risks they all faced, even in peacetime, in pursuing the rewards of a flying career. And it reinforced the importance of the whole community in dealing with these challenges, as Irene and the other spouses came together to support the grieving widow and her young family.

In September 1954, Skeets was transferred back to Rockcliffe Air Base on the edge of Ottawa. He was attached to Air Materiel Command (AMC) headquarters and appointed to the position of staff officer, Air Operations. This gave him continued opportunity to fly, and he took advantage whenever he could. The 'brass' needed to maintain their flying hours, too, and one of Skeets's regular companions was Air Vice Marshal John Plant, who was at the time the air member for Technical Services. He, also, was a decorated prewar and wartime pilot who preferred spending time in the airborne 'office' of a cockpit than sitting at his desk in headquarters, and who maintained his 'green' (instrument flying) ticket until he retired in 1956. Skeets logged many hours as aircraft captain with his boss sitting in the co-pilot's seat, a reversal of roles that perhaps more than anything else showed the kind of respect given to someone with Skeets' experience and skill.

Skeets was also a man of great modesty, well respected and liked. His aircrew colleagues enjoyed flying with him—he was experienced, competent and relaxed in the cockpit. Major General Roy Sturgess recalled the generosity and wisdom of many of the flyers of Skeets's generation:

> He was one of my heroes. He never talked much about his wartime experiences. But I flew with him, and I saw [the scars on] his back.
>
> When I first joined the squadron as a young pilot just out of training, I went down to check in with the experienced pilots. There were Hugh Cram, Skeets Ogilvie and Dave Adamson. I was handed a can of Aircraft Bright and told to get out and start polishing. I was amazed to watch these senior, experienced pilots out there polishing the airplane [sic] with the ground crews. I got a big dose of humble from those guys.

Skeets's sense of humour was also something of a legend—if anything, it had been sharpened by his wartime record. General Dave Adamson, who often shared the cockpit with him, recalled a classic example of his wry and self-effacing view of the world:

> Skeets and I were sitting on the patio of the officers' mess at Rockcliffe. [The beautiful stone mess and its famous chandelier, the site of many 'swingings,' are now gone. It used to sit at the top of the bluff overlooking the runways of the Rockcliffe Air Base and the adjacent Ottawa River.] We heard the sound of a Dak slowly approaching the airport, and watched as it came gracefully over the end of the field. The pilot touched down a little before he had intended, with the result that he bounced high in the air before he finally settled down onto the runway.
>
> We sat in silence for a moment or two. Then Skeets turned to me and said, 'That can't be me. I'm up here.'

35

NEW ROOTS

In addition to the flying opportunities for Skeets, the Ottawa postings gave our family another gift—the opportunity to connect regularly with what would become for us kids the quintessential vision of Canada: the pine trees, steep rocks and clear lakes of the heavily glaciated Laurentian shield. Each summer, without fail, the family packed up for three weeks at a place known simply as Hillier's at Camp's Bay on Big Gull Lake. The route came quickly back into memory every time we made the trip. Out of the city and up Highway 7 past Perth, through farm country, long games of 'I spy' and scrub brush that was full of wild blueberry plants offering delicious picking in the late summer, finally turning off the highway at Arden for the last part of the now seemingly interminable journey (for a kid, anyway) through Henderson and on to the potholed, tree-lined dirt road that would suddenly open up into a vision of bright sunshine, blue water and the weighty promise of summer vacation.

Hillier's was a collection of simple wooden cottages perched on the edge of the lake, offering noisy protection from the occasional rainstorm that beat on their tin roofs and almost no relief from the evening swarms of mosquitoes or the mice constantly trying to gain entry into the vacation food supplies. But the swimming was fantastic and I remember many peaceful sunsets viewed from the lake, sitting quietly in a hand-built rowboat with my father, trolling for an elusive pickerel for next morning's breakfast.

As he approached the RCAF's mandatory retirement age, Skeets accepted a last posting in November 1958 to RCAF Station Downsview. The base was north of Toronto—at that time, out on the edge of the city proper. The base, attached to Air Transport Command, was at the north end of the same airport system shared with the De Havilland of Canada Company's major manufacturing operation. Skeets took over as base operations officer, still taking advantage of the operational nature of the station to fly as much as he could. Again, the unusual was mixed with the routine; one of his trips was the subject of a letter of thanks from the Rehabilitation Foundation for his assistance in getting special equipment to Toronto to treat a baby suffering from polio.

At first the family settled into an apartment near the base and later moved into the sheltered and warm environment of permanent married quarters. The event that made that posting especially memorable for me occurred in May 1961. It was one thing to listen to the grown-ups talking about flying adventures, past and present, but never having been in the air made it difficult for me to really understand the thrill that was so evident in these conversations. The increasing formality of RCAF rules meant that family members weren't allowed in military aircraft except under exceptional circumstances, an ongoing disappointment for me.

But on this day in the warm early summer of that year, Skeets thought it was about time to bend the rules a bit and after an early supper suggested that I put on my scouting uniform, at least paying lip service to the requirements for some kind of formality. I had no idea why. We drove to the hangar line. Along with several servicemen who were going to Camp Borden, north of Toronto, I was strapped into a passenger seat on a C45 Beechcraft Expeditor for the short half-hour hop to Borden.

My memories of the trip north are mostly noise and feeling out of place among the adult passengers. But the return flight was nothing short of magic. There were no other passengers so I sat in the co-pilot's seat with an oversized headset fitted over my scout cap, carefully keeping my hands off anything that moved and staring dry-mouthed out the front of the aircraft. As we moved forward to take off, the aircraft swung left and right until the tail came up and the runway came into view, and we were off into the still evening air. It was one of those quintessential southern Ontario summer evenings, calm, warm and with an undefinable soft clarity in the air. Approaching Toronto in the deepening dusk, we watched the lights of the city come on. We flew out over the end of

Lake Ontario and turned into the brilliant colours of the fading sunset, making our way back to Downsview for a perfect landing—as far as I could tell, anyway.

The whole experience became an indelible memory for me, and one with a postscript. Years later, I was the proud possessor of a private pilot's licence and had been fortunate enough, with a partner, to purchase a surplus ex-RCAF de Havilland Chipmunk. It was an aircraft that was a joy to fly. Seventeen years after my first flight with my father from the same airport that housed the factory at which this Chipmunk had been built, I was able to return the favour by talking Skeets—who had ceased flying altogether on leaving the RCAF—into coming for an hour's flight from Rockcliffe. We flew up over the Gatineau hills, again in the calm, warm air of an early August evening. In all his time in the pilot's seat, Skeets had never flown a Chipmunk—it was, after all, only a basic trainer during its military service heyday, when Skeets was enjoying flying in much more sophisticated machines. But unknown to me, his well-thumbed log book was amended that day to add another type to the list of twenty-eight aircraft he had already flown: 'Chipmunk.' Hopefully, the gift of that day's flight brought back many memories and went some way to repaying my own joy and awe on being introduced to flying so many years before.

After a last big effort organizing the RCAF's participation in Toronto's Canadian National Exhibition Air Show, Skeets retired with no little regret in 1962, with nearly 5,000 hours of flying in his log book—including 300 in Spitfires. The date he chose for his retirement was just after the anniversary of the Battle of Britain. It was linked to a final act of service—representing the RCAF at the annual church service in Westminster Abbey in London and at a reunion at RAF Fighter Command headquarters. The long return flight on the RCAF Yukon must have been an occasion for much introspection.

Other than airline flights, he flew only a couple of times after his departure from the life he loved best; when an aneurism took away the sight in one eye, he was unable to medically qualify to fly any longer. But it would also be easy to believe it was at least partly a conscious choice on his part. After all, what could compare in civilian flying to the extraordinary rewards of the life he had been leading?

So Skeets and Irene settled into a home near the Ogilvie family house in Ottawa's Glebe neighbourhood and he took up the more plebeian tools of a public servant: pens, pencils and erasers. His modest pension from the RCAF and the princely award of £854s 0d per annum from the British Ministry of Pensions and National Insurance in compensation for disability caused by 'gunshot wound shoulder and humerus left' was not quite sufficient for a luxury retirement at the age of forty-eight, but it did not tempt Skeets to seek adventure at that stage of his life. He felt he had had quite enough challenges by then and chose a smoother path, joining a clerical office deep in the bureaucratic machinery of the Canadian government. For the rest of his working career, he oversaw a harem of mostly female clerks who adored him and who were always somewhat in awe of this unassuming man who had had such a colourful history. His modesty, sense of humour and genuine appreciation of the people he worked with gave him the tools to survive the years before he retired fully from the paying workforce.

Irene went to work as well, as a supervisor with Mutual Life, finally able to pursue a rewarding career of her own with her children now old enough to look after themselves. Even with a full-time job, she continued to volunteer with her church, St Matthew's—the place where she and Skeets had been married—with Meals on Wheels, the King's Daughters and anyone else who seemed to need her support.

Skeets even managed to put to rest the wry assessment of his boyhood mathematical abilities by Abe Sonley, his old trigonometry teacher. While he didn't do much trigonometry in later life, one of his ongoing passions—perhaps stemming from his early career working in a brokerage office—was following the stocks in which he had made small but consistent investments over the course of his working career. He kept better records on his investments than many a bookkeeper and, rarely, if ever, made a mistake in his accounting.

Not long after his retirement from the RCAF, Skeets received from his old 609 Squadron friend, Bisdee, a real-estate listing describing the availability on the market of 'a romantic ruin in the heart of the Highlands, with restoration possibilities.' Enclosed was a picture of Forter Castle, the Ogilvie family seat. The (half) joke was that for an offer over £10,000—about $25,000 Canadian at the time—Skeets could have retired to 'the pile,' as he put it, as the head of the Ogilvie clan. Well, it never came to pass—or was even seriously considered, to the family's regret—but the clan could have done worse.

When they had finally both fully retired, Irene and Skeets turned their attention south, spending time with a cluster of old RCAF friends and fellow retirees in Florida during the winter months. They always enjoyed sharing their experiences, but even those opportunities may have been in decline. Skeets's response to a request to recall some of his stories was, 'Stories? I guess you need a few drinks . . . and I'm not allowed to drink much any more.' Besides, the best stories had been shared so many times that they didn't need retelling. He was approached often for interviews, especially around the annual Remembrance Day ceremonies and the commemoration of the fiftieth anniversary of the Great Escape. His overwhelming modesty and genuine awe at having had these experiences, and having survived them, was always evident. After watching Hollywood's not very accurate Great Escape movie for the umpteenth time, he said, 'Gee, I knew those guys.' But in truth, he was one of 'those guys.'

He was not one for travel after he settled in Ottawa, but Skeets kept up a more or less regular and always affectionate correspondence with many of his old 609 Squadron comrades, like 'Joe' Atkinson, 'Squire' Winch and 'Bish' Bisdee. Then in June 1986, Skeets opened a letter from the Ministry of Defence in London. Air Commodore V.L. Warrington, director of Personal Services for the RAF, was inviting him to be one of six escorts for the Battle of Britain Roll of Honour at the annual commemorative ceremony in Westminster Abbey. It was a signal honour and one he accepted, for some unknown reason deciding to go on his own. It was a bittersweet occasion for Skeets, now seventy-one, to physically reconnect with men he had last seen when they were in their twenties.

Four years later, in September 1990, the Royal Air Force commemorated the fiftieth anniversary of the Battle of Britain and Skeets once again was talked into participating, this time with Irene at his side. It was a gala affair, with events in Buckingham Palace and Westminster Abbey, a formal ball and any number of chances to link up with his old 609 Squadron mates. Irene was also able to find the time to renew contact with her friends Helen and Dora. For each of them, the occasion refreshed memories and friendships that had endured but not been dusted off for years.

Skeets also kept in touch with 'those guys' as an active, if occasional, member of the Prisoner of War Association that met in Ottawa. One of the regulars was Wally Floody, the former 'tunnel king' who, after all his work on the tunnel, had been transferred—perhaps fortunately for him—to another camp just before the Great Escape. In a CBC interview, Wally recalled: 'The biggest thing about being an ex-prisoner of war is that every day is a plus, because if you're flying an airplane [*sic*] and you're alive and well forty years after, that's a plus . . . because you weren't supposed to be here. The day you were shot down, only 14% of us survived. All the rest are dead.'

And that was also what amazed Skeets for his entire life. In a post-war letter to Ziegler, 609's former intelligence officer, he wrote that in Görlitz, during repeated interrogations, 'I stuck to my story that I was a career officer. This must have registered with the Teutonic mind, because I was one of eight returned to camp—the other sixteen, as you know, were shot.' Keith characteristically concluded his letter: 'And that, old Spy, is I hope my last debriefing—until the big one.'

The 'big one' came in May 1998, after what Skeets would in all conscience consider a pretty full life of eighty-three years. A final tribute to him in 609 Squadron's Tally Ho quarterly newsletter, of August 1998, recorded: 'One of "The Few," we doubt his like will be seen again. They were an elite, men of high spirit, their comradeship forged by shared hazards and the intoxication of manning intricate, almost invincible, machines.'

In September of that year, Irene, my sister Jean and I travelled to Britain to visit some of the old haunts and meet several of hers and Skeets' old 609 Squadron colleagues. We stayed for a while with Helen Baker, Irene's old flatmate and putative saviour in the incident of the bombing and the grand piano. It was a memorable occasion, starting with a ceremony commemorating the anniversary of the Battle of Britain and highlighted by a day trip to Biggin Hill, the base from which Skeets had been flying when he was shot down. There, in a simple remembrance, some of Skeets's ashes were interred in the rose garden behind the chapel, in the presence of some of the men who had been his youthful colleagues. It was a privilege beyond counting to see the survivors, all in their smart blazers with the RAF crests, and reminiscing—Bisdee, Atkinson, the others, all now old and fragile but still sitting straight, with clear eyes, deep memories and an undeniable and unbreakable bond between them. Atkinson admitted he often thought of their days together, and of 'Keith's kindly wit and his modesty about his considerable successes.' But in one way or another this seemed to describe all of these men who had shared those same experiences.

We interred the rest of Skeets's ashes in the Canadian National Military Cemetery at Beechwood in Ottawa, almost in sight of the runway from which he had taken off so often and to which he had successfully returned every time. The family had arranged for the Anglican archdeacon (a 90lb woman from Belfast, of all places, full of energy, humour and a real charmer) of St Matthew's to lead a short, informal, family-only get-together. It had started to rain the evening before and by morning, it was coming down like Ottawa had never seen rain. It was smack dab in the middle of the remnant weather system from Hurricane Frances, and many parts of Ottawa were already under water.

Regardless, we went to the cemetery. Our umbrellas were not doing any earthly good and we were sopping, soaking wet from the waist down from the nearly sideways deluge. The water at the very top of the knoll around the big memorial stone was three-quarters of an inch deep and being replenished from the heavens faster than it could run away down the hill. The cemetery crew were frantically trying to bail out the prepared hole with a couple of big plastic pails. It was a daunting challenge, with the water running in more quickly than they could scoop it out. Skeets's grandson, Casey, was finally able to place the container with the ashes in the ground. One attendant immediately started throwing shovels full of sand and earth on top, before the rising water could float the urn back up and off into the water feature at the bottom of the hill. Irene was in tears and laughing hysterically—in fact, the whole family were. After seven or eight minutes of this battle, confident that the urn would stay put, we managed to get back into our cars and headed home to dry out after scrubbing the planned lunch at a local restaurant with Her Archdeaconship.

'Memorable!' said the Archdeacon as she left.

'Macabre—he didn't want to leave the warm bookshelf!' said Irene.

I think it was my father having the last word, laughing his socks off at us. He was the only dry one there.

EPILOGUE

After Skeets passed away, Irene spent part of her winters with family—son, daughter-in-law and grandchildren—in Victoria. For her, it was a kind of coming home, seeing the places where she had lived as a child and only since returned to once or twice for brief visits. Always independent, she rented the same condominium every year from a couple who went south for the winter. It overlooked a golf course and the Olympic mountain range on the US side of the Strait of Juan de Fuca, a spectacular and treasured view that she appreciated every day. She had a surfeit of friends to keep her busy, including her childhood best friend, Joan, whom she always delighted in seeing. She loved the golf course outside her window and took frequent advantage, whether it was playing or picking up errant balls from the front lawn.

At some point, we finally convinced her to apply for her overseas service medals, which she had always thought were trivial compared to Skeets's collection. They arrived in due course and became a source of great pride for her. In 2013, the Queen Elizabeth II Diamond Jubilee Medal was added, in recognition of the energy and effort she had put into her volunteer activities and her service to her country over many years.

But time takes its inevitable toll. Health challenges eventually put an end to the transcontinental trips and the golf games. The damage to her legs from her wartime accident finally caught up with Irene, leaving her in a wheelchair. She had the pleasure of being able to move into a wonderful residence, the Perley Veteran's Health Centre, thanks to her wartime service in the RCAF. She was well taken care of. In addition to loving care by her daughter, Jean, she was regularly visited by family, old friends and the children of old friends, now themselves in their sixth or seventh decades. It was not just for the family ties that they came for these visits, but I think because Irene was one of the last connections to a generation who paid so much and to whom we, their successors, owe such a great deal. It is thanks to their sacrifices and commitment that we in the West, for the most part, have been able to enjoy the relative peace and stability that has characterized at least our part of the world in the period since the end of the Second World War. Irene's callers also came because she was an extraordinary example to them all, keeping her humour, never complaining, and taking and genuinely appreciating the best of whatever each day offered.

She had lots of opportunity for reflection. During a visit with her family, she wistfully observed, 'Everything I see nowadays seems so much smaller than it did then, seems so tiny.' For her, too, it was an amazing life, a gift to be treasured to the very last. She is now at peace beside her beloved Skeets.

Most of her generation is also at rest, their experiences now mostly lost. There are not many Kriegies left, and none who participated in the Great Escape. But for those who survive, the memories are clear. Two former inmates, Andy Wiseman and Charles Clarke, attended the ceremonies commemorating the seventieth anniversary of the Great Escape at Zagan. It was a poignant event, taking place on a grey, windy and rainy day at the edge of the North Compound, where tunnel 'Harry' broke out of the ground just short of the surrounding forest. The day before the formal ceremonies Andy and Charles visited the spot, in the company of fifty young RAF personnel who would play a role in the next day's emotional occasion. This cold and grey day they gathered around the two elderly gentlemen, who were seated on either side of the stones marking the path of the tunnel, in front of a rebuilt section of barbed-wire fencing and a replica 'goon tower.'

As they told their stories, the servicemen and women around them became more and more engrossed. Suddenly there was a tinkling sound that repeated two or three times. Charles looked about and said, 'It's an ice cream truck!' The sound went on. Finally, one of the RAF onlookers put his hand on Charles's arm and told him, 'I believe it's your phone, sir.' Andy disagreed. 'It's someone in the tunnel,' he said, to great laughter. Charles fumbled in his pocket for a bit, pulled the still ringing instrument out and, blushing a bit, told his granddaughter he would call her back. He put the offending phone back in his pocket and, apologized, saying, 'I never realized it was loaded.'

The dry and humorous dialogue between these two old soldiers was a fine illustration of the resilience of the human spirit, and of the importance of memory. Here, at the site of the prison camp—abandoned nearly seven decades earlier, surrounded by the slow reassertion of the supremacy of the pine woods over the concrete pads, fallen chimneys and half buried relics—they could pass their stories on to a new generation.

History is being preserved and people continue to remember.

ACKNOWLEDGEMENTS

There have been many contributors to this journey of discovery, which has taken a long time. History isn't real until it is understood in personal terms, and so much of this account has been possible thanks to the inputs of people whose experiences and memories have brought it alive.

It has also been possible due to the encouragement and forbearance of Francine Hallé, my much-loved partner and best supporter who, along with Mika and Casey, has pushed me to make this project real.

I was the great beneficiary of a lot of family lore and of course of my parents' dusty archives, which my sister Jean spent hours sorting and boxing up for posterity. She offered many suggestions and ideas that have become part of the book.

And surprises came from nowhere. A neighbour of Irene and Skeets's in Ottawa, Anne Hennessy, made a roundabout and fortuitous electronic introduction to George Sweanor, a thoughtful and articulate survivor of the camp. This led to connections with Marilyn Walton and Barb Edy, both inveterate and knowledgeable researchers, preservers of memories and offspring of veterans of Stalag Luft III, who have been generous in sharing their knowledge. They were wonderful in connecting me with other children and relatives of those involved in the Great Escape who have shared stories from their own families. These connections also led to an invitation from the welcoming and thoughtful organizers and hosts of that event's seventieth anniversary commemorations in Zagan in March 2014. My sister Jean, son Casey and I were able to attend and we owe them all a great debt of thanks for the treasure trove of information and memories this provided. It also led to a meeting with publisher Steve Darlow, of Fighting High Ltd., the UK publisher of the first edition of this book, without whose assistance and advice this book would have remained just a project.

After the memorial for Irene in September 2014, I was presented with an original tape recording of a couple of hours or so, made clandestinely by Irene's cousins at their cottage during a summer visit of Skeets and Irene, who had been coerced by a glass of sherry or two into sharing their recollections. Many thanks to Jill for preserving this bit of history and for making it available.

Johanna Bisdee, daughter of 'Bish,' was very helpful and a gracious host during a rather tentative visit to the UK early in the process of pulling together information for the book.

Ian Darling, author of *Amazing Airmen*, was very open and accommodating in sharing the research he did for his book. The library at Canadian Forces Base Comox provided open access to John Colwell's diary, which describes so much of the day to day experience of the camp and includes John's record of the Long March. Harold Johnstone had the foresight and commitment to assist John in organizing his papers and getting them into an accessible form. And a major contribution to the piecemeal collection of wartime accounts was made by the late Tony Little, a former POW himself and president of the Ottawa chapter of the Canadian Prisoners of War Association. Tony encouraged Skeets, Wally Floody and many others to meet often at the Black Swan pub under the guise of preserving and sharing their stories and memories.

Family members and friends Bruce and Del Carson went over the manuscript and all offered excellent suggestions for improvement.

Just before the 70th Anniversary commemorative ceremony, we spent a few quiet moments at the site of the Great Escape memorial while one of the local women, Jadwiga Jastrzebska, set up an arrangement of flowers. She and the people of Zagan who have worked over the years to preserve this memorial deserve a special mention.

The encroachment of the forest on the site of Stalag Luft III and the fading of that part of history has been halted, at least for a while, through the remarkable efforts of Marek Lazarz, the curator of the museum there. He and his colleague, Mirek Walczak, have been wonderfully effective in attracting interest and funding to preserve this valuable piece of the past.

Most importantly, they are welcoming and open in providing access to the growing archive of records on the camp, a treasure trove for families of inmates and interested researchers. More visitors are coming each year to the museum in this quiet town in Silesia, curious about what ordinary people can do in extraordinary times.

RECORD OF SERVICE   A.K. 'Skeets' Ogilvie

August–October 1939 .... Hatfield, Hertfordshire, UK
(De Havilland School of Flying).

November 1939–May 1940 .... Hullavington, Wiltshire, UK
(No. 9 Flying Training School).

May–June 1940 .... Meir, Staffordshire, UK
(No. 1 Flying Practice Unit).

June–July 1940 .... Upavon, Wiltshire, UK
(Central Flying School).

July–August 1940 .... Aston Down, Gloucestershire, UK
(No. 5 Operational Training Unit).

August–November 1940 .... Middle Wallop, Hampshire, UK
(609 Squadron).

November 1940–February 1941 .... Warmwell, Dorset, UK
(609 Squadron).

February–July 1941 .... Biggin Hill, Bromley, UK
(609 Squadron).

July 1941–May 1945 .... prisoner of war in hospital and Stalag
Luft III, Zagan, Poland.

October–November 1945 .... Rockcliffe, Ontario, Canada.

November 1945–September 1946 .... Lachine, Quebec, Canada.

October 1946–March 1948 .... Trenton, Ontario, Canada
(control tower).

March 1948–November 1950 .... Centralia, Ontario, Canada
(SFCO and IFS course).

November 1950–November 1952 .... Rockcliffe, Ontario, Canada
(412 (T) Squadron).

December 1952–September 1954 .... Trenton, Ontario, Canada
(Acceptance and Test Flight—6RD).

September 1954–November 1958 .... Rockcliffe, Ontario, Canada
(staff officer, Air Operations, AMC).

November 1958–September 1962 .... Downsview, Ontario, Canada
(Base Operations officer).

NOTES

1. The *Letitia* was a passenger steamship that was requisitioned by the British Admiralty in September 1939, immediately after Skeets arrived in England at Liverpool.

2. Just under seven years later, the ill-starred *Athenia* became the first ship to be sunk at the outset of the Second World War, with the loss of 118 passengers and crew out of more than 1,100 on board. The U-boat captain had mistaken the *Athenia* for a British armed merchant cruiser.

3. The aircraft of choice for basic training was naturally a de Havilland product, the open-cockpit Tiger Moth. A biplane, it was slow, forgiving and a delight to fly, introducing thousands of trainees to the joys of flying. All of Skeets's basic training was done on this aircraft.

4. The Comet pub, which still stands in Hatfield as part of the Ramada Hotel, is an art deco building fronted by a statue commemorating the de Havilland Comet DH88 racer. The aircraft was purpose designed and built in the 1930s as a race plane. One of three produced, the aircraft memorialized outside the pub was given the registration G-ACSS and won the 1934 MacRobertson air race from Mildenhall, England, to Melbourne, Australia, in a record time that still stood in 2010. The same aircraft set a number of other records. The aircraft has been restored and is presently in the Shuttleworth Collection.

5. Norm Hurd, his friend from Ottawa, who ended up flying Blenheims.

6. The question mark is Skeets's diary notation—evidently there is some question as to whether all this was considered to be 'work.'

7. 'Jumbo' Down would later drop out of advanced multi-engined training.

8. Probably Betty Plewes, a friend from Ottawa.

9. Marj Taggart, a high-school friend in Ottawa.

10. In 1942, this evolved into MI12.

11. De Havilland Tiger Moth, the training aircraft.

12. Volunteer Reservist.

13. Wing Commander Clement 'Clem' Pike was a flying instructor who was instrumental in putting the whole training system for the profession on a sound basis, leading to the establishment of the RAF Reserve Flying Training Schools, of which this was one. He served with the RAF from 1939 to 1947 and later became the manager of Hatfield Aerodrome.

14. Ronnie and Monnie (Veronica and Monica) were the twins the Canadian volunteers had met on the *Letitia* during the August crossing of the Atlantic.

15. Had he been accepted into the Royal Canadian Navy, Jim, the youngest of the three Ogilvie brothers, would have rounded out tri-service representation from the family. It was not to be, however; in the end he joined Emerson's regiment and was wounded in action in Italy.

16. G-ADHV was the aircraft designation.

17. George Petty is most famous for his pin-up drawings that appeared in *Esquire* magazine in the 1930s and the covers for many Ice Capades programmes. Skeets's collection of personal papers includes a couple of racy copies. They must have indeed 'brightened up' the room!

18. The band at Willerby's was probably led by Ken 'Snake Hips' Johnson, from Georgetown, Guyana. He would later be killed in an air raid that Irene and Chili were altogether too close to.

19. Marshal of the Royal Air Force, Hugh Montague Trenchard, 1st Viscount Trenchard, GCB, OM, GCVO, DSO, was known as the 'Father of the Royal Air Force.'

20. Frank H. Ziegler, *The Story of 609 Squadron: Under the White Rose*, p. 158. An OTU is an Operational Training Unit that prepared aircrew for specific operational roles.

21. Initially equipped on its formation in March 1940 with a few Gladiators and Blenheims, this unit was soon in possession of some 40 Hurricanes, 24 Blenheims as well as Masters and Defiants. One account notes that 'a few Spitfires were used between May and August 1940,' to his good fortune right at the time Ogilvie arrived.

22. Ziegler, op. cit., p. 158. Squadron Leader H.S. 'George' Darley was Skeets's commanding officer during 609's extraordinary showing in the Battle of Britain.

23. David Crook, *Spitfire Pilot*, p. 22.

24. James Holland, *The Battle of Britain—Five Months that Changed History: May–October 1940*, p. 515.

25. Ziegler, op. cit., p. 98.

26. An interesting irony, considering that Irene's mother first brought her to Leeds in search of her father. This was of course unknown to Skeets at the time he began to keep his diary.

27. This was 18 August 1940, and was the last time the Luftwaffe sent Ju87 (Stuka) dive bombers over England in any kind of force. German losses that day were far too high to support repeated use of these aircraft.

28. Ziegler, op. cit., p. 137.

29. His briefer account of this says he was flying Red 3.

30. Max Arthur, *Last of the Few: The Battle of Britain in the Words of the Pilots Who Won It*, p. 93.

31. The Dornier 215 was a version of the Do17 originally intended for export, but which ended up serving in the Luftwaffe. The two aircraft versions are almost identical.

32. Ian Darling, *Amazing Airmen*.

33. Ogilvie's scrapbook also has stills taken from his film camera that show the aircraft on fire and at least one of the crew baling out, barely missing Ogilvie's propeller.

34. Ziegler, op. cit., p. 135.

35. R. Bracken, *Spitfire—The Canadians*.

36. Ziegler, op. cit., p. 371.

37. This figure was the number claimed by the Air Ministry in a press statement. In fact, the German losses were about one-third this figure, but still more than double the RAF's losses of the day.

38. Ziegler, op. cit., pp. 157–58.

39. The critical Supermarine works, where the RAF's Spitfires were assembled, was in Woolston, near Southampton.

40. Fighter Command 'were asleep,' according to the notes in his training diary. One of the responding squadrons was 601, a training squadron. Ziegler (p. 148) credits the lack of RAF fighter presence to the successful diversionary tactics on the part of the Luftwaffe.

41. His log book notes, 'A flamer, crashed in field west of Poole.'

42. The combat notes at the back of the flying school diary also admit that they 'got lost coming home and barely had enough petrol to make the 'drome.'

43. The Me109 had a two-stage supercharger that allowed it to outperform the Spitfire above 25,000 feet. The new Luftwaffe tactics took full advantage of this superiority to place their fighters above the RAF patrols.

44. A curious addendum on Zurakowski's extensive experience can be found on http://www.combatsim.com/htm/dec99/Zura2.htm, whose editor says, 'Mr. Zurakowski, despite being hired as the chief test pilot on the Arrow, in fact never did have a pilot's license [*sic*], let alone experimental Jet test endorsement.' He did, however, graduate from the Empire Test Pilots' School in January 1945. When the Arrow programme was cancelled by the

Canadian government in 1959, Zurakowski was so disgusted that he never flew again, retiring to his lovely lodge near Barry's Bay, Ontario.

45. Ziegler, op. cit., p. 158.

46. This action took place on 7 October.

47. Heytesbury is in southern central England, just south of Bath, Wiltshire, not far from Stonehenge and the River Avon. It is some way from Middle Wallop, and it is not clear why Skeets chose this area for his leave. In any case, he must have taken with him his notes on his experiences since joining the squadron and rewritten his 'formal' diary to this point, over the course of his leave.

48. Central Flying School.

49. Holland, op. cit. According to Holland, the Luftwaffe began the summer with 3,578 aircraft and lost 3,701 irredeemably destroyed in various ways. Production did not keep up with losses, leaving the Luftwaffe with a 'combat strength by the end of October 1940 . . . somewhere in the region of 75 per cent less than it had been before the western campaign.'

50. Ibid., p. 810.

51. No. 782 Naval Air Squadron, Fleet Air Arm, had nine Harrows it used as transports. It was likely one of these involved in the 'experimental job.'

52. Ziegler, op. cit., p. 23.

53. Skeets likely meant the expected invasion of the continent.

54. Group Captain.

55. Skeets was leading Red section. In the squadron operational log, he says, 'Red 2 thinks he saw a small white dot first before the plane hit and the pilot may have jumped at a low altitude. I saw a trawler proceed to the green patch in the water.'

56. The squadron aircraft were all designated PR-A, PR-B, PR-C, etc. and the Drones were given these designations as a joke, since they didn't exactly live up to the Spitfire's standards.

57. Ziegler, op. cit., p. 182.

58. Excerpts from the Form 540 Operations Records Book of 609 (West Riding) Squadron, found at http://www.609wrsquadron.co.uk/Archives/Biographies/PDF_Files/Alfred%20Ogilvie.pdf.

59. The Prunier and Suivi were well-known nightclubs, the latter a squadron favourite and Stéphane Grappelli's home club. No. 609's pilots became personally known to the staff and had the run of the place.

60. Ziegler, op. cit., p. 189.

61. Realizing this must have brought home with some certainty that the long-term chances of 'survival' were remote. Many did, however, like Skeets's friends Bisdee, Joe Atkinson and many others.

62. The squadron log notes that the incident 'amused them both, in retrospect.'

63. Skeets apparently mixed up this entry in his diary with the previous account of the action in which he himself had taken part. It must indeed have been a good, relaxing period of leave!

64. Mercer was killed trying to force-land on the beach of St Margaret's Bay, also referred to as 'Hell's Corner.'

65. The Chance light was a portable unit used to illuminate the threshold of the runway.

66. These were the fighter 'sweeps' that increasingly became part of the RAF's tactics, aimed at unpredictably disrupting the peace for the Germans by seeking targets of opportunity.

67. Curchin was lost on June 4. It was unclear whether he had been shot down or collided with an Me109 during aerial combat.

68. Gravesend, less than 20 miles to the northeast of Biggin Hill, functioned initially as a training base and then during the Battle of Britain as a satellite of Biggin Hill. It later developed into a fully fledged fighter base in its own right. It has since been developed for housing.

69. An article by Lloyd Hunt in the July/Aug/Sept 1990 issue of *Airforce* magazine records that after being shot down, 'he now had a lot of time to reflect ruefully about the next posting he had just received. He had been selected for a Canadian squadron where he would be given a position of command.' It was RCAF 401 Squadron, also operating from Biggin Hill at the time.

70. Ziegler, op. cit., pp. 203–04.

71. This was the July 4 Eagle Club 'do,' for which Irene had procured precious tickets. Irene must have made mention of it in her earlier letter.

72. In his book *Goon in the Block*, Don Edy attributes the name to 'the comical appearance of the guards up in their sentry boxes. In the wintertime they wore enormous long greatcoats, heavy caps with a scarf wound around the neck and lower face, thick gloves and huge fleece-lined boots. With nothing but their eyes and noses showing they looked for all the world like Alice the Goon in the old Popeye comics.' Other sources attribute the name to an unpleasant Disney character with very hairy legs and an unintelligible language. Whatever the origin, the term was clearly not complimentary.

73. By the time he left three years later, there would be close to 15,000.

74. Andrew Wiseman, interviewed in the BBC film on the Great Escape, *Going Underground*, on Youtube at http://www.youtube.com/watch?v=0bgiqKbnuyM.

75. Paul Brickhill, *The Great Escape*, p. 42.

76. From A.K. Ogilvie, 'Tigers in the Tunnel,' *The Roundel*, Vol. 13, No. 7, September 1961.

77. Wiseman, in *Going Underground*, on YouTube at http://www.youtube.com/watch?v=0bgiqKbnuyM.

78. The Women's Royal Canadian Navy Service (WRCNS) was commonly referred to as the WRENs.

79. 'Veteran Led Orchestra at Prison Camp Stalag Luft III,' *Edmonton Journal*, May 7, 2010.

80. Arthur, op. cit., p. 339.

81. H.P. Clark, *Wirebound World—Stalag Luft III*.

82. Arthur, op. cit., p. 330.

83. Ibid., p. 337.

84. Reported in the back story to a CBC interview with Wally Floody, http://www.cbc.ca/archives/categories/war-conflict/second-world-war/general-22/wally-floody-and-the-great-escape.html, last visited June 13, 2005.

85. Arthur, op. cit., pp. 336–37.

86. B.A. James, *Moonless Night*, p. 194.

87. Arthur Crighton was one of those who declined to be considered, perhaps recognizing the importance to those remaining in the camp of the musical and theatrical presentations in which he had played such a key role.

88. Roger Bushell.

89. Major Dodge was an army officer who had escaped several times from custody and had been turned over at one point to Luftwaffe guards, who subsequently interred him in the Luftwaffe's 'escape proof' camp that was Stalag Luft III.

90. Interview with Bruce Urquhart, *The Ottawa Citizen*, April 2000.

91. The place where he was picked up was near Halbau, about 80 kilometres from Zagan. It was quite a lot of ground to have covered under those conditions.

92. Ogilvie, 'Tigers in the Tunnel,' op. cit.

93. Von Lindeiner was later court-martialled for having allowed the escape to take place. He had found approximately 100 tunnels during his tenure as camp Kommandant, but missed finding the 101st.

94. James, op. cit., p. 223.

95. http://www.cbc.ca/archives/categories/war-conflict/second-world-war/general-22/wally-floody-and-the-great-escape.html, last visited 13 June 2005.

96. From BBC news coverage of the release of files by the Public Record Office in Kew, set out on https://news.bbc.co.uk/hi/english/uk/newsid_71900/719289.stm

97. *Morituri te salutant* was the cry attributed to gladiators. It is generally translated as 'Those who are about to die salute you.'

98. Ogilvie, 'Tigers in the Tunnel,' op. cit.

99. Brickhill, op. cit., p. 219.

100. Shortly after, Al Hake was observed by another prisoner being taken away from Görlitz in a dark car by Dr Wilhelm Sharpwinkel, head of the Breslau Gestapo and his associate Lux.

101. Ogilvie, 'Tigers in the Tunnel,' op. cit.

102. British documents held in the Zagan museum record the discovery after the war that the memorial had been broken open and many of the urns smashed, apparently by Russian troops looking for gold or other treasure. The ashes were removed from the cairn and reburied at the Poznan Old Garrison military cemetery, but the cairn still stands in Zagan, carefully maintained by the local population.

103. *Mail Online* article at www.dailymail.co.uk/news/article-1246442/British-veterans-forced-gruelling-Long-March-Poland-enact-journey-65-years-later.html

104. The barn is still standing. It was visited again sixty-five years later by some former POWs who had participated in the march.

105. Brickhill, op. cit., p. 246.

106. Group Captain D.E.L. Wilson, in an article in *The Camp*, June 1988, p. 11.

107. Brickhill, op. cit., p. 246.

108. Colwell, op. cit., p. 114.

109. http://ww2talk.com/forums/topic/7129-question-about-unit-at-Lübeck-1945/, last visited June 24, 2013.

110. Hansard, as recorded in http://hansard.millbanksystems.com/commons/1944/jun/23/officer-prisoners-of-war-germany-shooting, last visited June 24, 2013.

111. In memory of Wing Commander Hugh Malcolm, a Blenheim pilot who was shot down under pressing circumstances during a hazardous bombing mission in North Africa on December 4, 1942.

112. Wartime—and immediate post-war—friendships being what they were, they lasted a very long time. Irene was to keep in touch with Audrey until Audrey's death in the 1990s.

113. Josef Kramer was the Kommandant of Bergen-Belsen concentration camp. Irma Grese was the head guard in the women's section. Both were hanged after their trials, Grese at the age of twenty-two years and nine months.

114. Delirium tremens, the result of alcohol withdrawal. It seems to have been quite a party period.

SELECTED BIBLIOGRAPHY

Air Ministry (1943), *The Battle of Britain*, Great Britain Air Ministry Pamphlet 156.

Andrews, Allen (1978), *Exemplary Justice*, London: Corgi Books.

Arthur, Max (2005), *Lost Voices of the Royal Air Force*, Great Britain: Hodder & Stoughton Paperbacks.

Barris, Ted (2013), *The Great Escape: A Canadian Story*, Toronto: Thomas Allen Publishers.

Bashow, David L. (1996), *All the Fine Young Eagles*, Toronto: Stoddard Publishing.

Bishop, Arthur (1994), *The Splendid Hundred: The True Story of Canadians Who Flew in the Greatest Air Battle of World War II*, Whitby, Ontario: McGraw-Hill Ryerson.

Bishop, Edward (1968), *Their Finest Hour: The Story of the Battle of Britain 1940*, London: Ballantine Books.

Bracken, Robert (1995), *Spitfire: The Canadians*, North York, Ontario: Stoddart Publishing Co. Ltd.

Brickhill, Paul (1971), *The Great Escape*, London: Faber and Faber Limited.

Buckham, Robert (1984), *Forced March to Freedom*, Stittsville, Ontario: Canada's Wings, Inc.

Clark, H.P., *Wirebound World*, London: Alfred H. Cooper & Sons, Ltd.

Clayton, Tim and Craig, Phil (2002), *Finest Hour: The Battle of Britain*, New York: Touchstone.

Collier, Richard (1966), *Eagle Day*, Great Britain: Hodder & Stoughton.

Crook, David (1943), *Spitfire Pilot*, London: Faber and Faber Limited.

Dancocks, Daniel G. (1983), *In Enemy Hands: Canadian Prisoners of War 1939–1945*, Edmonton: Hurtig Publishers.

Darling, Ian (2009), *Amazing Airmen*, Toronto: Dundurn Press.

Deighton, Len (1977), *Fighter: The True Story of the Battle of Britain*, London: Jonathan Cape.

Edy, Don (1961), *Goon in the Block*, Aylmer, Ontario: Aylmer Express Ltd.

Gill, Anton (2002), *The Great Escape*, London: Headline Book Publishing.

Goss, Chris (1994), *Brothers in Arms*, Great Britain: Crécy Books Ltd.

Greenfield, Nathan M. (2013), *The Forgotten*, Toronto: HarperCollins Publishers.

Haining, Peter (1990), *Spitfire Summer: The People's Eye-View of the Battle of Britain*, London: W.H. Allen & Co. Plc.

Holland, James (2011), *The Battle of Britain: Five Months that Changed History May–October 1940*, Great Britain: Corgi Books.

Hough, Richard and Richards, Denis (1989), *The Battle of Britain: The Greatest Air Battle of World War II*, London: W.W. Norton & Company.

Johnson, J.E. (1957), *Wing Leader*, New York: Ballantine Books.

Johnstone, Harold (2001), *John Colwell*, Nanaimo, British Columbia: Harold Johnstone.

Kaplan, Philip and Collier, Richard (1990), *The Few: Summer 1940*, The Battle of Britain, London: Seven Dials.

Lagrandeur, Philip (2006), *We Flew, We Fell, We Lived*, St Catherines, Ontario: Vanwell Publishing Limited.

Mahoney, John E. *Life in Stalag Luft III* (self-published).

Nichol, John and Rennell, Tony (2002), *The Last Escape: The Untold Story of Allied Prisoners of War in Germany 1944–45*, Great Britain: Viking Books.

Ogilvie, A.K. 'Tigers in the Tunnel,' *The Roundel*, Vol. 13, No. 7, September 1961.

Orde, Captain Cuthbert (1943), *Pilots of Fighter Command*, London: George G. Harrap & Co., Ltd.

Ramsey, Winston G., ed. (1980), *The Battle of Britain: Then and Now*, London: After the Battle.

Rees, Ken (2004), *Lie in the Dark and Listen*, London: Grub Street.

Royal Canadian Air Force Air Historical Section (1948), *Among the Few: A Sketch of the Part Played by Canadian Airmen in the Battle of Britain*, AFP 49.

Sweanor, George (1981), *It's All Pensionable Time*, Colorado Springs: Adman Publishers.

Vance, Jonathan (2000), *A Gallant Company: The Men of the Great Escape*, California: Pacifica Military History.

Wallace, Graham (1958), *R.A.F. Biggin Hill*, London: Four Square Books.

Wynn, Kenneth G. (1989), *Men of the Battle of Britain*, Norwich: Gliddon Books.

Ziegler, Frank H. (1993), *The Story of 609 Squadron: Under the White Rose*, Great Britain: Crécy Books Ltd.

INDEX

ABOUT THE AUTHOR

Born in Belleville, Ontario, Keith Ogilvie is the son of Keith "Skeets" Ogilvie and Irene Ogilvie (née Lockwood). The younger Keith grew up as a "service brat," moving with his family around southern Ontario as his father pursued his career as an RCAF pilot. He graduated from Royal Military College with an engineering degree in 1969 and then went into the RCAF as an aerospace engineer. While posted to Ottawa's Uplands air base, he earned his BA in English Literature from Carleton and pursued post-graduate engineering studies. He left the RCAF in 1974 to work on Canada's space program, then moved into the consulting field, initially in technical areas and later in the fields of information technology, governance and public administration. Since the late 1980s, he has worked in the field of international development, supporting governance- and economic-development-related projects. Keith is also a former pilot (he owned an ex-RCAF trainer, a Chipmunk, for ten years), a sailor, a walker, an explorer and a lover of the west coast. He lives in North Saanich on Vancouver Island with his wife, has two children also living in greater Victoria, and one spoiled, curly-haired granddaughter.